CONTEMPORARY SCREEN ETHICS

CONTEMPORARY SCREEN ETHICS

Absences, Identities, Belonging, Looking Anew

Edited by Lucy Bolton, David Martin-Jones
and Robert Sinnerbrink

EDINBURGH
University Press

Edinburgh University Press is one of the leading university presses in the UK.
We publish academic books and journals in our selected subject areas across the
humanities and social sciences, combining cutting-edge scholarship with high editorial
and production values to produce academic works of lasting importance. For more
information visit our website: edinburghuniversitypress.com

© Editorial matter and organisation, Lucy Bolton, David Martin-Jones and
Robert Sinnerbrink, 2023, 2024
© The chapters their several authors, 2023, 2024

Edinburgh University Press Ltd
13 Infirmary Street,
Edinburgh, EH1 1LT

First published in hardback by Edinburgh University Press 2023

Typeset in 10/12.5 pt Sabon by
IDSUK (DataConnection) Ltd

A CIP record for this book is available from the British Library

ISBN 978 1 4744 4758 4 (hardback)
ISBN 978 1 4744 4761 4 (paperback)
ISBN 978 1 4744 4759 1 (webready PDF)
ISBN 978 1 4744 4760 7 (epub)

The right of Lucy Bolton, David Martin-Jones and Robert Sinnerbrink to be identified
as editors of this work have been asserted in accordance with the Copyright, Designs
and Patent Act 1988, and the Copyright and Related Rights Regulations 2003 (SI No.
2498)

CONTENTS

List of Figures	vii
Acknowledgements	ix
Notes on Contributors	xi

Introduction: Absences, Identities, Belonging: Looking Anew at
Screen Ethics   1
Lucy Bolton, David Martin-Jones and Robert Sinnerbrink

PART ONE   HISTORIES AND ABSENCES

1. Domestic Work, Gender, Race, Class and the Ethical Paradox of
   the Big House in Brazilian Cinema   23
   Alessandra Soares Brandão and Ramayana Lira de Sousa

2. Cinematic Ethics and a World of Cinemas: A Reason to Believe in
   this World's History in Hu Jie's *Wo sui si qu/Though I am Gone*   42
   David Martin-Jones

3. Memory, Witnessing and Re-enactment: *The Look of Silence, S21:
   The Khmer Rouge Killing Machine* and Cinematic Ethics   60
   Robert Sinnerbrink

PART TWO   BODIES AND IDENTITIES

4. Becoming Beyoncé: Disidentification and Racial Imaginaries   83
   Tina Chanter

5. Race, Bodies and Altered Identities in *Sleight* and *Us* 100
   Mary K. Bloodsworth-Lugo

PART THREE LOVE AND BELONGING

6. A Planetary Whole for the Alienated: John Akomfrah's
   Vertigo Sea through Jameson and Deleuze 117
   Jakob A. Nilsson

7. Mermaids and Superpigs: Loving Nature under Global Capitalism 133
   Chelsea Birks

8. Dreaming of Joyce Vincent's Life: Carol Morley's Intersectional
   Ethics of Care 151
   Lucy Bolton

PART FOUR LOOKING ANEW

9. Empathy Machines, Indifference Engines and Digital Extensions
   of Perception 171
   Nick Jones

10. Do You See what I See? The Ethics of Seeing Race in *Get Out* 188
    Berenike Jung

11. Don't Look Away: Production-assemblages of Rape Culture in
    Midi Z's *Nina Wu* 204
    Jiaying Sim

Index 225

FIGURES

3.1	Moral blindness and ethical witnessing	65
3.2	Adi Rukun: the look of silence	66
3.3	Historical trauma and political propaganda	67
3.4	Amir Siahaan: denying responsibility and threatening Rukun	70
6.1	*Vertigo Sea*, 2015	120
6.2	*Vertigo Sea*, 2015	120
6.3	*Vertigo Sea*, 2015	121
6.4	*Vertigo Sea*, 2015	128
7.1	Eco branding in *Okja*	136
7.2	Spectacle of global capitalism in *The Mermaid*	137
7.3	Environmental suffering in *The Mermaid*	138
7.4	Superpig feedlot in *Okja*	140
7.5	Domestic tranquillity at the end of *Okja*	147
8.1	Alix Luka-Cain plays young Joyce gazing longingly after her father	154
8.2	Some of the very few photographs of Joyce that Morley found and which act as traces of Joyce in the film	155
8.3	Zawe Ashton plays Joyce recording a demo tape	160
8.4	A photograph of Joyce Vincent	163
9.1	*The Last Goodbye* screengrab	175
9.2	*Clouds Over Sidra* screengrab	177
10.1	Protagonist Chris Washington, seen through a white gaze	196
10.2	Former photographer Jim Hudson, viewed on a grainy television image	197

10.3	Chris, captured and in close-up	197
10.4	Falling into the Sunken Place, from Chris's point of view	198
11.1	Nina putting on make-up before livestreaming	208
11.2	Nina in the midst of her livestream session	208
11.3	Marco convinces Nina to take the role	213
11.4	Silhouette of a lizard writhing under the heat of a lamp	213
11.5	Nina breaks the fourth wall and points a knife at the camera	218
11.6	Director enacting physical and verbal abuse on Nina in order to get her to perform her lines to his satisfaction	219

ACKNOWLEDGEMENTS

The editors would like to thank all the contributors for their patience and perseverance whilst this volume was collated over several years. Thanks also to Gillian Leslie and all her colleagues at Edinburgh University Press for their unwavering support throughout, along with the work's anonymous peer reviewers.

The volume was informed in part by research undertaken by Robert Sinnerbrink which was funded by an Australian Research Council Discovery Grant, 'Film as Philosophy: Understanding Cinematic Thinking' [DP1092889, (2010-2013)] and an Australian Research Council Future Fellowship, 'Cinematic Ethics: Exploring Ethical Experience through Film' [FT130100334 (2014-2018)]. This includes the chapter 'Memory, Witnessing and Re-enactment. . .' by Robert Sinnerbrink. The University of Glasgow, College of Arts, also supported the volume through the funding of two bespoke events on cinema and ethics, in Film and Television Studies. Our thanks to both funders for enabling this project so generously.

The chapter 'Domestic Work. . .' by Alessandra Soares Brandão and Ramayana Lira de Sousa is part of an individual project (Ramayana Lira de Sousa) funded by *Instituto Ânima* (https://www.institutoanimaeducacao.org.br/). The project is titled *Imagens políticas: gênero, raça, sexualidade [atravessamentos]*. Jakob A. Nilsson's chapter 'A Planetary Whole . . .' is one outcome of a larger individual research project called 'Modern Essay Films as Thought-Maps of Globalization' (2015–18), which was generously funded by the Swedish Research Council. The research underlying Chelsea Birks's chapter 'Mermaids and Superpigs . . .' was made possible by funding from the College of Arts at the University of Glasgow, for the doctoral project 'Limit Cinema: Bataille and the Nonhuman in Contemporary Global Film' (2017).

Finally, the editors wish to thank Carol Morley, Cairo Cannon and Dogwoof Limited for permission to use the cover image of Zawe Ashton from *Dreams of a Life* (2011).

NOTES ON CONTRIBUTORS

Chelsea Birks is the Learning and Outreach Director at The Cinematheque in Vancouver, Canada, and a sessional instructor in Film Studies at the University of British Columbia. Her first book, *Limit Cinema: Transgression and the Nonhuman in Contemporary Global Film*, was published in 2021 as part of Bloomsbury's 'Thinking Cinema' series. She won the 2017 SCMS Student Writing Award and has been published in *Cinema Journal* (now *JCMS*), *Film-Philosophy*, *New Review of Film and Television Studies* and *Journal of Gender Studies*.

Mary K. Bloodsworth-Lugo is professor of Comparative Ethnic Studies and graduate director of American Studies and Culture in the School of Languages, Cultures, and Race at Washington State University. Her teaching and research spans narratives of disease and contagion, race and racism in US popular culture and film, theories of embodiment, and 9/11 cultural and rhetorical production. She is the author or co-author of seven published books and forty journal articles and book chapters, and she has presented her scholarly work at seventy national and international venues.

Lucy Bolton is Reader in Film Studies at Queen Mary University of London, and the author of *Contemporary Cinema and the Philosophy of Iris Murdoch* (Edinburgh University Press, 2019), and *Film and Female Consciousness: Irigaray, Cinema and Thinking Women* (2011). She is the co-editor of *Lasting Screen Stars: Images that Fade and Personas that Endure* (2016; winner

BAFTSS Best Edited Collection), and co-editor, with Richard Rushton, of the book series *Visionaries – Thinking Through Female Filmmakers*, published by Edinburgh University Press. Lucy is currently writing a monograph on *Philosophies of Hollywood Stardom: Ethics, Aesthetics and Phenomenologies* and compiling an anthology of feminist film philosophy.

Tina Chanter has published on contemporary French philosophy, drawing inspiration from a range of sources, including feminist theory, race theory, psychoanalysis, art, politics, film and tragedy. Her most recent books are: *Whose Antigone? The Tragic Marginalisation of Slavery*, and *Art, Politics and Rancière: Broken Perceptions*. Her work is 'indisciplinary' in Rancière's sense, and her thinking is informed by Rancière, though not uncritically. Current and forthcoming work focuses on questions of politics and aesthetics. It includes a consideration of Rancière's conception of politics in the context of the Black Lives Matter movement, and an analysis of Sylvia Wynter's discussion of Shakespeare's *The Tempest* in the context of a consideration of Kant's aesthetics and Kristeva's notion of abjection. Other essays include a reflection on the political implications of Kristeva on art and the veil, an article on Sara Kofman's feminist, Freudian inspired reading of Kant's aesthetics, an essay on Levinas, Shakespeare and the *il y a*, and an essay that focuses on the question of violence against women and the racialisation of mourning, drawing on Wynter and Irigaray. Chanter taught in the US, most recently in Chicago, before returning to the UK, where she worked and taught in Bristol and London before joining Newcastle University.

Nick Jones is Senior Lecturer in Film, Television, and Digital Culture at the University of York. He is the author of *Hollywood Action Films and Spatial Theory* (2015), *Spaces Mapped and Monstrous: Digital 3D Cinema and Visual Culture* (2020) and *Gooey Media: Screen Entertainment and the Graphic User Interface* (2023). His work on action filmmaking, VFX, digital media, spatial theory and 3D has also been published in a wide range of journals and edited collections.

Berenike Jung is a Lecturer in Film Studies at the University of Southampton. Previously, she taught Film Studies at King's College London, University of Groningen and University of Tübingen. She received her PhD in Film and Television Studies from the University of Warwick in 2016. Her research centres around the cinematic representation of violence and the politics of memory; cinemas of Latin America and the Global South; decolonising film education; auditory, visual and kinaesthetic aesthetics in contemporary digital media formats. She is the author of *The Invisibilities of Torture: The Presence of Absence in US and Chilean Cinema* (Edinburgh University Press, 2020), and co-editor with Stella Bruzzi of *Beyond the Rhetoric of Pain* (2018). Recent articles include 'De-marginalising and de-centring film studies in bodies, places and on screens' in *Film Education Journal* (June 2022), with Derilene Marco. She contributed a book chapter on TikTok for the forthcoming anthology *Traveling Music Videos*.

Ramayana Lira de Sousa is a Professor of Film and Literary Studies in the Graduate Program in Language Sciences at the Universidade do Sul de Santa Catarina, Brazil. She has written on Brazilian and Latin American cinemas and on issues of gender and feminist theory for a number of journals and has contributed to the book *Human Rights, Social Movements and Activism in Contemporary Latin American Cinema* (2018). Her recent research, 'Political images: crossings [gender, race and sexuality]' investigates the politics of lesbian desire in contemporary cinema. She is also a curator.

David Martin-Jones is Professor of Film Studies, University of Glasgow, UK. His specialism is film-philosophy, and his research engages with world cinemas. He is the author/editor of ten books, including *Deleuze and World Cinemas* (2011) which was shortlisted for the BAFTSS Annual Book Award, *Cinema Against Doublethink* (2018), and *Columbo: Paying Attention 24/7* (Edinburgh University Press, 2021) which was shortlisted for the MeCCSA Best Monograph Award. He has published in numerous journals including *Cinema Journal*, *Screen* and *Third Text* amongst others. He is co-editor of various anthologies and special editions of journals, along with the Bloomsbury monograph series Thinking Cinema. He is a member of the editorial boards of *Deleuze and Guattari Studies*, *Film-Philosophy* and *Transnational Screens*.

Jakob A. Nilsson is Assistant Professor of Film Studies at the Department of Media and Communication Studies, Örebro University. He is the author of the book *Cinecepts, Deleuze and Godard-Miéville. Developing Philosophy through Audiovisual Media* (Edinburgh University Press, forthcoming 2023). He has published articles in *Journal of Aesthetics & Culture; Journal of French and Francophone Philosophy; Cinema. Journal of Philosophy and Moving Image; Theory, Culture & Society; Cinema & Cie. International Film Studies Journal*. He is also the co-editor, with Sven-Olov Wallenstein, of the anthology *Foucault, Biopolitics, and Governmentality* (2013).

Jiaying Sim is an Assistant Professor of Humanities and Social Sciences at DigiPen Institute of Technology, Singapore. She received her PhD in film and television studies from the University of Glasgow, UK. Her research interests include transnational Chinese cinemas, Southeast Asian Cinemas, transnational migration in film and film philosophy. Focusing on different types of body assemblages that are produced with consideration to historicity, modernity, urban spaces, race, class, gender and sexuality, she has written on circuits of transnational sensoria and affects that are embedded within the dynamic processes of capital, labour, socioeconomic markets and political contexts. Jiaying is currently working on a monograph on affective non-normative care assemblages in media texts.

Robert Sinnerbrink is Associate Professor of Philosophy and former Australian Research Council Future Fellow at Macquarie University, Sydney. He is the author of *New Philosophies of Film (Second Edition): An Introduction to Cinema as a Way of Thinking* (2022), *Terrence Malick: Filmmaker and Philosopher* (2019), *Cinematic Ethics: Exploring Ethical Experience through Film* (2016), *New Philosophies of Film: Thinking Images* (2011) and *Understanding Hegelianism* (2007; 2014). He has edited two books (*Emotion, Ethics, and Cinematic Experience: New Phenomenological and Cognitivist Perspectives* [2021] and *Critique Today* [2006]), as well as special issues of the journals *Projections: The Journal of Movies and Mind*, *Film-Philosophy*, *SubStance* and *Screening the Past*. He is also a member of the editorial boards of the journals *Film-Philosophy*, *Film and Philosophy* and *Projections: The Journal of Movies and Mind*.

Alessandra Soares Brandão is a Professor of Film and Literary Studies in the Graduate Program in Literature at the Universidade Federal de Santa Catarina, Brazil. She has written on Brazilian and Latin American cinemas for a number of journals and has contributed to the book *Human Rights, Social Movements and Activism in Contemporary Latin American Cinema* (2018). Her recent research, 'Women on the move and women's movements: narratives of im/mobility and in/visibility', focuses on issues of domestic labour and lesbian desire in cinema and literature from a decolonial perspective.

INTRODUCTION: ABSENCES, IDENTITIES, BELONGING: LOOKING ANEW AT SCREEN ETHICS

Lucy Bolton, David Martin-Jones and Robert Sinnerbrink

This edited collection emerged due to a shared sense amongst the editors that more needed to be said about how cinematic ethics is intertwined with the sociopolitical. This sense arose from the observation of a growing focus on this topic within the field, as seen in, for example, recent conference papers and publications in journals focusing on film-philosophy. With the turn to ethics in scholarship at the interdisciplinary intersection of film and philosophy now firmly established, it became clear that we should foreground the complex contextualisations, associations, imbrications, combinations and assemblages combining the ethical with the sociopolitical. Alongside this realisation was the growing awareness that cinematic ethics also requires a broader understanding of *screen* ethics to include examples of screen media 'types' which proliferate in our media-saturated world. Not a provincialising of cinematic ethics, but a recognition of the need to broaden the panorama to include television, digital media, virtual reality technology, and so on.

The contributions in *Contemporary Screen Ethics* together indicate how *political* the examination of screen ethics is. The manifestation of such politics, however, typically focus on the *sociopolitical* as opposed to the political strictly speaking (as in the politics of government, for example). Thus, collected in this anthology are chapters which examine screen ethics in relation to a range of topics which can be understood to be sociopolitical. It is worth outlining a few examples.

Feminist-informed explorations of screen ethics herein lead to three distinct contexts. First, considerations of decolonial analysis of the figure of the housemaid in a range of Brazilian cinematic genres and modes (intersectionally considering gender, race and class), which gesture towards an ethics of relationality that could be more inclusive of such otherwise marginalised figures. Second, the teasing out of what an ethics of care might look like in terms of documentary filmmaking practice, once more recognising of the nuanced intersectional nature of such practices and their subjects. Third, the affective nature of the ethical gaze when films explore sexual and gendered violence in the media and film industries.

We might equally consider the various approaches to race which open up discussion of, for instance, how televised stand-up comedy can make an ethico-political intervention into the circulation of stereotypes, or, how popular genre films may encourage people to ethically encounter otherness anew in a context which has normalised alignment with a constructed, racialised gaze. Environmental concerns, similarly, indicate the intertwining of ecological issues with ethics in the engagement of the human with the non-human on-screen, whether specifically in terms of the animal other or the planet as a whole. The remembrance of histories of political violence, furthermore, indicate how an ethics of witnessing becomes vital to the on-screen remembrance of things past. In these various ways the sociopolitical is foregrounded throughout this collection.

We shall come to the genesis and development of the volume momentarily, but suffice it to say that this is a collection which began to take shape prior to the recent global pandemic, and which was therefore shaped by a tumultuous period of history. As the contributions indicate, we might consider this historical 'moment' to have been brought into focus by such recent events as: the election of Donald J. Trump as the President of the USA and the geopolitical turmoil of the UK vote to leave the European Union (both in 2016), the #MeToo movement (especially in 2017), the COVID-19 pandemic (declared as such in 2020) and resulting global recession, the renewed spotlight on Black Lives Matter after the murder by police of George Floyd (also 2020), the attack on the Capitol Building of the USA by a section of its own populace in January 2021, all alongside ever-increasing evidence of the climate crisis.

Admittedly, it might be argued that the preceding is a Westocentric range of indicators of momentous events. In fact, the roots of this historical 'moment' in which screen ethics finds such resonance are much deeper than these recent events may immediately suggest. As the three chapters which constitute the first part of this book indicate, in other parts of the world it might be, for example, the Cold War – which continues to decompose across parts of Asia (Kwon 2010) – that informs the present's emphasis on recognising the history of the excluded other in the ethical encounter. Reaching even further back than this is the world history of coloniality after 1492, that continues to shape relationships between those included and excluded sociopolitically in various parts of the world. To recognise the other ethically is to also recognise this history of global structural inequality which underpins so many recent sociopolitical developments.

Accordingly, the intertwinements of the sociopolitical with the ethical that are explored within this volume are at once context-specific and resonant with other examples, and thus are indicative of the global panorama of contemporary screen ethics. Whilst we cannot rack such an image into sharp focus with one volume of essays, it can be evoked by glimpsing the resonances which emerge when context-specific examples are explored, in spite of their very different locations worldwide.

Along with the sociopolitical, the second defining feature of this collection is that it addresses the proliferation of screen media which are now receiving scholarly attention. The emphasis remains on fiction film, including contributions focusing on 'art' (or 'festival' films) – such as *The Second Mother* (Anna Muylaert, 2015), *Nina Wu* (Midi Z, 2019), *Three Summers* (Sandra Kogut, 2019) – as well as popular genres (which range from Brazilian *chanchadas* [musical comedies] and *pornochanchadas* to Jordan Peele's Hollywood hits *Get Out* (2017) and *Us* (2019), to the contemporary Stephen Chow Chinese blockbuster rom-com *The Mermaid* (2016). This work is joined, however, by explorations of: short films (the Brazilian *Babás*), movies made directly for consumption on screening platforms which many may regard as being like television (i.e. Bong Joon-ho's *Okja* [2017] which is distributed on Netflix), various forms of documentary which circulate in different ways, including via festivals and/or the internet (*S21: The Khmer Rouge Killing Machine* [Rithy Panh, 2003], *Though I am Gone* [Jie Hu, 2006], *Dreams of a Life* [Carol Morley, 2011], *Housemaids* [Gabriel Mascaro, 2012], *The Look of Silence* [Joshua Oppenheimer, 2014]), a BBC television recording of Luisa Omelian's stand-up comedy (2017) now available on YouTube, the video installation *Vertigo Sea* by John Akomfrah (2015), Alejandro G. Iñárritu's virtual reality experience *Carne y arena* (2017), and different forms of digital media, from Google Earth to military drone footage. This proliferation is especially pertinent now that the interdisciplinary areas of film-philosophy increasingly turn to examine the screens it has inadvertently excluded. Once again, it is impossible to actualise the global diversity of such screen media in twenty-first century life. However, it is possible to at least incorporate a broader range of examples so that something of the scope of a more all-encompassing screen ethics can begin to be conceived.

Finally, we should address the fact that *Contemporary Screen Ethics* emerges during the move to decolonise knowledge (and by extension, the academy) which has gathered pace since at least the Rhodes Must Fall movement of 2015 (in the same year as #OscarsSoWhite). This brings into focus something of the contribution this volume makes to the continuing development of screen ethics, which is explored further below.

In addition to its intellectual engagement with directly related issues (especially decolonial feminism and perspectives on race), *Contemporary Screen Ethics* offers its own small contribution to the decolonisation of the academy in three ways. First, in the attention it has paid to inclusivity in its constitution of authors, who are based in eight countries across five continents (eight women, four men), and who include both early career and established scholars. Second, and in part a result of this array of authors, in its analysis of examples from around the world. For example, the anthology commences with a chapter on Brazilian cinema, whilst a particular emphasis on Asian examples soon emerges across the piece (including exploration of works emanating from China, Indonesia, South Korea, Taiwan and Thailand, whether nationally specific or international co-productions), alongside likely more well-known examples from the USA and Europe. The anthology includes analysis of several films directed by women – Carol Morley's *Dreams of a Life*, Anna Muylaert's *The Second Mother*, Sandra Kogut's *Three Summers* – and discussion of the on-screen performance of Black, Asian, and Latina women of colour. Third, the names of thinkers which have become commonplace in explorations of film-philosophy broadly speaking, if not cinematic ethics per se – such as Deleuze, Irigaray, Jameson, Kierkegaard, Rancière and Žižek – are joined by a range of different voices which might not typically be expected to 'speak' in such discussions, including: María Lugones, Françoise Vergès, Denise Ferreira da Silva, Kalpana Sheshadri-Crooks, Talila Milroy and José Esteban Muñoz, amongst others.

More broadly with respect to decolonisation, as the collection's subtitle and thematic parts indicate, this is a book which engages with the ethical ramifications of the structural inequality which shapes our contemporary world into the uneasy coexistence of Global North and South. However the origins of this contemporary moment are understood, its screen ethics focuses our attention on: the *Absences* of those excluded (whether this is the eradication of the victims of colonial or political violence who have since been written out of history, or the ongoing exclusion of certain sections of populations to ensure that others who have more perpetuate these same histories); and, the *Identities* of those whose inclusion depends greatly on how they are represented (for instance, the struggle for equality of visibility on the part of racialised bodies in settler colonist countries like the USA). These are the topics covered in Parts One and Two of the book, entitled 'Histories and Absences' and 'Bodies and Identities' respectively.

As important as this, perhaps, is the search for a sense of communal *Belonging* to the world as a planetary whole which is demanded of humanity by the current climate crisis: how to overcome the dichotomy of human/nature being the subject of screen ethical investigations into both video installations and genre movies; or again, how to cross the human/human separation of atomised lives under neoliberal globalisation which is explored in documentaries, each of which, in their own ways, confronts head-on the challenge of living in the Anthropocene/ Capitalocene. A world at once divided in the most apparently irretrievable of ways, must, nevertheless, seek to re-imagine itself inclusively if it is to avoid catastrophe. This quest for belonging requires, finally, *Looking Anew*. Whether this is in terms of what new digital technologies make visible about the world, or, through new ways of visualising racial difference which challenge existing constructions of a racialised gaze, or, again, new ways of understanding the gender and sexual violence which accompanies the construction of so many film and media images. These are the topics covered in Parts Three and Four of the book, entitled 'Love and Belonging' and 'Looking Anew' respectively. The complexities of this context, as it is encountered in myriad ways around the world, is the overarching subject of *Contemporary Screen Ethics*.

Genesis and Development

This collection developed over nearly a decade, its origins tracing back to two one-day conferences co-organised by David Martin-Jones and Robert Sinnerbrink at the University of Glasgow in 2013 and 2017 respectively. The first of these, 'Proliferating Ethical Encounters in Film and Media', contained the seeds of the volume's emphasis on a variety of screen media forms. The second, 'Cinematic Ethics and Globalization', brought into focus the need to explore this topic as one which is intertwined with the sociopolitical in various contexts internationally. These events included speakers who contributed pieces to this volume and were together envisaged as attempts to broaden the focus on film, ethics and philosophy to encompass the more global and political concerns which were central to important strands of film theory prominent during the 1990s and 2000s. It was at the latter event that Lucy Bolton joined the project, as we three together developed the proposal for the ongoing work. When we held these conferences, the possibility of 'film as philosophy' was still a topic of debate. There were lively exchanges and experiments that sought ways to explore how a productive encounter between film and philosophy could transform how we understand both film and philosophy. At the same time, there was increasing interest in ethics and film, from both 'Analytic' and 'Continental' philosophical perspectives, coupled with intense interest in the ethical dimensions of embodied spectators, the body, affect and increasing diversity in the kinds of films, traditions, genres and cultural contexts analysed from philosophical and ethical perspectives. Our idea was to bring together these developments and see how the exploration of cinematic ethics could be promoted and enhanced in philosophical, cultural and sociopolitical directions, taking existing debates further and linking up with similar trends within film theory and media studies. The underlying intuition was, and remains, that a broader, more diverse approach remains essential within the wider film-philosophy movement, with the nexus between ethics, the sociopolitical and various screen media still a key area to be explored.

In the years that followed this original idea underwent significant changes as the project developed. As is perhaps typical, one key reason for this was the shifting intellectual terrain. Far less common, however, was the second reason – the COVID-19 pandemic. First, the intellectual. Important shifts in the field have occurred over the past decade (see Sinnerbrink 2016, 2022). We could mention here that the turn to ethics broadly construed has coincided with – and contributed to – such developments as a renewed concern with identity politics, an increasing emphasis on diversity, on non-binary and trans identities, critiques of colonialism, of Eurocentrism, and the rise of critical race theory applied to film, alongside ecocritical concerns. This is to name only some of the most prominent ideas which have informed recent scholarship. During this time, questions of ethics and aesthetics have perhaps become more closely intertwined, alongside more political questions of class, race, identity and transnationality. Intersectional feminism, for example, has called for a response to issues of race and gender through a more matrix-like analysis, whilst, concurrently, developments in and widespread take up of digital technology necessitate increased attention to non-cinematic forms of visual experience.

The project's orientation was influenced by these broader intellectual concerns, recognising the importance of diversity and the contribution of contemporary ethico-political debates. At the same time, we thought it was important to keep the philosophical and ethical dimensions of these developments firmly in view: maintaining an attitude of questioning, of reflection, dialogue and experimentation, rather than dogmatic assertion or critical denunciation. We were also convinced that close film analyses and critical interpretation of cinematic aesthetics should remain paramount: a focus that has been characteristic of film-philosophy since its inception.

The second key influence on the project's development, towards it latter stages especially, was the COVID-19 pandemic. As is well known, not only did people suffer illness and bereavement, but working situations in academia, film production and every other industry were radically transformed. Geopolitical responses to and experiences of the COVID- 19 virus emerged as diverse and multifarious, and it became apparent that the pandemic would have a dramatic effect on the production, distribution, exhibition and consumption of the visual arts. In such a context, a scholarly collection pales in significance. Delays became inevitable, as authors faced huge rebalances to their work/life commitments, alongside all the other issues which came with the pandemic. Some original contributors left the project during or in the wake of the pandemic. New contributors came onboard, their inspiring works inevitably transforming the volume's shape once again. The collection's twin drivers – proliferating media, emphasising the sociopolitical – ensured that it had a chance of keeping track of (if not pace with) the rapidly evolving trends and modes of ethical experience which are engaged by various screen media, despite the changing context. Having thus 'survived' the pandemic, albeit in a transformed state, this collection addresses the contemporary stage of screen ethics, 'looking anew' by revisiting previous assumptions and relationships, expanding the range of media explored, and addressing wider international contextual diversity.

Cinematic/Screen Ethics

What, then, of the place of such a work in the interdisciplinary field of film-philosophy? The emergence of a body of work on film and ethics since the noughties indicates a clear consensus that film has an ethical potential for exploring moral issues, ethically charged situations, or moral 'thought experiments'. This has been taken up by film theorists and philosophers from a variety of philosophical perspectives (see Wartenberg 2007; Flory 2008; Mulhall 2008; Tersman 2009; Jones and Vice 2011; Shaw 2012; Choi and Frey 2014; Sinnerbrink 2016). Concurrently, scholars have elaborated the ways in which cinema can be read alongside philosophical approaches to ethics, or how certain filmmakers can be understood as engaging in ethics through film (Cooper 2006; Stadler 2008; Wheatley 2009; Downing and Saxton 2010; Sinnerbrink 2016, 2019; Bolton 2019; Martin-Jones 2019). Indeed, film-philosophy has become so engaged by the question of ethics and cinema that it can accurately be described as having undergone an ethical turn over the last fifteen years or so – reflecting upon cinema as a distinctive way of thinking through ethical concerns or even exploring the idea of cinema *as* ethics (see Stadler 2008; Downing and Saxton 2010; Jones and Vice 2011; Chaudhuri 2014; Choi and Frey 2014; Grønstad 2016; Sinnerbrink 2016; Raviv 2020).

This ethical turn in film theory/philosophy of film is an important development that enables the tradition of film theory concerned with politics and ideology to be reappropriated in new ways. It also broadens the reach of philosophical engagement with film beyond abstract questions of ontology and metaphysics as well as more technical and formal questions concerning epistemology and film aesthetics. Philosophers and film theorists are now finally giving the question of ethics and film due attention within aesthetics, philosophy of film, as well as film theory, although most approaches remain concerned with ethical themes or else applying philosophical ethical theories to cinema (drawing on Deleuze, Cavell or Levinas, for example). This field of exploration is now so vibrant and diverse that any three different scholars – such as the three editors of this volume – might all see it rather differently. Even so, whilst summarising the main trends and emphases, as well as the lacunas, is not a straightforward task, it is imperative to attempt such a summary.

One helpful way to summarise things is to map some of the ways in which cinema and ethics have been related. We can describe ethical approaches to cinema as focusing on one of three aspects of the relationship between film, spectator and context. The most familiar example is (1) ethics *in* cinema (focusing on narrative content including dramatic scenarios involving morally charged situations, conflicts, decisions, or actions). Many analyses of individual films will explore cinematic works in terms of their narrative content, moral thematics, or interplay between cinematic, dramatic, and moral-ethical concerns. The other influential approach, spanning both fiction and non-fiction film, concerns (2) the ethics (and politics) *of* cinematic representation (focusing on the ethical issues raised by elements of film production and/or audience reception, such as studies on the ethics of documentary representation concerning issues of consent or truthful depiction, or the ongoing debates over the effects of screen violence in narrative film and computer gaming). This can be broadened out into the cultural-ideological domain, which tackles (3) the ethics of cinema *as* a cultural medium expressing moral beliefs, social values, or ideological perspectives (such as feminist film analysis of gender representations, Marxist analyses of ideology, or critical theory analyses of race and ethnicity in popular cinema). To this we could add recent interest in ecocritical approaches to the question of cinema and the environment, the depiction of animals, ecological themes, and the question of the Anthropocene in relation to cinema.

What are the dominant philosophical ways of exploring cinema and ethics today? We can identify the following theoretical approaches, which also span the oft-overstated Continental philosophy/Analytic-cognitivist film theory divide. Since the retreat from so-called 'Grand Theory' (during the late 1990s and 2000s), the *Deleuzian* perspective has become highly influential in film theory and film-philosophy (see Rodowick 1997, 2010; Flaxman 2000, 2011; Rushton 2012, 2020; Del Rio 2012; Martin-Jones and Brown 2012; Pisters 2012; Rizzo 2012; Boljkovac 2013; Deamer 2016; Martin-Jones 2019, for representative texts). Deleuzian cinematic ethics has been championed by Rodowick in particular (n.d., 2010, 2014, 2015), who takes Deleuze's cinephilosophy as a predominantly ethical mode of thinking (cinema as exploring what Deleuze calls immanent 'modes of existence', as communicating thought, or giving us 'reasons to believe in this world' through new forms of movement- and time-image cinematic narration (Rodowick n.d.: 1; Deleuze 1989: 171–2). From a philosophical perspective, there is more attention being given to *Cavellian* film-philosophy (cinema as exploring scepticism, philosophy and the everyday, and moral perfectionism), which Cavell first introduced in the 1970s during the highpoint of so-called psychoanalytic-semiotic film theory (see Read and Goodenough 2005; Sinnerbrink 2014; Rugo 2016; Shaw 2019; Wheatley 2019; LaRocca 2020). Since the 2010s, *phenomenological and post-phenomenological film theory* (focusing on subjective and intersubjective experiences of affect, perception, emotion, embodiment, and how these relate to moral-ethical experience in cinema[1]) has become increasingly prominent, with numerous studies focusing on the ethical dimensions of cinematic affect and embodied spectator engagement – emphasising the intersecting axes of gender, race and historico-political context – with cinematic worlds (see Sobchack 1992, 2004; Shaviro 1993, 2010; Marks 2000, 2002; Barker 2009; Bolton 2009, 2019; Chamarette 2012; Yacavone 2015; Walton 2016; Ince 2017). Finally, *cognitivist film theory* has emerged as an alternative paradigm to theorising cinematic experience, focusing on emotional engagement, moral imagination, and the ethical evaluation of cinema (see Bordwell 1985, 1989; Carroll 1990, 1998, 2003, 2008; Currie 1995; Smith 1995, 2017; Tan 1995; Bordwell and Carroll 1996; Plantinga and G. Smith 1999; Plantinga 2009, 2018; Shimamura 2013; Nannicelli and Taberham 2014). Cognitivist film theories tend to adopt 'naturalistic' accounts of cognition to theorise our affective and emotional response to film, along with more reflective, higher-order cognition, which taken together provide an account of moral allegiance with character and broader ethical evaluation in response to narrative cinema.

With such distinct approaches already apparent, what is the significance of the ethical turn in recent film-philosophy? One response is to point out that cinema has always been concerned with ethics, or that moral concerns have always been brought to the study of cinema. Early film theorists, for example, were concerned with the ethical potential of cinema, either as an aesthetically powerful way of cultivating moral sensibilities or as a pernicious, morally corrupting form of mass distraction (see Sinnerbrink 2013). These ethical and moral concerns were displaced during the 1960s and 70s by a turn towards more explicitly political and ideological agendas, a tendency manifested by the rise of Lacanian-Althusserian 'psycho-semiotic' and feminist film theory. With the historical collapse of communism and decline of Marxism as a theoretical paradigm during the 1990s, a renewed focus on ethics – on questions of human rights, democracy, concern for the Other and our responsibilities towards nature and the environment – became a distinctive feature of many forms of social, cultural and political discourse. Within the academy, the reigning paradigm of film theory came under attack during the 1980s and 90s, being subjected, as Rodowick remarks, to 'a triple displacement – by history, science, and finally by philosophy' (2015: 6). Reports of the death of theory, however, are much exaggerated. At the same time, ethical questions concerning cinema became more prominent and continued to reverberate with the emergence of film-philosophy, most notably in, and as a result of, the work of Cavell and Deleuze, which ushered in the movement we now recognise as 'film-philosophy' (see Sinnerbrink 2011; Rodowick 2015; Elsaesser 2019).

Such a shift could also be discerned in contemporary cinema across the globe, which is rife with films dealing with ethical issues, moral problems or cultural-political concerns. Indeed, contemporary cinema is where many socially charged ethical problems and cultural-moral debates are most creatively explored; it is where cultures across the globe can find imaginative narrative ways to address, reflect upon, question and explore some of the most important moral-ethical and cultural-political issues of our times. This is evident in the rise of new ethically and politically engaged cinema, particularly within diverse cultural traditions and social contexts, amidst the dissemination of what is often loosely called world cinema, world cinemas, or a world of cinemas (see Martin-Jones 2011, 2019; Nagib 2011; Chaudhuri 2014). It is also evident in the rise of a plurality of documentary forms and styles, again part of the broad and diverse sweep of world cinemas (see Marcus and Kara 2016), some examples of which feature in this volume.

The idea of cinema as medium of ethical experience offers a way of understanding what cinema can do: its transformative potential to sharpen our moral perception, challenge our beliefs through experiential means, and thus enhance our understanding of moral-social complexity. In some cases, it can also provoke philosophical thinking through morally confronting or provocative forms of ethical experience conveyed and evoked through film. It can thereby bring together the three important aspects of the cinema-ethics relationship: ethical content in narrative cinema; the ethics of cinematic representation (from filmmaker and spectator perspectives); and the ethics of cinema as symptomatic of broader cultural, social and ideological concerns. We should also underline the *aesthetic dimension* of cinema – in particular the role of aesthetic form in intensifying our experience, refining and focusing our attention, and thus of conveying complexity of meaning through manifold means – as a way of *evoking ethical experience* and inviting critical reflection. This aesthetic dimension is an integral features of film studies, and, as noted earlier, has been vital to the interdisciplinary field of film-philosophy since its inception in the 1990s. In sum, the question of ethics in cinema, or of cinema as ethical, is not exhausted by narrative explorations of ethics, or questions of production and consumption, or by the ethics of spectatorship, or by the ideological-political dimensions of cinema. Rather, we should acknowledge how aesthetics and ethics are productively related: how aesthetic features of a film are articulated with each other, and how these together serve to communicate ethical meaning via aesthetic means.

What then, finally, of the contribution of *Contemporary Screen Ethics* to this field? The contributions in this volume illustrate how a concern with screen ethics, coupled with a sensitivity to cultural and historical contexts and dedicated attention to the aesthetic dimensions of individual works, can contribute to the broadening and diversification of ways of reflecting upon contemporary sociopolitical concerns Hence the advance to knowledge which our intervention offers is twofold: (1) to continue to reconsider and advance existing understandings of cinematic ethics (e.g. interrogating the world historical ramifications of the Deleuzian understanding of cinema's ability to rejuvenate a belief in this world); and (2) to integrate existing concerns in film studies and film-philosophy with the consideration of ethics (in particular around race, decolonisation, feminism, ecology), thereby advancing our understanding of such emerging ideas as an ethics of witnessing or an ethics of care in filmmaking. This advance to knowledge offered by the collection is achieved due to the twin drivers which propel it, the expansion of the consideration of screen ethics into various contexts internationally, and, of its various proliferating forms.

Shape of the Collection

The volume consists of four parts: 'Histories and Absences', 'Bodies and Identities', 'Love and Belonging' and 'Looking Anew'. Each part collates contributions that explore contemporary concerns and movements, whilst recognising that such specific case studies are situated in more expansive contexts (for example, that a chapter on the dynamics between humans and nature, in the context of the climate crisis, also opens out onto much broader concerns, such as love and belonging). This arrangement is thus intended to enable these essays, and indeed this whole volume, to be both productive at the 'micro' level, as well as evocative and generative at the 'macro' level.

The three contributions to Part One, 'Histories and Absences', all consider those typically excluded from, or marginalised within, the historical record. In Chapter 1, Alessandra Soares Brandão and Ramayana Lira de Sousa explore a topic which became extremely pertinent during the COVID-19 pandemic, that of the recognition, or lack of it, afforded to domestic labour. Soares Brandão and Lira de Sousa take a decolonising feminist approach to representations of the housemaid in films depicting the Big House – an architectural phenomenon synonymous with colonial plantations – in Brazilian cinema, from the 1940s and 1950s to the present. Their primary focus is films of the 2010s, including *Doméstica/Housemaids* (Gabriel Mascaro, 2013), *Que horas ela volta?/The Second Mother* (2015), and *Três Verões/Three Summers* (2019). Engaging with the philosophy of Jacques Rancière alongside thinkers like Françoise Vergès, María Lugones and Denise Ferreira da Silva, Soares Brandão and Lira de Sousa's chapter explores the 'invisibility' of the black woman housemaid in this cinematic heritage. Examining this figure at the intersection of gender and sexuality, the 'invisibility' which is perpetuated today is shown to have roots deep within the colonial history of Brazil, and colonial modernity more generally.

Chapters 2 and 3 examine documentaries from different parts of Asia which explore histories of political violence during the Cold War for which survivors and their descendants still seek justice. In Chapter 2, David Martin-Jones examines the Deleuzian conceptualisation of a cinematic ethics, which suggests the potential of films to restore a reason to believe in this world. Examining the Chinese documentary *Wo sui si qu /Though I Am Gone* (Hu Jie, 2006), Martin-Jones questions whether it is this world, or in fact its histories, which cinema may restore belief in. This is due to Deleuze's formulation of such an ethical potential for cinema with respect to the time-image, a cinematic figure found, precisely, throughout *Though I Am Gone*. Situating the political complexities of this particularly harrowing documentary about a murder which took place during the Cultural Revolution (1966–76) within a broader understanding of the cinemas of the world, a further question is explored: of the extent to which it is possible to understand the specificities of history which films frame from all around the world in their own particular ways, when representing the past. In Chapter 3, Robert Sinnerbrink explores the documentaries *The Look of Silence* (Joshua Oppenheimer, 2014) and *S21: The Khmer Rouge Killing Machine* (Rithy Panh, 2003), in terms of the ethical experiences they offer to viewers. Sinnerbrink draws out this cinematic ethics with a particular emphasis on the aesthetic strategies which each film uses to elicit and depict memories of violence and trauma. These complementary examples, focused on Cold War pasts marked by political violence in Indonesia and Kampuchea respectively, together illustrate the potential of cinema to provide a form of ethical witnessing: an ethics of solidarity aligned with a survivor's perspective in *The Look of Silence*, a performative release of bodily memory through re-enactment in *S21*.

Together these three initial contributions indicate the *Absences* which explorations of cinema and ethics are so often engaged in revealing. This is a paradoxical task which requires the uncovering of those marginalised and excluded from the official record of the past from the memories, physical traces, and recorded glimpses of their passing, and, indeed, the revelation of the structuring absences of their lives and deaths in the present-day perpetuation of the same systems which excluded them in the first place.

Part Two, 'Bodies and Identities', moves from the recognition demanded by those absented from the past – the emphasis of Part One – to the physical presence of bodies in the present. In Chapter 4, Tina Chanter commences by analysing the racial stereotyping which surrounded the women tennis stars Serena Williams and Naomi Osaka after the final of the US Open in 2018. By contrast, an ethico-political intervention in the circulation of stereotypes of this kind is then uncovered by Chanter, in a stand-up routine by UK comedian Luisa Omielan, *What Would Beyoncé Do?* Omelian's routine was recorded at the Edinburgh Fringe, before airing on the BBC, and, finally, circulating on the internet. It is found to offer a divergent racial imaginary through Omelian's identification with the lyrics and dance moves of the US pop star. Like Soares Brandão and Lira de Sousa in Chapter 1, as well as Lucy Bolton in Chapter 8,

Chanter's approach is intersectional, drawing in this case on such thinkers as Luce Irigaray, Kalpana Sheshadri-Crooks and José Esteban Muñoz to explore comedic performance as a form of ethico-political intervention in the otherwise habitual, (stereo)typical construction of difference. For her part, in Chapter 5, Mary Bloodsworth-Lugo analyses two films by black directors, *Sleight* (J. D. Dillard, 2017) and *Us* (Jordan Peele, 2019), as allegories of the political stakes surrounding race in Trump-era USA. These films illuminate how closely entwined are ethical and political considerations around race in such a context. These important films explore such tensions through the depictions of black bodies, which, more broadly, indicate the recognition, indeed the compassion, demanded by those whose more debased lives serve to prop up those more privileged. Taken together, these two chapters show how these films can engage with the ethical complexities concerning the *Identities* of those whose recognition depends on the politics of their representation. From those absented historically, in Part One, to those whose contemporary presence is a struggle for equal recognition, often against (stereo)type, in particular with regard to gendered and racialised bodies.

The second half of the book builds upon the preceding examinations of *Absences* and *Identities*. The first half established, through specific case studies, the global situation of structural inequality, evidenced in ways which illustrate at once deep historical roots in coloniality, more recent political structures lingering from the Cold War particular to late capitalism, and contemporary engagements with the continuation of widespread disparity. In Part Three, 'Love and Belonging', three chapters ask that we consider what it might mean to understand *Belonging* – both in terms of the planet which humanity resides upon, and, indeed, within globalised human society. This requires further depth to be added both to the previous examinations of history – to recognise histories like that of the Anthropocene, or, more expansively, of the planet itself – as well as development of our analyses of what screen media illustrate regarding the ethics required of our contemporary world. The emphasis on *Belonging* in Part Three, 'Love and Belonging', following on from *Absences* and *Identities* in Parts One and Two, thus begins the second half of the book's process of *Looking Anew* which continues in Part Four.

In Chapter 6, Jakob Nilsson considers how the video installation work of John Akomfrah, *Vertigo Sea* (2015), can be understood as an ethico-ecological response to the currently pressing challenge of realising our existence as part of a planetary whole. Drawing on Deleuze, along with Fredric Jameson, Nilsson teases out how Akomfrah's work assists those who encounter it in grasping their existence within a planetary whole. At once historical and yet also visionary, its montage works to foster an immersive experience which contrasts with a prevailing sense of alienation from nature felt by modern subjects (after Bruno Latour). Thus, this powerful example of screen media is shown to use a form of ethical planetary cartography to answer the urgent need for humans to better comprehend the inextricable ties between humanity and nature of the Anthropocene/Capitalocene which the environmental crisis brings into sharp focus. Accompanying Nilsson's ecological focus, in Chapter 7, Chelsea Birks examines two Asian popular genre movies of the mid-2010s, *The Mermaid* (Stephen Chow, 2016) and *Okja* (Bong-Joon-ho, 2017), which examine what it might mean to talk of love between the human and the non-human in this current age of globalised capitalism. In her exploration of the ethical decentering of humanity in these works of eco-cinema, Birks draws on the philosophical writings on love of Søren Kierkegaard (divine love) and Slavoj Žižek (the neighbour) to consider their visual reimagining of the Anthropocene/Capitalocene offered by the films. Such imaginings emerge in spite of the challenge – which the films themselves address – facing any serious attempt to address the climate crisis, due to the incessant demands of multi-national corporate capitalism for constant consumption of the Earth's dwindling resources.

Rounding off Part Three, Lucy Bolton's exploration of *Dreams of a Life* (Carol Morley, 2011) develops further our understanding of how screen ethics engages with *Belonging*, encouraging us to consider how we belong under global capitalism not only in terms of the planetary (the relationship, or love, between the human world and the natural world), but also the societal (the relationship, or again the love, between people in the human world). Bolton offers an intersectional consideration of Morley's documentary as demonstrating an ethics of care. This is developed in part through initial analysis of Morley's approach to the research and production of the film. As importantly, Bolton analyses what is seen on screen: through the editing and montage; the film's blending of fact and fictional recreations in its representation, or 'dream' of another person's life; and the memorable performance of Zawe Ashton as deceased dual-heritage Londoner, Joyce Vincent (a still of which adorns the cover of the book). This aesthetic analysis is positioned in relation to contemporary feminist ethics and is informed by the thinking of Olena Hankivsky and Talila Milroy. Bolton's contribution indicates how *Belonging*, in a global city like London, may require a more ethical form of interaction, perhaps understood as love, or care, between people living separate and separated lives.

Finally, in Part Four, 'Looking Anew', three contributions offer different ways of understanding what it might mean to look anew via screen ethics. The three examples consider: new technological means of looking; new ways of seeing what has been normalised onscreen through hierarchical alignment with the cinematic apparatus (here, depictions of race); and revelatory visions of what lies behind the onscreen image (in this case, sexual and gendered violence in the screen industries).

Nick Jones provides an expansive Chapter 9 which explores what the new digital visuality means in terms of screen ethics. By contrast to claims that virtual reality (VR) offers an immersive 'empathy machine' for its users, Jones analyses VR projects like *Carne y arena* (Alejandro G. Iñárritu, 2017), alongside their promotion and reception, to illustrate how VR's ethical potential is being overstated. VR may in fact only offer the illusion of such intimacy. This may prove a potentially appropriative act, privileging instead the invitation to marvel at how technology is seemingly able to take us close to the other for whom we should feel empathy (e.g. the refugee, in *Clouds Over Sidra* [Gabo Arora and Chris Milk, 2015]). The extent to which this is an ethical encounter facilitated by screen media is thus as debatable as it was in older debates about the role of television in a similar process. Like Nilsson previously in the volume, Jones is also interested in the cartographic nature of screen ethical concerns. In this instance, in how the digital gaze extends over an algorithmically-generated world to provide the VR-esque experience of Google Earth and Google Street View, as is deconstructed in such artworks as *Postcards from Google Earth* (Clement Valla, 2010–ongoing), *Anonymous Gods* (Marion Balac, 2014) and *The Nine Eyes of Google Street View* (Jon Rafman, 2010–ongoing). Finally, the proliferation of screen media continues in a concluding account of how existing accounts of VR's ethical potential to take the viewer closer to the other is thrown into stark relief by consideration of how unmanned drones used in warfare function similarly. Such a comparison illuminates the power asymmetries – reminiscent of colonial hierarchies of visual control – and resulting lack of empathy which may in fact surround the new digital visuality.

In Chapter 10, Berenike Jung explores how *Get Out* (Jordan Peele, 2017) meditates on the politics of the racialised gaze. The film is analysed as an intervention which seeks at once to expose the normative manner in which black bodies are depicted in US films (which is itself indicative of how cultural norms shape our field of vision), and, in so doing, to simultaneously offer viewers an opportunity for a formative viewing experience by the way of a cinematic ethics (as formulated by Sinnerbrink). Jung outlines how this influential film reconsiders tropes familiar to the horror genre in order to invert normative binaries which detract from the racial violence which underpins white dominance of the status quo. Thus *Get Out* offers audiences an opportunity to observe the potential terrorising effect of encountering wealthy white US suburbia when seen through the eyes of an outsider of African-American heritage. The collection closes with Jiaying Sim, in Chapter 11, examining the affective register through which *Nina Wu* (Midi Z, 2019) confronts viewers with the sexual and gendered violence of the media and film industries. Sim carefully contextualises the film in terms of the Taiwanese context of production, noting that director Midi Z states that *Nina Wu* is not a #MeToo film. Sim then considers *Nina Wu*'s ethical potential to viscerally prompt viewers to rethink rape culture in the specific context of the Asian media and screen industries, with dedicated focus on Taiwan. Sim's analysis of the film's aesthetics, its metacinematic reflexivity, demonstrates how the viewer is invited to look anew at the assemblages and affects which produce the sexual and gendered violence which not only appears on screen, but also underpins production.

This final section on 'Looking Anew', then, epitomises the dual aims of *Contemporary Screen Ethics*. To propel the examination of cinematic ethics beyond film towards a more inclusive exploration of a range of screen media (Jones), whilst emphasising the closeness between the ethical and the sociopolitical (the two case studies by Jung and Sim respectively) in analysis which is firmly embedded in context.

Throughout, screen ethics is shown to be adept at revealing the historically rooted *Absences* which structure contemporary inequality, and again, the struggle for acknowledgement of different *Identities*. It is also able to (re)conceive of human/non-human *Belonging* in the face of alarming climate change. But above all else, it encourages a more positive *Looking Anew* at life and the role we play in it, a feature highlighted by all the contributions to *Contemporary Screen Ethics*.

Note

1. A related strand concerns the Levinasian ethics of responsibility towards the 'alterity' of the Other as applied to our experience of cinema (see Cooper 2007; Girgus 2010; Raviv 2020).

References

Barker, Jennifer M. (2009), *The Tactile Eye: Touch and the Cinematic Experience*, Berkeley: University of California Press.
Boljkovac, N. (2013), *Untimely Affects: Gilles Deleuze and an Ethics of Cinema*, Edinburgh: Edinburgh University Press.
Bolton, L. (2009), *Film and Female Consciousness: Irigaray, Film and Thinking Women*, London: Palgrave Macmillan.
Bolton, L. (2019), *Contemporary Cinema and the Philosophy of Iris Murdoch*, Edinburgh: Edinburgh University Press.
Bordwell, D. (1985), *Narration in the Fiction Film*, Madison, WI: University of Wisconsin Press.
Bordwell, D. (1989), 'A case for cognitivism', *Iris*, 9: 11–40, <http://geocities.com/david_bordwell/caseforcog.1.htm> (accessed 14 May 2009).
Bordwell, David and Noël Carroll (eds) (1996), *Post-Theory: Reconstructing Film Studies*, Madison, WI: University of Wisconsin Press.
Carroll, N. (1990), *The Philosophy of Horror; or, the Paradoxes of the Heart*, London and New York: Routledge.
Carroll, N. (1998), *A Philosophy of Mass Art*, Oxford: Oxford University Press.
Carroll, N. (2003), *Engaging the Moving Image*, New Haven, CT and London: Yale University Press.

Carroll, N. (2008), *The Philosophy of Motion Pictures*, Malden, MA: Blackwell Publishing.

Chamarette, J. (2012), *Phenomenology and the Future of Film: Rethinking Subjectivity Beyond French Film*, Basingstoke: Palgrave Macmillan.

Chauduri, Shohini (2014), *Cinema of the Dark Side: Atrocity and the Ethics of Film Spectatorship*, Edinburgh: Edinburgh University Press.

Choi, Jinhee and Mattias Frey (eds) (2014), *Cine-Ethics: Ethical Dimensions of Film Theory, Practice, and Spectatorship*, Abingdon and New York: Routledge.

Cooper, Sarah (2006), *Selfless Cinema? Ethics and French Documentary*, London: Legenda.

Cooper, S. (2007), 'Introduction', in 'The Occluded Relation: Levinas and Film Studies', Special Issue of *Film-Philosophy*, 11: 2, i–vii.

Currie, G. (1995), *Image and Mind: Film, Philosophy, and Cognitive Science*, New York: Cambridge University Press.

Deamer, D. (2016), *Deleuze's* Cinema *Books: Three Introductions to the Taxonomy of Images*, Edinburgh: Edinburgh University Press.

Deleuze, Gilles (1989), *Cinema 2: The Time-Image*, trans. H. Tomlinson and R. Galatea, Minneapolis: University of Minnesota Press.

Del Rio, E. (2012), *Deleuze and the Cinemas of Performance: Powers of Affection*, Edinburgh: Edinburgh University Press.

Downing, Lisa and Libby Saxton (2010), *Film and Ethics: Foreclosed Encounters*, Abingdon and London: Routledge.

Elsaesser, T. (2019), *European Cinema and Continental Philosophy: Film as Thought Experiment*, New York and London: Bloomsbury Academic.

Flaxman, G. (ed.) (2000), *The Brain is the Screen: Deleuze and the Philosophy of Cinema*, Minneapolis, MN: University of Minnesota Press.

Flaxman, G. (2011), *Gilles Deleuze and the Fabulation of Philosophy*, Minneapolis, MN: University of Minnesota Press.

Flory, D. (2008), *Philosophy, Black Film, Film Noir*, University Park, PA: Penn State University Press.

Girgus, S. G. (2010), *Levinas and the Cinema of Redemption: Time, Ethics, and the Feminine*, New York: Columbia University Press.

Grønstad, Asbjørn (2016), *Film and the Ethical Imagination*, London: Palgrave Macmillan.

Ince, K. (2017), *The Body and the Screen: Female Subjectivities in Women's Cinema*, London and New York: Bloomsbury Academic.

Jones, Ward E. and Samantha Vice (eds) (2011), *Ethics at the Cinema*, Oxford: Oxford University Press.

Kwon, Heonik. (2010) *The Other Cold War*. New York: Columbia University Press.

LaRocca, D. (ed.) (2020), *The Thought of Stanley Cavell and Cinema: Turning Anew to the Ontology of Film a Half-Century after* The World Viewed, New York and London: Bloomsbury Academic.

Marcus, Daniel and Selmin Kara (eds) (2016), *Contemporary Documentary*, London and New York: Routledge.

Marks, Laura U. (2000), *The Skin of the Film: Intercultural Cinema, Embodiment, the Senses*, Durham, NC: Duke University Press.

Marks, Laura U. (2002), *Touch: Sensuous Theory and Multisensory Media*, Minneapolis, MN: University of Minnesota Press.
Martin-Jones, David (2011), *Deleuze and World Cinemas*, London and New York: Continuum.
Martin-Jones, David (2019), *Cinema against Doublethink: Ethical Encounters with the Lost Pasts of World History*, London and New York: Routledge.
Martin-Jones, David and Brown, William (eds) (2012), *Deleuze and Film*, Edinburgh: Edinburgh University Press.
Mulhall, Stephen (2008), *On Film*, 2nd edn, Abingdon and New York: Routledge.
Nagib, Lúcia (2011), *World Cinema and the Ethics of Realism*, New York and London: Continuum.
Nannicelli, Ted and Paul Taberham (eds) (2014), *Cognitive Media Theory*, London: Routledge.
Pisters, Patricia (2012), *The Neuro-Image: A Deleuzian Film-Philosophy of Digital Screen Culture*, Stanford, CA: Stanford University Press.
Plantinga, Carl (2009), *Moving Viewers: American Film and the Spectator's Experience*, Berkeley, CA: University of California Press.
Plantinga, Carl (2018), *Screen Stories: Emotion and the Ethics of Engagement*, Oxford: Oxford University Press.
Plantinga, Carl and Greg M. Smith (eds) (1999), *Passionate Views: Film, Cognition, and Emotion*, Baltimore, MD: Johns Hopkins University Press.
Raviv, Orna (2020), *Ethics of Cinematic Experience: Screens of Alterity*, London: Routledge.
Read, Rupert and Jerry Goodenough (eds) (2005), *Film as Philosophy: Essays on Cinema after Wittgenstein and Cavell*, Basingstoke and New York: Palgrave Macmillan.
Rizzo, Teresa (2012), *Deleuze and Film: A Feminist Introduction*, London and New York: Bloomsbury.
Rodowick, David N. (1997), *Gilles Deleuze's Time Machine*, Durham, NC and London: Duke University Press.
Rodowick, David N. (ed.) (2010), *Afterimages of Gilles Deleuze's Film Philosophy*, Minneapolis, MN: University of Minnesota Press.
Rodowick, David N. (2014), *An Elegy for Theory*, Cambridge, MA and London: Harvard University Press.
Rodowick, David N. (2015), *Philosophy's Artful Conversation*, Cambridge, MA and London: Harvard University Press.
Rodowick, David N. (n.d.), 'Ethics in film philosophy (Cavell, Deleuze, Levinas)', 1–21, <www.academia.edu/36412056/Ethics_in_film_philosophy_Cavell_Deleuze_Levinas_> (accessed 5 August 2019).
Rugo, Daniele (2016), *Philosophy and the Patience of Film in Cavell and Nancy*, London: Palgrave Macmillan.
Rushton, Richard (2012), *Cinema After Deleuze*, London: Bloomsbury Publishing.
Rushton, Richard (2020), *Deleuze and Lola Montès*, London: Bloomsbury Publishing.
Shaviro, Steven (1993), *The Cinematic Body*, Minneapolis, MN: University of Minnesota Press.
Shaviro, S. (2010), *Post-Cinematic Affect*, Winchester: Zero Books.

Shaw, Dan (2012), *Morality at the Movies: Reading Ethics through Film*, London and New York: Continuum.
Shaw, D. (2019), *Stanley Cavell and the Magic of Hollywood Films*, Edinburgh: Edinburgh University Press.
Shimamura, A. P. (ed.) (2013), *Psychocinematics: Exploring Cognition at the Movies*, Oxford: Oxford University Press.
Sinnerbrink, Robert (2011), 'Re-enfranchising film: towards a romantic film-philosophy', in H. Carel and G. Tuck (eds), *New Takes in Film-Philosophy*, London: Palgrave Macmillan, pp. 25–47.
Sinnerbrink, Robert (2013), 'Early film-philosophy: a dialectical fable', *Screening the Past, Special Dossier: Thinking Cinematically*, 38, <http://www.screeningthepast.com/2013/12/early-film-philosophy-a-dialectical-fable/>.
Sinnerbrink, Robert (ed.) (2014), Special Issue, 'On Stanley Cavell', *Film-Philosophy*, 18.
Sinnerbrink, Robert (2016), *Cinematic Ethics: Exploring Ethical Experience through Film*, Abingdon and New York: Routledge.
Sinnerbrink, Robert (2019), *Terrence Malick: Filmmaker and Philosopher*, London and New York: Bloomsbury Academic.
Sinnerbrink, Robert (2022), *New Philosophies of Film: An Introduction to Cinema as a Way of Thinking*, London and New York: Bloomsbury Academic.
Smith, Murray (1995), *Engaging Characters: Fiction, Emotion, and the Cinema*, Oxford: Oxford University Press.
Smith, Murray (2017), *Film, Art, and the Third Culture: A Naturalized Aesthetics of Film*, Oxford: Oxford University Press.
Sobchack, Vivian (1992), *The Address of the Eye: A Phenomenology of Film Experience*, Princeton: Princeton University Press.
Sobchack, Vivian (2004), *Carnal Thoughts: Embodiment and Moving Image Culture*, Berkeley: University of California Press.
Stadler, Jane (2008), *Pulling Focus: Intersubjective Experience, Narrative Film, and Ethics*, New York and London: Continuum.
Tan, Ed S. (1995), *Emotion and the Structure of Narrative Film: Cinema as an Emotion Machine*, Marwah, NJ: Lawrence Erlbaum Associates, Inc.
Tersman, Folke (2009), 'Ethics', in Paisley Livingston and Carl Plantinga (eds), *The Routledge Companion to Philosophy and Film*, London and New York: Routledge, pp. 111–20.
Walton, Saige (2016), *Cinema's Baroque Flesh: Film, Phenomenology and the Art of Entanglement*, Amsterdam: University of Amsterdam Press.
Wartenberg, Thomas. E. (2007), *Thinking on Screen: Film as Philosophy*, Abingdon and New York: Routledge.
Wheatley, Catherine (2009), *Michael Haneke's Cinema: The Ethic of the Image*, New York and Oxford: Berghahn Books.
Wheatley, Catherine (2019), *Stanley Cavell and Film: Scepticism and Self-Reliance at the Cinema*, London: Bloomsbury.
Yacavone, Daniel (2015), *Film Worlds: A Philosophical Aesthetics of Cinema*, New York: Columbia University Press.

PART ONE

HISTORIES AND ABSENCES

1. DOMESTIC WORK, GENDER, RACE, CLASS AND THE ETHICAL PARADOX OF THE BIG HOUSE IN BRAZILIAN CINEMA

Alessandra Soares Brandão and Ramayana Lira de Sousa[1]

In the foreword to the Brazilian edition of her book *A Decolonial Feminism*, published during the COVID-19 pandemic in 2020, Françoise Vergès observes that domestic labour, like care work and cleaning jobs in general, are a corollary of colonialism and slavery. At the same time that they are necessary and indispensable for a 'racial neoliberal capitalism', these jobs – and thus the people who perform them, mostly racialised women – must remain invisible (2020: 17). In fact, according to Vergès, slavery has produced superfluous lives, and the paradox of the economy of the superfluous lives lies in the fact that black women are both dispensable and intrinsically necessary in capitalist societies; they are both needed and made invisible/ostracised. Vergès thus calls for a decolonial feminism that might unveil such disparities and contradictions in Western societies and contribute to the historical struggles of the underprivileged fighting for their right to exist. Race and the colonial legacy become, under Vergès's scrutiny, essential terms for the understanding of domestic work. Race and coloniality,[2] thus, intersect with gender and class in the construction of the social position and the imagery of domestic work.

It is precisely the interwoven relationship between Brazil's colonial past and how slavery has helped shape systemic racism, ethnocentrism, sexism and classism – and has developed as informal work in modern society – that informs our reading of the figure of the housemaid in contemporary Brazilian cinema. We point out the coloniality of power[3] embedded in the employer/housemaid relationship in modern Brazil that constitutes what we will define as the ethical paradox of the Big House: the denial of relationality, that is, the suggestion that employers and housemaids exist autonomously from each other. This denial, consequently, also encompasses the relation between coloniality and modernity as well as the intersection of gender and sexuality that constitutes the colonial/modern gender system, as proposed by María Lugones (2007; 2010). From the employer's point of view, the Big House includes practices of erasure and denies agency and subjectivity at the same time that it has naturalised submission and hierarchical relations to the point that the housemaid can be often treated as property that can be disposed of and replaced, and even sexually harassed. Following Vergès and Lugones, we argue that the depiction of the domestic worker in Brazilian cinema gives a twofold response to the ethical problem created by the historical legacy of the Big House: on the one hand, focusing on the permanence of the colonial (un)gendering processes,[4] films might reproduce the notion that a white/European femininity is private, delicate, passive, while women of colour are dehumanised exactly for the absence of such traits; on the other hand, a few recent films can be seen as works of resistance to this legacy, even if in rather ambiguous terms.

We argue that the paradox at the root of the ethics of the Big House is that it commands the forms of appearance and disappearance of the figure of the housemaid in order to regulate relationality and thereby manage the distribution of the sensible. The idea of the distribution of the sensible is developed by Jacques Rancière (2004) both as a change in the perception of the in/visible and as a political reordering of exclusion/inclusion which might lead to the formulation of a new apparatus, regime or device. Rancière argues that 'Politics revolves around what is seen and what can be said about it, around who has the ability to see and the talent to speak, around the properties of spaces and the possibilities of time' (2004: 13). In this chapter we will discuss how the racial/colonial/heteropatriarchal apparatus materialised in the architectural structure of the Big House and the slave quarters, which spans centuries and symbolically extends into contemporary relations as a mechanism for maintaining the domination of the elites over the working class and the domestic space, is examined in Brazilian cinema.

We examine in particular the ways in which contemporary Brazilian cinema deals with the dialectics of the housemaid's in/visibility as a remnant of the gender, race and class problematic that was established by the processes of colonisation, and which still resonates in the present. As an echo of the past that extends into the present, carrying ghosts of a historically unequal relationship, the image of the housemaid develops in ways which range from indifference to centrality: from laughter and the construction of stereotypes for comic relief, starting in mid-twentieth century, to a more sensitive expression of the housemaid's subjectivity as a marginal existence ruled by subordination, a perspective that will only be reached with more maturity in the second decade of the twenty-first century. While it is true that by the early 2010s 'the drama of domestic servitude had already established itself as a favorite genre in Brazilian art cinema' (Nagib 2017: 354), in films such as *O Som ao Redor*/*Neighbouring Sounds* (Kleber Mendonça, 2012) and *Aquarius* (Kleber Mendonça, 2016), the dialectics of in/visibility are hampered by the fact that the characters are marginal to the narrative. Instead, we focus on recent productions where the housemaid's centrality allows for a reading that highlights the characters' agency exactly because they reflexively bring to the fore historical injustices and inequality, tackling the colonial wound that perseveres in our society and, thus, exposing the ethical pitfalls of the Big House.

The Big House and the Housemaid as an Object of Laughter

Nelson Maldonado-Torres, when commenting on Frantz Fanon's *Black Skin, White Masks*, reminds us that 'in the colonial context what happens at the level of the private and the intimate is fundamentally linked to social structures and to colonial cultural formations and forms of value' (2008: 126). Domestic work, located in the liminal space between the public and the private spheres, still shapes social and architectonic spaces and conserves the othering of women (especially women of colour). Hence, at the intersection of questions of gender, race, class, spatiality and affects, the ethical problem of the Big House, as presented in Brazilian cinema, delineates broader cultural, social and ideological issues. Indeed, the Big House is a spatial element that is crystallised in social relations in Brazil. As discussed by Brazilian anthropologist and sociologist Gilberto Freyre (1986: xvi), the Big House (*Casa Grande*) and its counterpoint, the slave quarters (*Senzala*), 'suggest the antagonism and social distance between masters and slaves, whites and blacks, Europeans and Africans' (1986: xvi). The home of the plantation's owners, the Big House accumulated several functions: fortress, bank, cemetery, school (Freyre 1986: xxxiii). It was also the centre of Brazilian patriarchalism, a symbol of male European dominance. The Big House is a paradigm of how social relations are materialised in architecture and, although absent from contemporary urban spaces (chock-full of vertical condos and skyscrapers), it still remains as an organising principle for spatiality, subjectivity and alterity in Brazilian culture. Brazilian architect Guilherme Wisnik argues that Brazilian condominiums are stacks of miniaturised colonial mansions, vertically reproducing the patriarchal family structure (2006). Wisnik compares early modern architecture in Europe, in which the bourgeois manor, dependent on the abundant work of servants, is replaced by compact spaces (thus eliminating the need of servants), with current trends in Brazil, where increasingly smaller apartments tend to compartmentalise their spaces while maintaining an (almost) uninhabitable counterpart to the slave quarters (the 'housemaid's room'[5]) next to the kitchen, properly isolated from the areas of socialisation.

In a social–economic context where the housemaid is necessary but also made invisible, as suggested by Vergès (2020), it comes as no surprise that Brazilian cinema has not taken the housemaid seriously until very recently, as two historical examples can briefly illuminate. The housemaid first becomes a character to be noticed by the audience in Brazilian cinema in the form of a caricature in comedy films or *chanchadas*[6] of the 1940s and 1950s, such as *O Petróleo é nosso* (Watson Macedo, 1954), *O Camelô da Rua Larga* (Eurides Ramos, 1958), and *Cala a boca, Etelvina* (Eurides Ramos and Hélio Barrozo Netto, 1959), to name just a few.

Unable to deal with the vexed question of the housemaid in Brazilian culture, cinema developed a strategy to present them more as a laughable type, thus avoiding tackling the sensitive issue of national identity and its economic and social issues. By assimilating the housemaid into the humour of the scene, such films offer, instead, an indifferent attitude toward her subaltern position, naturalised by laughter. These comedies create a type, a stigma that is widely accepted by the audience because it escapes the complexity of socio-economic implications at the same time that it avoids the racial problematic as the maids are played by white female comedians. In other words, in the realm of representation, the domestic worker reflects her paradoxical existence in the limbo of capitalism: she is at the same time necessary, as an object of laughter, and invisible, as a form of life that is situated at the margins. Comicality emerges as a symptom of the denial of reality, of the gender, race and class oppressions that define the employer–housemaid relationship. Such erasure is a trace of the strategies established during colonial times, as Grada Kilomba argues, and persists well into the present: 'denial is used to maintain and legitimate violent structures of racial exclusion' (2010: 18).

The stereotypes reinforced in the *chanchadas* are further explored in *pornochanchada* in the figure of the hypersexualised housemaid who threatens the integrity of the traditional family. The *pornochanchada* was another popular genre in Brazilian cinema, comedies produced from the late 1960s to the early 1980s with strong sexual overtones. The term is derived from *chanchadas* (the popular musical comedies of the 1940s to 1960s), with the added prefix *porno* to indicate sexual content. The prefix, however, may be misleading, because only a small part of the *pornochanchadas* was overtly pornographic. The whitewashing of the housemaids as they were portrayed in the *chanchadas* is replaced, in the *pornochanchadas*, by the hypersexualised and racialised body. As in the *chanchadas*, laughter both foregrounds and buffers the severity of the social conflicts concerning domestic work. A good example of the way the image of the housemaid was hypersexualised by the *pornochanchadas* is *Como É Boa Nossa Empregada* (Victor di Mello and Ismar Porto, 1973). The film is divided into three segments where the male protagonist is invariably a young man, the son in a white middle- or upper-class family, who harasses the housemaids. This plot reverberates the narratives of sexual initiation of the young male colonisers with enslaved women in colonial times, reinforcing the continuity between the figure of the slave and the housemaid.

Thus, such films illustrate, domestic work predominantly carried out by women reflects, in the public sphere, the subjection of women to the domestic, familial, private space, in which the housemaid, as a kind of extension of the (house)wife, is, on the one hand, hypersexualised, and, on the other hand, takes on a maternal role to her employer's children. This is as discussed by Lélia González (1984), who notes that *mulata* (the mulatto woman) and *doméstica* (housemaid) are attributions of the same subject, the black woman (1984: 228). Gilberto Freyre cites a colonial maxim that evinces the degree of sexualisation of the *mulata*: 'White woman for marriage, mulatto woman for f—, Negro woman for work' (1986: 13). The *mulata* is often praised in Brazilian popular culture, mainly during *carnaval*, for her seductiveness. However, as González puts it, 'the other side of the deification during *carnaval* occurs in this woman's everyday life, in the moment she is transfigured into the housemaid. That's where the culpability caused by her deification is exerted with strong traces of aggressiveness' (1984: 228). The housemaid, for González, is also indirectly linked to the *mucama*, the slave responsible for domestic work and for raising the coloniser's children. In Gonzáles's words:

> As for the housemaid, she is nothing more than the allowed *mucama*, provider of goods and services, that is, the pack mule that carries his family and that of others on her back. Hence, it is the opposite of exaltation; because it is in everyday life. (1984: 230)

According to González, if, on the one hand, black women's sexuality is explored in the figure of the *mulata*, the mixed-race woman object of the coloniser's desire and exalted in many expressions of Brazilian culture, on the other hand, the *mucama* is made invisible for playing indispensable roles in society, including the maternal figure. In this sense, González argues that the care of children, performed by the *mucamas* (and, later, by the housemaids and nannies), needed to be made invisible, so that the figure of the white woman as a mother is not problematised. She says:

> The white woman, the so-called legitimate wife, is precisely the other who, impossible as it may seem, only serves to give birth to the master's children. She does not exercise the maternal function. Therefore, the 'black mother' is the mother. (1984: 235)

Challenging the Figure of the 'Black Mother'

The short film *Babás* (*Nannies*, 2010), directed by Consuelo Lins, helps us think about the *mucama* in relation to the nanny employed by contemporary middle and upper classes. In *Babás* Lins uses archival photographs and videos as well as historical documents to reflect on her own experience as a white middle-class woman who was raised by nannies, and as a mother who often had to resort to employing housemaids. Lins also connects her present and past to Brazilian history, tracing a line from the work of *mucamas* in colonial times to the nannies of twenty-first century Brazil. Indeed, the very word in Portuguese used to designate nannies, *babás*, is of African origin. The film begins with a photograph taken in Recife in 1860 which shows a well-dressed white boy leaning on his black nurse with 'affection and intimacy', as described by the voice-over narration. The film's narration, though written in the first person, is delivered not by Lins, but by Flávia Castro, another Brazilian documentary filmmaker. Over the image of the white boy and his black nanny the voice-over says: 'When I saw this photo for the first time I thought that if one day I was to make a film about nannies it would start with this image.' Indeed, Castro's voice is laden with affect as her delivery, intonation and pauses create modulations that work alongside the more sociological rhetoric of the film to connect the personal and the political, subjectivity and alterity. It carries with it some of the boy's 'affection and intimacy' towards his nurse. Still, the choice for a voice-over narration of a first-person account performed by another filmmaker imposes a certain distance that disturbs this intimacy. Castro's voice, thus, performs a forged alterity, detached from Lins's private experience, but at the same time aligned to it in terms of class and race through the filmic medium.

Following this archival image, *Babás* shows present-day nannies in Rio de Janeiro, pushing strollers and playing with the children at the beach. They are invariably dressed in white. After that, we are shown a line of five women wearing regular clothes and we hear the narrator naming them: Vera Lúcia, Denise, Vera, Creusa and Andreia. A cut then presents these women in the same line-up, but now wearing white t-shirts. The film suggests that the image of the nanny, in the twenty-first century, carries with it centuries of oppression of black women in Brazil. It is given to us, therefore, as an image of the past embedded in the present. The white uniform, which prevents the nanny from expressing herself culturally and subjectively through her clothes, both denies her existence as a subject and communicates cleanliness, discretion, conformity, in addition to alluding to the sanitisation of race so that the nanny can be accepted to live with the white family. The same colour was worn by the *mucamas* from the past. It is necessary, first of all, to remove any cultural/racial mark, any signs of excesses and luxuries, to reconfigure the nanny in her place of invisibility inside the home, in proximity to the family.

But Lins also tries to make amends for the depersonalisation of the white uniform by giving voice to the five women and talking about their roles in her life. She shows each of them in medium shots and close-ups, disconnecting them from the line and emphasising their singularities expressed in their individual faces. Nevertheless, their stories are told through Lins's perspective, from her experience as an employer, which eventually reduces the women's role to that of the nannies who look after her family's children. The narrator expresses her discomfort with the situation when she tells Denise's story. Denise has looked after Joaquim, Lins's son, for twelve years. When he was three years old, Eduarda, Denise's daughter, was four. The voice-over says:

> From Monday to Saturday [Denise] was away from her daughter, who was being looked after by her grandmother. I couldn't fathom having a job that made me stay away from my son for 6 days. I preferred not to think about her situation at the time. It became increasingly discomforting for me.

The film seems to be confronting the director's privileges while acknowledging how her own interest in the production of home movies and family photographs rendered Denise almost invisible. We see Denise ironing clothes and feel her awkwardness at realising she is being filmed by Lins and, more importantly, we watch a scene where baby Joaquim is being taught to dance and Denise is kept at the margins of the shot. The narrator expresses her realisation that she filmed her son but produced few images of the woman 'who was by his side all those years'. In this particular shot, the camera follows Joaquim in his uncoordinated dance while Denise observes the boy. The editing again connects the personal archive with a broader history by introducing scenes from a 1920 movie that shows a little girl learning to dance the Charleston with her (black) nanny by her side. Lins uses this association to reflect upon the lack of images of nannies in the public archives. She comments that nannies are rarely present in movies and when they do appear it is because they are accompanying a white family's children.

Throughout the film, we have many candid shots of nannies and the children interacting. It is clear that Lins chose to emphasise tenderness and patience in these moments. Tenderness and patience that could easily be read as maternal gestures, but could also reveal an effort to attenuate the complex and sensitive class and race domination that the film exposes. Therefore, it can be argued that the way the nannies are addressed is akin to what Donna M. Goldstein calls ambiguous affection:

> Many middle- and upper-class Brazilians talk about their domestic workers with a mixture of love and appreciation. They express familial like affections or a fondness for that special domestic worker who lived with their family for many years and devoted her life to serving the family, or the nanny they had as a child, who pampered them in special ways, such as by cooking their favorite foods or comforting them in times of sorrow. (Goldstein 2003: 85)

Hence, familial bonds are commonly extended to nannies and housemaids throughout the years, as if they were a member of the family. In such cases, the conjunction 'as if' establishes a false belonging, marked by difference, as in the case of the 'black mother', a term that designates an extended motherhood determined by racial difference. The 'black mother' is always the 'other', the outsider from the natural order of the white family. The ethical challenge that the expression 'as if' poses is that of a specific kind of misrecognition: under the pretence of acknowledging the status of personhood for the 'black mother' based on a lineage, the expression (and the social practices) denies the status of a full partnership society and prevents the nannies and housemaids from fully participating as peers in social life (Fraser 1997: 280).

Indeed, one of the nannies interviewed in the film is an older black woman who recalls being called the 'black mother'. Her testimony reveals the permanence of the figure of the *mucama* as described by Lélia Gonzáles; after all, only a few of the nannies shown in *Babás* are not women of colour, which suggests that Gonzáles's assessment is still valid. The 'black mother' is also a strong reminder of how housework and caregiving in Brazil confound the borders between the public and private spheres. The nanny, when seen as the 'black mother', is considered almost as a part of the family. Almost. At the borders of the frame in Lins's film, she is neither totally inside familial relations nor completely excluded from them. She inhabits the 'housemaid's room', a liminal space that is simultaneously located inside and outside the home, in the in-betweenness of in/visibility. For the bourgeois family, displays of affection work to conceal this liminality, as if, by acknowledging the 'black motherhood', they could erase the fact the true nature of the relationship: paid labour. Most importantly, affection works as an emotional bonding that disguises the economic abyss which separates these women, a form of involuntary compensation for one woman's success at the expense of the other's 'conformed' subalternity. Affect, after all, 'can be an element in the exploitation of domestic work', as Debora Diniz concludes (Instagram photo, March 2022). Lins's film exposes this wound, and in this gesture of exposure rests its ethical commitment.

Domestic Work and Affects

It is also from the affective perspective of this relationship between employers and housemaids that the film *Doméstica* (Gabriel Mascaro, 2013) presents the view of seven teenagers from different regions of the country in conversation with the housemaids with whom they have lived since childhood. The film's premise is simple: Mascaro handed over the camera to the teenagers to record the interviews, which were subsequently edited by the film's team, resulting in an aesthetics that, as suggested by Mariana Souto (2012: 71), resembles home movies. Because the preferred point of view is that of the families the housemaids work for, Mascaro's film emphasises the power imbalance between classes and, often but now always, race. The camerawork employed by the amateur teenage cinematographers varies from an observational attitude (a fixed camera that captures the housemaid's daily routines) to a more intrusive and inquisitive posture (daily close-ups during interviews) and it frequently causes discomfort in the people being filmed. The final editing oscillates between focusing on the housemaids themselves and giving more space for the employers, mostly women for whom the housemaid's work is essential for their own professional careers. The combination of footage produced by non-professional operators, the interviews and personal narratives and Mascaro's editing, while accentuating the intimacy of personal relations, reveals the othering of the housemaids, kept in the liminal space between public and private spheres in order to pacify the social gaps, racial tensions and gender inequalities that mark the way Brazilian society organises domestic work.

As in *Babás*, it is common for the employers in *Doméstica* to refer to their housemaids 'as if they were family'. In a testimony laden with affection, one of the young women, Juana, says about Lena, the housemaid: 'we usually say that Lena lives here, helps at home, is like family', only to casually announce afterwards that Lena's room is in the back of the house. Lena is the continuity of the colonial system in the present. The boss and Juana's mother, Lucia, explains: 'Lena's parents always lived in our smallholding, you know, our farm, there with my parents. There was Lena and there was another person also related to another worker from the farm.' The power asymmetry in rural spaces, itself forged in the colonial past, is thus preserved in the urban reality of the housekeeper's work, exposing the social gap between employers and housemaids and their distinct trajectories. Another clear example of this difference is given by the relationship between Lucimar, a black housemaid from Rio de Janeiro, and her white employer, Fernanda, of whom she was a childhood 'friend'. 'My great-grandmother's housekeeper's daughter, [. . .] I've known Lucimar all my life', Fernanda declares. But, at fourteen, Lucimar came from the countryside to be employed by her 'friend', to fulfil her role in the Brazilian social structure characterised by violent racial difference. 'But at the beginning it was difficult, you know, because I had to impose myself as a boss and she is Lucimar, my old friend', Fernanda goes on, revealing the historical and social traps that make her reorganise her affections in the grand chain of gender and class roles that both she and Lucimar have to play.[7]

The command of the *mise-en-scène* in *Doméstica* replicates the disproportion of power, since those who benefit the most from the housemaids' work have control both over the camera and over the workers. Neto, a teenager from the north of Brazil, for example, films three of the housemaids while they are having a meal. Initially, the three women are visibly uncomfortable with being filmed until Neto tells them to start talking. They do so, although we are never really sure if the stilted conversation that ensues is something that the housemaids would be doing had the camera not been there. Furthermore, the camerawork is an allegory of this complicated mesh of affects, for throughout the film it both interweaves the characters behind and in front of the camera and works as a mediation that separates them. The camera takes part in the production of affects as many shots are clearly intended as a way to get closer without actually touching them, with a plethora of zoom ins and close-ups of faces and hands. It is as if the teenagers, by operating the camera, could, possibly for the first time, see those hand and those faces as pure hands and faces and not the socially marked countenances to which they had grown accustomed. However, such moments of affect are juxtaposed – sometimes synchronously – with verbal narratives of condescension and attempts at erasing the load of affective labour that the housemaids have to carry. As Encarnación Gutiérrez-Rodríguez reminds us, both employer and housemaids

> are affected by this labor in similar but also different ways, at the same time that this labor is textured by their affects. The vital character of this labor as living labor is sustained by the affects produced and absorbed within it. (2010: 2)

The way the teenagers film their housemaids, thus, brings to the fore the survival in the present of past colonial experiences. The 'pure' affect of close-ups cannot be separated from these residues of meaning. Affects are

> haunted by past intensities, not always spelled out and conceived in the present. Immediate expressions and transmissions of affects may indeed revive repressed sensations, experiences of pain or joy. Although not explicitly expressed as such, they are temporal and spatial constellations of certain times, intricately impressed in legacies of the past and itineraries of the present/future. (Gutiérrez-Rodríguez 2020: 4)

What is at stake here is the realisation that domestic work involves more than tasks such as cleaning, washing and sweeping: it concerns affects and subjects. And, as argued by Goldstein (2003), such affects are ambiguous, as exemplified by the spatial distribution within the homes, where the 'room in the back' occupied by the housemaid, is the most remarkable figuration of this ambiguity. Brazilian cinema, nonetheless, has also created narratives that seem to counter this dominant mode, albeit in still rather ambiguous ways, resulting in varying strategies and results. To start with, the recent films we discuss below address the problem directly, showing housemaids as protagonists, and, more importantly, they tackle class issues in a much more open way. Generally speaking, the first two decades of the twenty-first century are marked by an increasing awareness of the ethical issues raised by the persistence of the elements of the

Big House we have discussed above. In what follows we bring to light how these films reconfigure social relations and put into question the othering of the maid.

Resisting the Big House

In *Que horas ela volta?/The Second Mother* (2015), Val (Regina Casé) is a housemaid of a wealthy family in São Paulo. In addition to the household chores of cleaning and cooking, she also plays the role of surrogate mother – a projection of the *mucama*, as discussed above – to the family's spoiled teenage son. Val has left her own daughter behind in north-eastern Brazil, a region that is a source of a cheap labour for more industrially developed regions such as São Paulo. Years after being left by her mother, Val's daughter Jéssica (Camila Márdila), now a teenager, arrives in São Paulo to spend a few days with Val and announces that she will take the entrance exam for the School of Architecture and Urbanism (FAU) of the University of São Paulo (USP). USP is one of the most prestigious universities in Latin America, and a place of difficult access for the unprivileged classes. The news surprises Val's employers, due to the girl's boldness in aiming at being accepted at FAU and due to the spontaneity with which Jéssica announces it, making it seem a natural consequence of her trajectory as a student. The film clearly sets Jéssica's position – defiant, independent, enlightened and self-assured – against the previous logic of dependence that immobilises Val in the colonialist entanglements of the Brazilian upper-class family.

Jéssica destabilises the initial order of the house, which is an environment that establishes an abysmal dynamic between Val and her employers. Her presence compresses the spaces of in/visibility, functioning as a mechanism that disorganises the employers' comfort zone – which renders Val invisible under the pretence of belonging to the family. Jéssica's arrival also provokes a change in Val's worldview, which ignored the violence of oppression, disguised by the cordiality of her relationship with the family, which was greatly fuelled by the affection for the boy Fabinho, the person who filled the gap in Val's heart in Jéssica's absence. Jéssica condenses and flattens the hierarchies, refusing her mother's role against the inaction of the employers. Her attitude is not a melodramatic expression of jealousy for her mother, but an acute awareness of class that triggers the conflict, as if to insistently declare that the Brazil she inhabits today is in clear disagreement with the classist and colonial exploitation of domestic work.

From the beginning, Jéssica roams freely around the rooms of the house, as a visitor, not as a stranger. Much to the desperation of Barbara, the employer, she is caught playing in the pool with Fabinho and some friends from school, not bothering to ask permission because she already feels authorised since her mother lives in the house. Jéssica becomes an intruder, therefore, confusing the spaces of the house previously preserved by class relations. Jéssica does not yield to this spatial restriction, as her arrival also establishes another temporality that clashes with the traditional temporality of the city. Her presence contaminates the environment with the power of the impure, which precisely functions as 'resistance to the logic of control, the logic of purity' (Lugones 2003: 144). The pool is then emptied, as a way of preventing the upper and lower classes from congregating, for the pool has become a dangerous symbol of the inclusion of Jéssica, or indeed the exclusion of Val, who probably never enjoyed its waters. It is worth remembering the opening scene of the film, in which little Fabinho swims in the pool while Val waits for him, in her white uniform, standing outside, obediently playing the role of the nanny who knows her place in the equation of difference. Jéssica's stance, on the contrary, repoliticises difference, appropriating it, resignifying the order of things. She refuses the Big House/Slave Quarters duality replicated in the modern employer/housemaid relationship and muddles the spatiality of difference by claiming to belong to that house as guest, rejecting the subaltern position expected from her due to her mother's employment. Jéssica's storyline proves that 'a logic of resistance can involve a refusal to take up the dominant logic and a denial of the relationships it designates, a resistance to animating the self constructed there' (Hoagland 2007: 106).

Val, on the other hand, is portrayed in the traditional role of the benevolent housemaid, her body contained within the limits of the house where she works and lives, occupying the restricted space of a small room at the back of the house. When seen in other spaces, Val is usually framed by windows in medium shots or close-ups, as if she were confined to the frame in the same way that she is confined in the house, where she is denied the leisure of the pool. She moves around the city, on public transport, and her small face is framed by the bus window as she watches the outside world without expectations. A small respite from this confinement is given in a brief scene showing Val in a bar with friends. Val's liberation from this restriction will only occur by the end of the film, when she moves with her daughter to her own home.

Jéssica's presence disturbs the family dynamics particularly deeply when she passes the entrance exam while Fabinho fails it, and relationships are ruptured for good. With Jéssica's success and the imminent move to São Paulo with her baby daughter, Val envisions another life, disentangling herself once and for all from the chain of dependence materialised by the back room. She even goes clandestinely into the semi-emptied pool, from where she calls Jéssica, in search of recognition and complicity for her small misdemeanour. This symbolic gesture, compared to Jéssica's complete plunge into the waters, still suggests that Val's liberation is in process. The film will insist, in the end, on her presence inside a house. Freed from the restrictions imposed by paid domestic work, Val finds herself again in the confining space of domesticity, assuming the role of mother and now grandmother to Jéssica's daughter. Nevertheless, she now seems convinced that she can no longer inhabit a house that is not her own, that the bond to the Big House has been broken and the subaltern condition in the context of domestic work is not the only possible condition for her existence.

The film's ending, thus, is bittersweet. Whereas Val is able to finally experience some sense of freedom in as much as her own identity is no longer dependent on her role as a maid, she is still caught in a broader structure that keeps her as the confined caregiver (now to her daughter and granddaughter). Also, the image that synthesises this recently acquired freedom is a shot of Val and Jéssica looking outside from the window: the world they see is that of a long stretched slum. This ending implies an incomplete liberation: like Russian dolls, processes of oppression seem to emerge one after the other at increasingly larger scales.

In *Três Verões* (2019), directed by Sandra Kogut, Casé again plays a housemaid.[8] The film centres on the working class of a mansion by the sea in Rio de Janeiro. Casé plays Madá, the housekeeper who supervises domestic work in the property. The narrative follows Madá during three different summers at the house as she strives to maintain some semblance of order in a home that is disintegrating due to a national corruption scandal. After Edgar, her boss, is arrested and his wife, Marta, moves abroad, Madá and the other workers stay at the mansion and keep working despite not being fully paid. Madá and her colleagues are soon forgotten by their employers, disregarded by Edgar and Marta as if they were pieces of the furniture left by the departing family. The workers, however, realising that they have been disregarded, reconfigure their belonging to that mansion, inventing other ways to occupy it and make a living out of what was left behind. Madá is the central organising element in this reinvention, designing strategies of survival which eventually solidify the bonds among the workers.

When questioned about the repetition of successive roles as a housemaid, Casé clearly identifies the invisibility of domestic work, bringing to the fore a history of representation with a focus on the elites: 'Since the nineteenth all you see are the employers.' She pinpoints the erasure of the housemaid from the social fabric while calling attention to the role of cinema and television in the dismissal of the housemaid in representation as she questions: 'In Brazil, are there more employers or more housemaids? The number of housemaids is incomparable. So what is wrong is the fact that they have not been protagonists.'[9]

Madá is definitely a protagonist in *Três Verões*. The story revolves around her life and relationship with the house, with the family for whom she works, and with her co-workers during a recent controversial context in Brazil. The three summers to which the title refers are the years 2015, 2016 and 2017, when a set of investigations by the federal police, which became known as Operation Car Wash, started to dismantle corruption schemes involving Brazilian businessmen and politicians. This culminated in the imprisonment of more than a hundred people, including former President Luiz Inácio Lula da Silva (2002–10), although without proof of his participation in the scheme.[10] In the film narrative, Edgar stages a common stratagem of corrupt elites that ignore the boundaries between the public and the private spheres and confidently safeguards a patriarchal culture based on asset and property ownership which dates back to pre-Republic times and enhances women's subordination. The employer uses Madá's personal cell phone, for instance, to close shady deals, ignoring the existence of barriers between professional and personal relationships. This gesture, moreover, reproduces the co-option of enslaved people's assets by the owners of the Big House, since the slaves, once denied the condition of subject of rights, did not enjoy the same guarantee of the right to property that protected the colonisers.

This division into three years seems to portray three acts that range from the full privileged life of Edgar's family in the summer of 2015 to his imprisonment in 2016, and then an open end in 2017. By the second summer, the family is no longer on the scene; rather, it is the group of workers, led by Madá, who occupy this second act. Only Seu Lira, Edgar's elderly and debilitated father, remains, temporarily living at his son's mansion while his own apartment in Copacabana is being renovated. Madá continues to take care of him in Marta and Edgar's absence and she eventually creates a bond of complicity and friendship with the ageing man that defies the norms of dominant relations of the contemporary Big House. Although the roles designated to the opposing social classes – Madá, an employee, and Seu Lira, a substitute for the son in the position of boss – remain, punctuating the social distinction between the two characters, the coexistence and, mainly, the condition of abandonment in which they find themselves in the house, gradually blurs the boundaries that separate them.

Seu Lira does not question the fact that Madá and her colleagues sell part of the family's belongings as a way to support themselves. The man, who at this point more resembles the figure of the *agregado*[11] than of the employer, is ashamed of the actions of his son, with whom he has little affinity. Accordingly he starts to contribute to the strategies created by Madá to earn money by selling the goods left in the house. He suggests, for example, that they rent the house for short stays and events as an alternative so that they will not have to sell the art pieces scattered around the mansion. The Big House is thus appropriated by the working class in order to make a living from it.

It is during the third summer that Madá's past life comes to the fore, when a film crew rents out the house to record a television commercial for Christmas 2017. The domestic workers and the film crew intermingle in the new order of the house, with housemaids helping the commercial production, as if they were part of the same environment. This stages an approximation of classes that could never be configured in the old dynamics of the house, when the bosses and their guests still lived there. In the old order, the workers were restricted to the kitchen and the housemaid's quarters. Only Madá, who had free access to the family, could move around the house and among the guests. In the third act, Madá is invited to act in the TV production. After several attempts to follow the script, she decides to improvise a speech that reveals her tragic past. Her husband and daughter died, close to Christmas, victims of the collapse of the shack in which they lived, on a very rainy night when she had gone out to get help for her sick daughter. Acting to the camera inside the film, Madá gives a heart-breaking performance with her tale of woe. But, recorded by the apparatus of commercial television, this testimony can also be seen as a gesture of capture by Madá of the sensationalistic audiovisual language used to represent social vulnerability. Although Casé delivers this soliloquy with great pathos, there remains a vestige of a possible pretence, as if the narrative she is now staging could be another part of her strategy of survival, eliciting pity and playing to the guilty consciences of the film crew. The film creates a complex opacity where the fictional character self-reflexively makes use of the media in order to induce sympathy under a regime of the visible created to victimise the other, thus short-circuiting this very regime for those who are watching the film. Madá's conscious use of the audiovisual apparatus touches on a very important ethical question: how can the oppressed be visible without being transparent for the easy consumption of their misery? Kogut's film does not focus on this issue; on the contrary, one could easily argue that its aesthetic is one of transparency. This sequence, however, stands out as brief foray into the difficulties created when the performances of the oppressed in front of the camera resist capture and exceed their function in the distribution of meaning.

Madá's revelation touches everyone, especially Seu Lira. Without a home and without a family, one can better understand why she ended up caring for Edgar and Marta's house. Moved by her narrative, Seu Lira, who dies at the end of the film, leaves his Copacabana apartment to Madá. Such a narrative solution, however, does not place Madá as a victim. Unlike Val in *Que horas ela volta?*, Madá seems very aware of her position in the social structure of the house and what she can extract from the privilege that the long years she has dedicated to working for the family of Edgar and Marta have given her. She is honest and dedicated without being naive or subordinate. By the end of 2017, on the verge of Edgar's return home, Madá moves to Copacabana. From the infertile existence at the beach house, without the vigour of the rich summer, the film takes us to the turn of 2018 where Madá, in the company of her co-workers, celebrates her new address and the promise of a new life.

Conclusion

The ethics of the Big House command the forms of appearance and disappearance of the figure of the housemaid in order to regulate relationality and thereby manage the distribution of the sensible. The racial/colonial/heteropatriarchal apparatus materialised in the architectural structure of the Big House and the Slave Quarters spans centuries and symbolically extends into contemporary relations as a mechanism for maintaining the domination of the elites over the working class and the domestic space.

In Brazil, given its colonial past, precariousness is directly related to historical structures that mobilise race, class and gender. María Lugones, however, refuses to minimise the potentialities of the colonised:

> And thus I want to think of the colonized neither as simply imagined and constructed by the colonizer and coloniality in accordance with the colonial imagination and the strictures of the capitalist colonial venture, but as a being who begins to inhabit a fractured locus constructed doubly, who perceives doubly, relates doubly, where the 'sides' of the locus are in tension, and the conflict itself actively informs the subjectivity of the colonized self in multiple relation. (2010: 748)

The fractured locus where the colonised lives is the interstitial space where those who have been denied humanity and voice exercise some type of resistance. We looked for these moments in Brazilian cinema: not only how cinema imagines the performance of a coloniality of power, but also how the characters of domestic workers redraw possible spaces of existence. Our reading of recent Brazilian films emphasises the colonial and racial engineering that is produced in the present figures of domestic workers. What these films ultimately confront is the unpayable debt that, according to Denise Ferreira da Silva (2019), expresses the impossibility of quantifying the exploitation of slave work and the expropriation of indigenous lands. The notion of an unpayable debt captures 'the unfolding of the perverse logic that occludes the way in which, since the end of the 19th century, raciality operates as an ethical arsenal – inside, beside, and always-already – before the legal-economic architectures that constitute the State-Capital pair' (Silva 2019: 33). The ethics of the Big House, originating in colonial forms of racial oppression, is directly linked to this unpayable debt. The Big House, as a colonial space that survives in Brazilian architecture and imaginary, provides us with a powerful tool to understand the ethical problems which arise with modernity. In the films we discussed, the Big House regulates the inclusion and exclusion of the domestic worker in the realm of humanity. It is, therefore, at the very core of an ethics of humanity: the right to be seen and treated as humans and the acknowledgement that their work matters precisely because their lives matter and must be seen with dignity and respect not with fear or subordination. This ethical recognition of the human, however, can be reframed: the criteria used to acknowledge a life, a human life and its work, can actually reinforce the norms that excluded this life in the first place. As Judith Butler points out, 'In fact, a living figure outside the norms of life not only becomes the problem to be managed by normativity, but seems to be that which normativity is bound to reproduce: it is living, but not a life' (2009: 8). In this sense, Val's rupture with the hierarchical structure of the Big House seems to tell us that her self-awareness and agency are crucial elements to subvert the oppressive dynamics of social and labour relations. Nevertheless, the political and ethical imagination in *The Second Mother* reframes Val's trajectory in the broader structures of capitalist exclusion by keeping her in the fringes of capitalism.

But the Big House also helps us understand how the interplay of affects might generate other possibilities: an ethics of relationality, where separability is confronted with entanglements. Because conciliation with the colonial past is not on the immediate horizon, an awareness of a necessary change in society needs to be collectively constructed. Contemporary Brazilian films, like those we discuss in the chapter, critically face this issue. Perhaps this is as yet a timid contribution to the work of imagining historical reparation, but these works do activate our political imagination while refusing to produce stigmatised perceptions of the maid. Even though it is not attainable to heal all the wounds of the colonial scene, it is still possible to find traces of humanity in the way affects are depicted in the films. *Doméstica*, for instance, counterposes the implicit violence of the portrayed social relations to the small, brief parcels of shared affects. This is perhaps the great paradox that the films invite us to face: even in the violence of the social fracture, affects and belongings will sometimes emerge. Affects, however, are paradoxical: they humanise the relationships but they reinforce oppression inasmuch as they represent a surplus labour that is exploited. They can also be a buffer that softens class, gender and racial conflicts. Thus, these films provide us with a view of the paradoxes we inherited with the Big House and how its imagery and structures still arrest the political imagination of a more ethical future.

Notes

1. Ramayana Lira de Sousa would like to thank Instituto Ânima for the funding provided for this research.
2. As Nelson Maldonado-Torres explains, 'Coloniality [. . .] refers to long-standing patterns of power that emerged as a result of colonialism, but that define culture, labor, intersubjective relations, and knowledge production well beyond the strict limits of colonial administrations' (2007: 243).
3. 'Coloniality of power', for Peruvian intellectual Aníbal Quijano (2000), is a constitutive element of the world pattern of capitalist power. It is supported by the imposition of a racial/ethnic classification of the world's population and operates in everyday social life. For Quijano, the modern/colonial world system, based on

the assumption of a naturalised inferiority that justifies the colonised's oppression, remains in force even after decolonisation.
4. For María Lugones (2007: 206), the colonial power that develops a gender system has a light side and a dark side. The light side, which defines the modern constitution of the genre, concerns the control of the lives of white bourgeois men and women. This light side of the gender system imposes the ideas of sexual purity and passivity as crucial characteristics of white bourgeois women, responsible for the reproduction of the colonial and racial position of white bourgeois men. In this order of affairs, white bourgeois women, represented as weak, are excluded from the spheres of authority, the production of knowledge and most of the control over the means of production.
5. It is worth noting that the ambiguity of the expression in Portuguese used to designate the housemaid's room in Brazilian architecture: *dependência de empregada*. Dependence refers to the room itself – usually an annex to the house – as well as the oppressive dynamic of both necessity and subordination.
6. Lisa Shaw explains this popular film genre in Brazil reminding us that 'term *chanchada* was initially used in a pejorative sense to refer to the film musicals of the 1930s and early 1940s which promoted carnival songs and took their lead from Hollywood, yet the term soon became synonymous with the light musical comedies produced by Atlântida studios' (2001: 17).
7. In *Cronicamente inviável* (2000), Sérgio Bianchi fictionalises a similar 'friendship' between the white boss, Maria Alice, and her black housemaid, Josilene, but he does so tinting this relationship with cynicism, placing on Josilene the metonymical burden of class resentment, as argued by Ismail Xavier (2018).
8. The actress also plays a housemaid in the soap opera *Amor de Mãe* (Rede Globo 2019–20).
9. Available at <https://g1.globo.com/pop-arte/cinema/noticia/2020/09/04/tres-veroes-regina-case-une-esquenta-e-operacao-lava-jato-em-novo-filme-de-sandra-kogut.ghtml> (accessed 10 October 2020).
10. Luiz Inacio Lula da Silva was imprisoned in 2018 charged with corruption and money laundering. In 2021 he was acquitted of all charges for lack of evidence and because the ruling judge who convicted him was considered biased by the Brazilian Supreme Court. A summary of the political instability in Brazil in this period can be found in a *Time* magazine piece on Lula's candidacy for president from May 2022.
11. As described by Roberto Schwarz, the culture of the 'favour' – epitomised in the figure of the *agregado* – constructed the bond of dependence of free men (and women) in post-slavery Brazil. Without property, the *agregados* made up a class of dispossessed people bound to the wealthy by the mechanism of the favour, an almost universal mediation in Brazil, 'thereby unwittingly disguising the violence that had always been essential to the sphere of production' (1992: 22).

References

'Brazil's most popular president returns from political exile with a promise to save the nation' (2022), *Time*, 4 May, <https://time.com/6172611/brazil-president-lula-interview/> (accessed 4 May 2022).

Butler, Judith. P. (2009), *Frames of War When Is Life Grievable?* London: New York: Verso.

Fraser, Nancy (1997), 'Heterosexism, misrecognition, and capitalism: a response to Judith Butler', *Social Text*, 52/53 (Winter 1997): 279–89.
Freyre, Gilberto (1986), *The Masters and the Slaves*, Berkeley and Los Angeles: University of California Press.
Goldstein, Donna M. (2003), *Laughter out of Place: Race, Class, Violence, and Sexuality in a Rio Shantytown*, Berkeley and Los Angeles: University of California Press.
González, Lélia (1984), 'Racismo e Sexismo na Cultura Brasileira'. *Revista Ciências Sociais Hoje*, São Paulo: ANPOCS. pp. 223–244.
Gutiérrez-Rodríguez, Encarnación. (2010), *Migration, Domestic Work and Affect: A Decolonial Approach on Value and the Feminization of Labor*. New York: Routledge.
Hoagland, Sarah L. (2207), 'Denying relationality: epistemology and ethics and ignorance', in Shannon Sullivan and Nancy Tuana (eds), *Race and Epistemologies of Ignorance*, Albany: State University of New York Press, pp. 95–118.
Kilomba, Grada (2010), *Plantation Memories: Episodes of Everyday Racism*, Münster: Unrest Verlag.
Lugones, Mari'a (2003), *Pilgrimages/Peregrinajes: Theorizing Coalition against Multiple Oppressions*, Lanham: Rowman & Littlefield.
Lugones, María (2007), 'Heterosexualism and the colonial/modern gender system', *Hypatia* 22: 1 (Winter 2007), 166–209.
Lugones, María (2010), 'Toward a decolonial feminism', *Hypatia*, 25: 4 (Fall 2010), 742–59.
Maldonado-Torres, Nelson (2007), 'On the coloniality of being: contributions to the development of a concept', *Cultural Studies*, 21: 2/3 (March/May 2007), 240–70.
Maldonado-Torres, Nelson (2008), *Against War: Views from the Underside of Modernity*, Durham, NC: Duke University Press.
Nagib, Lucia (2017), 'The horizontal spread of a vertical malady', in M. M. Delgado, S. M. Hart and R. Johnson (eds), *A Companion to Latin American Cinema*, Chichester: Wiley Blackwell, pp. 343–56.
Quijano, Aníbal (2000), 'Coloniality of power, Eurocentrism, and Latin America', *Nepantla: Views from South*, 1: 3, 533–80.
Rancière, Jacques (2004), *The Politics of Aesthetics: The Distribution of the Sensible*, London: Continuum.
Schwarz, Roberto (1992), *Ao vencedor as batatas*. São Paulo: Duas Cidade.
Shaw, Lisa (2001), 'The Brazilian chanchada of the 1950s and notions of popular identity', *Luso-Brazilian Review*, 38: 1 (Summer 2001), 17–30.
Silva, Denise Ferreira da (2019), *A dívida impagável*, São Paulo: Oficina de Imaginação Política and Casa do Povo.
Souto, Mariana (2012), 'O direto interno, o dispositivo de infiltração e a mise-en-scène do amador – Notas sobre Pacific e Doméstica', *Revista Devires*, 9: 1, 66–85.
Valente, Eduardo (2001), 'Domésticas – O filme', *Contracampo*, <http://www.contracampo.com.br/criticas/domesticas.htm> (accessed 10 October 2020).
Vergès, Françoise (2020), *Um feminismo decolonial*, São Paulo: Ubu.
Wisnik, Guilherme (2006), 'Cidade "casa-grande"', *Folha de São Paulo*, 21 August, <https://www1.folha.uol.com.br/fsp/ilustrad/fq2108200610.htm> (accessed 5 October 2020).
Xavier, Ismail (2018), 'Figuras do ressentimento no cinema brasileiro dos anos 1990', *Aniki*, 5: 2, 311–32.

2. CINEMATIC ETHICS AND A WORLD OF CINEMAS: A REASON TO BELIEVE IN THIS WORLD'S HISTORY IN HU JIE'S *WO SUI SI QU/THOUGH I AM GONE*

David Martin-Jones

This chapter critically reflects upon Gilles Deleuze's cinematic ethics, which considers cinema to have the potential to restore belief in humanity's ability to act upon the world, or, to put it in a more Deleuzian manner, to provide a reason to believe in this world. Through close analysis of the Chinese documentary *Wo sui si qu/Though I am Gone* (Hu Jie, 2006) – in which time-images are used to reconsider history – a key point of Deleuze's cinematic ethics is highlighted for further investigation: namely, in a world of cinemas broadly conceived, it may not always be *precisely* this world which a cinematic ethics asks us to rejuvenate our belief in, but this world's history. Or more precisely, to rejuvenate a belief in the possibility that other records of the past can potentially relativise the official version of history.

This nuancing of Deleuze's cinematic ethics is relevant to our globalised world for two reasons. First, due to the need to understand not the so-called 'end of history' but rather the elusive totality of world history. Second, due to neoliberalism globalisation's preference for authoritarian governance, especially the state of exception (Agamben 2005: 87). The second of these is of particular importance. Although the historical moment the documentary engages with – China's Cultural Revolution of 1966–76 – is politically far-removed from the present-day reality many experience worldwide, what it can nevertheless illuminate, which remains pertinent, is the way in which the state of exception shapes history. Neoliberal globalisation's attempted normalisation of the state of exception makes the emphasis on history in the time-image (which is so integral to Deleuze's cinematic ethics), extremely apposite. As the time-images in *Though I am Gone* indicate, histories obscured during a state of exception can remain 'alive' for the present. Thus, Deleuze's cinematic ethics, when understood in relation to both the engagement with world history found in a world of cinemas, and, more broadly, globalisation's emphasis on the eradication of alternative pasts in the state of exception (the return of which indicate the contingency of the present's norms), provides not only a reason to believe in this world, but also, in this process, emphasises the importance of believing in this world's history (the maintenance of its potential to relativise the official version of history). This, even whilst the complexities of world history, coupled with what many of the world's viewers might reasonably be expected to understand of its nuances, ensure that we can only glimpse a fraction of, and may only imperfectly understand, this historical context.

Deleuze's Cinematic Ethics and the State of Exception

Deleuze argues that cinema can be ethical in that it can offer us a reason to believe in this world (1985: 166). This relates to Deleuze's broader understanding of the world in terms of immanence (its forever coming into being), rather than with recourse to a transcendent other world from which moral absolutes have emanated. Ethics, understood in this context, relates to the 'mode of existence' of one who chooses to believe in this world (171). D. N. Rodowick clarifies: 'The ethical choice for Deleuze, then, is whether the powers of change are affirmed and harnessed in ways that value life and its openness to change, or whether we disparage life in *this* world in fealty to moral absolutes' (2010: 101). Belief in this world, for Deleuze, requires a link to be restored between humanity and the (often 'intolerable') modern world (1985: 164). This indicates, Robert Sinnerbrink notes, that Deleuze's recourse to cinema to develop his ethics should be understood as a reaction against a pervasive post-war Nietzschean cultural nihilism, at least in the West (2015: 58). In the face of a faltering belief that a person's actions may be able to transform an otherwise 'intolerable' situation (1985: 17), cinema may prompt a new kind of thinking to emerge (164), one which can potentially reconnect humanity to the world by rekindling belief in our ability to transform an 'intolerable' situation (166). In this process the importance of time becomes especially evident, for Deleuze, due to its ability to create new and surprising linkages which stimulate thinking. In time-image cinemas, Deleuze's ethics includes the role the past may play in the present for political reasons. Indeed, his ethics emerges in *Cinema 2* (1985) between the sections on the labyrinthine, temporal 'powers of the false' (historical) and modern political or minor cinema.[1] In practical terms, we might understand new thinking to potentially be prompted by a renewed engagement with the past through the 'powers of the false' which can offer an alternative informing past for the present from amidst myriad '*not-necessarily true pasts*', as just one example (1985: 127).

The historical situation explored in *Though I am Gone* is the Chinese Cultural Revolution (1966–76). Although a 'past' moment in Cold War history, this historical state of exception has resonances for our contemporary era. As Giorgio Agamben outlines, the state of exception is: 'a legal civil war that allows for the physical elimination not only of political adversaries but of entire categories of citizens who for some reason cannot be integrated into the political system' (2005: 2). Writing in the wake of the 9/11 attacks in the USA in 2001, and the subsequent introduction of the Patriot Act, Agamben argues that a 'permanent state of emergency' (in which civil rights are suspended for some portion of the populace) 'has become one of the essential practices of contemporary states' (2), a practice which he considers to have been growing since the First World War (86–7).[2] The relevance of *Though I am Gone* for our contemporary world, then, is not in any direct political comparison between Maoist China and the contemporary era of neoliberal globalisation. Rather, specifically, it is in what this documentary can illuminate with respect to how history is shaped during the state of exception. This is of relevance for a contemporary context in which neoliberal globalisation favours the normalisation of the state of exception. During such an exceptional situation – whatever the broader political forces at play in the respective historical moment – history is rewritten. This is precisely the subject of *Though I am Gone*, and the reason for the claim that this documentary offers lessons from the past which are pertinent for the present, in spite of the significant political differences between the two historical eras: the Cold War then, globalisation now.

By extension, analysing *Though I am Gone* can also shed new light on how an ethics like Deleuze's can relate to (world) history. This documentary explores the consequences, several decades on, of the erasing of other histories inherent to the state of exception, indicating thereby how a painful, ethical 'mode of existence' – which can be maintained in the face of an 'intolerable' sustained denial of justice – links directly to the state of exception's eradication of 'other' histories. Simultaneously, however, the film indicates the challenges thrown up by a world of cinemas to our ability to grasp the ethical import of the political suppression of other histories from contexts in which the finer points of this history may or may not be known to all viewers.

At the convergence of neoliberal globalisation's authoritarian politics, and the increased availability of a world of cinemas, then, a key point of Deleuze's cinematic ethics is thus highlighted in terms of the nuance it requires when confronting political history.

Wo sui si qu/Though I am Gone (2006)

Though I am Gone explores a historical injustice – a murder committed during the Cultural Revolution, for which the Red Guard perpetrators have never been brought to trial. A Beijing school teacher, Bian Zhongyun was killed by her students in August 1966. After a severe beating, Bian's unconscious bleeding body was left for several hours before she was taken to hospital. She later died. Bian was the vice principal of the girls' middle school attached to Beijing Normal University, and also the party secretary. The school's students included many children of influential party members, including, at that time, the daughters of Liu Shaoqui, Deng Xiaoping and Chairman Mao (MacFarquhar and Schoenhals 2006: 73 and 108; Zhang and Wright 2018: 40). The death of Bian is well-known in China, and has been the topic of much public debate in the ensuing decades. This seems, in part, due to the closeness of the death to the daughters of such high-ranking officials. Perhaps unsurprisingly, Hu Jie's documentary is banned in China (although it has been widely viewed on the internet[3]).

Though I am Gone focuses on Bian's grieving widower, Wang Jingyao, who has preserved the evidence (and memory) of his wife's brutal murder in the hope that it may one day be officially brought to trial (or failing that, he notes, it might inform an official museum of memory to victims of the Cultural Revolution). Wang preserved events of that time, primarily using a camera that he bought the day after Bian's death. He states that he was 'determined to record the truth of history'. The documentary incorporates many of Wang's photographs from the aftermath of his wife's murder, such as a picture of his daughters viewing the corpse of their mother, and pictures of the *dazibao* ('big character' posters) the Red Guard painted inside his home. Wang also kept physical mementos, including the bloodied, muddied, urine and excrement-soiled clothes his wife was wearing.

Wang's personal memories are 'captured' by Hu Jie, in the spaces where events happened in the past (including in walk-through recreations). Through Wang's personal memory we are granted access to an aspect of Chinese collective history that has been – to a large extent – erased from the state-approved national history. 'To a large extent' is important. There has been a 'Communist party apology, renunciation, and compensation for this Maoist movement, including public trials, rehabilitation of victims and restorations of jobs, lost property, and income' (Kraus 2012: 104). The Communist Party officially acknowledged that this period of history damaged 'the party, the state, and people' (104) of China. Nevertheless, for Wang an element of this history remains obscured: justice for Bian.

Wang retrospectively sought justice after the Cultural Revolution. He identified Yuan Shue (the ex-wife of one of Bian's colleagues) as having concocted rumours against Bian, which led to Bian being slandered, and then beaten (Zhang and Wright 2018: 42). The Supreme People's Procuratorate found Yuan Shue guilty of this but exempted her from prosecution on the grounds that too much time had elapsed (see also Zhang and Wright 2018: 81). Yet Wang notes that public prosecution and the court system broke down during the Cultural Revolution (another vice principal of the school, Hu Zhitao, tried to report the beatings of Bian and others at government offices, but found them empty). This, then, is part of the broader state evasion of the memory of the Cultural Revolution, which also discourages museums of memory (Kraus 2012: 113), denying a platform for personal stories to be heard publicly (112). The only attempt to run such a dedicated museum of memory, which opened in 2005 in Shantou (Guangdong Province, bordering on Hong Kong), was very deliberately 'covered up' by the state in 2016, on the fiftieth anniversary of the Cultural Revolution (the museum was obscured by concrete, scaffolding and banners [Tatlow]). After a limited period of public examination of the Cultural Revolution, then, it would seem as though any further memory work, including the preservation of past injustices, must be done individually and informally.

The state may perhaps fear the consequences of reminding people that politics can proceed through 'mass mobilization' (Kraus 2012: 112). Maoism, in particular, may imply constant revolution, and therefore be considered by some better left in the past. This, especially since the move towards marketisation of the Chinese economy after the Cultural Revolution meant a social 'depoliticization' along with the emergence of what Wang Hui calls a 'state-party' system (entirely woven throughout the state's bureaucratic apparatus) (2009: 8–10). In this context, to critically reconsider the past, especially the Cultural Revolution, is to raise questions not only about the Chinese Communist Party (CCP), but now also the fabric of the state. It might even undermine the veracity of the official narrative of the CCP's positive role in recent Chinese history (Edwards 2015: 92). Thus, the trauma of the Cultural Revolution, within living memory for many, remains structuring of society.

This tension surrounding the extent to which history is acknowledged by the state is evident in *Though I am Gone* in numerous everyday shots of present-day Tiananmen Square, empty of protestors or political rallies, interspersed with footage of the past. The Cultural Revolution included mass rallies of the Red Guard in this space, whilst the pro-democracy demonstrations of 1989 are similarly iconic. Both these moments of mass mobilisation haunt the documentary's images of the empty square. History as we know it, the official history of China, is thus shown to be a riven history. One dimension, or perhaps version, of it can be thus easily evoked whilst, paradoxically, it remains an officially unrecognised memory, surviving only in personal, private archives such as that of Wang.

Though I am Gone has received considerable scholarly coverage. Three works are specifically relevant for this discussion. First, Chris Berry and Lisa Rofel discuss the film as an 'alternative archive' in relation to the archival function of the New Documentary Film Movement. This includes storing oral histories, especially those at odds with, alternative or oppositional to the accepted view of history, which can be informing of the future (2010:

152). Second, and similarly, Jie Li discusses the documentary in terms of a 'Virtual Museum of Forbidden Memory', not unlike those on the internet, in the absence of a state approved *physical* museum memorialising the victims of the Cultural Revolution (2009: 3). Third, Dan Edwards, noting the lack of acknowledgement in official discourse of the violence perpetrated against educators, considers *Though I am Gone* 'a political gesture of resistance against a deliberate amnesia engendered through official accounts' (2015: 90). These representative texts, although not engaged with Deleuze, help us 'make sense' of the documentary's time-images.[4] Time-images, after all, function to recuperate 'lost' histories, particularly personal memories of 'erased' public pasts (Martin-Jones 2018: 151-78). More than this, though, *Though I am Gone*'s time-images indicate what this film can reveal regarding Deleuze's cinematic ethics and history.

Wang's mode of existence keeps alive the possibility of another thought, that of the past seen differently to the form in which it is officially recognised in the present (the possibility of justice being wrought via the virtual powers of the false). As Elizabeth Jelin (2003) observes, memories which survive in the private sphere with the potential to later (re-)inform the public, rarely form a single, coherent counter-narrative to the official story of history. Rather, various individual experiences of the past create 'multiple social and political' viewpoints' (29). Wang's mode of existence, his choosing to choose to believe in this (for him, painful) world, is thus that of the (personal) archivist acting in the (minoritarian) anticipation of a people yet to come. He maintains his personal past hoping that it can inform the public sphere anew. To be very accurate, then, his mode of existence embodies less a belief in this world than in the potential of this world's history. Accordingly, what is explored in *Though I am Gone* is not so much (private) memory against (public) silence, but, to follow Jelin, 'memory against memory' (xviii). Noticeably, Hu expresses this with time-images which would counter any attempt to eradicate the possibility of political opposition re-emerging from the past.

Crystalline Beijing

Hu's film is haunted by time. We hear a ticking clock intermittently, in transitions between locations, or more obtrusively, as dialogue fades out to be replaced by the sound of ticking. The opening shot is a clock pendulum, there are other scattered images of clocks, and two watches feature prominently in the conclusion (discussed below). As Li observes, the film emphasises that time is 'running out' for the witnesses of the atrocities of the Cultural Revolution (Wang was in his eighties when the film was made). The passing of this generation will close off access to this layer of history, at least in terms of what might be possible regarding social justice (542). Yet the foregrounding of time also reinforces the film's self-conscious construction of history via the time-image, and the omnipresence of the past in the present. The opening, for example, includes a foregrounded shift from black and white to colour – from a clock ticking now in the present, in colour, to the camera Wang used in 1965 in black and white – which demonstrates the coexistence of different historical periods in the present (the Deleuzian crystal of time). Moreover, we are repeatedly shown the present, then a transitional shot which is a close-up of Wang's camera lens, as though it were photographing us, and then the reverse shot is often a photo of the past. Transitions between layers of time, especially between present and past, thus take place through a standard shot/reverse shot pattern. In this way, Hu's film creates a giant crystal of time, with myriad entrances from the present into the virtual past.

The photos Wang took of Bian's corpse, including those featuring her children as mourning witnesses, provide one such way into the past. They suggest the coexistence of the present with an informing virtual layer of the past the consequences of which at the personal, familial level have been occluded within official memory. The remembrance of this past thus relies upon the documentary we are watching to keep it alive, a film which is itself drawing upon an unofficial archive, the museum of memory of an individual, Wang. This is clearest in the film's climactic, and almost unbearably emotional moments, in which Wang unlocks a suitcase containing his wife's personal effects. It is the first time Wang has opened it in thirty-nine years. As Wang opens a bag filled with the bloody gauzes, he emotionally explains that they were removed from Bian's mouth. The gauzes are one of several such material remnants of the past, including Bian's hair, and her torn and crumpled clothes. The latter still contain the inked-on words denouncing her, mud from when she was beaten unconscious and revived with water, her blood, urine and excrement. These items are handled carefully by Wang, Hu's camera providing close-ups to emphasise the visceral experience of his touch.

In this sequence, the documentary again plays with colour and black and white, creating a crystal of time. Up to this point, alternation between colour and black and white has occurred without much rhyme or reason – suggesting perhaps an ever-present temporal confusion in Wang's traumatised life. He has, after all, dedicated much of his life to memorialising his wife in private (keeping her ashes in an improvised shrine in the house when burying her was illegal; maintaining an archive of eye witness accounts of her death, his photos and Bian's personal effects). As Wang sorts through the clothes, the sequence is black and white until he unwraps the bundle of clothes and reveals Bian's underwear. The camera closes in on her excrement. Suddenly the documentary cuts to a colour close-up. A still image, appearing rather like the photographs of the past have until now, as a brief interruption to the story Wang is recounting of Bian's murder. The sudden colour close-up on Bian's excrement provides a physical remainder of her bodily existence from the past. Via the sudden shift to colour, as Wang unpacks his long unopened archive, we seemingly encounter a physical remnant of the past. What can we make of this visual effect, and what might it mean for Deleuze's cinematic ethics?

It is possible to understand this image following Damian Sutton's contention that 'the still image is the fold between two images of time – the rational order of the movement-image and the glimpsed duration of the time-image' (2009: 123–4). As such, we can interpret Hu's time-images as indicating that Wang's personal memory exists in the folds within official history, hidden away from official recognition, denying justice for such crimes against individuals. The still image, infused with colour, is somehow an image of our time. But it is also an image which provides the possibility of the return of an unaddressed aspect of the past – a return from the fold as conceived by Sutton – suggesting perhaps how the past may revivify and 'bring colour' to the present. Previously in the documentary we have been told by Wang's daughter, that it was when he was confronted with the excrement stained underwear of his dead wife, in 1966, that Wang lost control emotionally. Thus, the emotions the soiled clothes revive in Wang indicate precisely the potential of the past to revivify the present and potentially propel it into a new future.

Such an interpretation is confirmed by the film's conclusion. Throughout the documentary the insertion of the photographs of Bian provide access to an additional virtual layer of time to that of the present. Wang, after telling his story, packs away his camera. The camera is then shot, situated on some books, in black and white. From the black and white we dissolve to colour. Once again, the reality of the past, its subsistence within the folds of official history is evoked. Simultaneously, this colour footage, now of the original camera rather than the remnants of Bian's excrement, indicates that an unresolved injustice from 1966 is active, and present, in the present. These moments indicate the yet-to-come nature of what persists in the folds within official history, often with a visceral affect when experienced.

Thus, in *Though I am Gone*'s time-images the personal becomes a conduit into the obscured aspect of national history. The occasional archival footage of newsreel and radio broadcasts used (such footage from this period is not readily available in the public sphere in China [Li 2009: 547]) stands in contrast to the personal footage that Wang collected. His personal archive, along with witness testimonies and other found footage indicates what is missing from the approved history. Seemingly a work of modern political or minor cinema, *Though I am Gone* appears in line with Deleuze's cinematic ethics in its attempts to foreground the immanence of the justice for past crimes that is yet to come.

Yet, on closer inspection, the film also reveals something of the complexities of the broader political situation framing the personal story. The political biases involved in retelling history thus become evident in the documentary's construction, political history nuancing how the Deleuzian ethics should be understood. On the one hand, Wang's photographs, documents, the testimony of other witnesses and survivors, and the artefacts preserved for nearly four decades, together resemble exhibits at a trial. Thus, the ethical mode of existence and its relationship to a historical injustice are apparent, the injustice Wang feels being over the death of a loved one. But on the other hand, what of the political history we are also told, of which he and his wife were a part prior to the Cultural Revolution? Wang and his wife had been – the documentary reveals – loyal party members through the Sino-Japanese war, and the Civil War, before they attained the roles they had when the Cultural Revolution erupted. Wang's familial history (the majority of the photographs are of the family unit) ensures that his and Bian's revolutionary lives prior to the Cultural Revolution demonstrate as much the betrayal of the *history of the party* and the national history constructed by it, which they had worked for, as they do the injustice of Bian's murder for her family.

The interlinked and unanswered questions which we are then left with are several. What experiences in the biographical past of a loyal party member led Wang to purchase the camera the day after his wife's death? Why did he record her corpse as one would a body in a crime scene? How did his experience of political history prior to the Cultural Revolution inform his decision-making? Through such questioning, the nature of the injustice Wang feels is here rendered more complex, further nuancing, by turns, how recognising the past through cinema may be understood to be ethical. To consider this further we first need to understand the extent to which we can claim the Cultural Revolution to have been a state of exception in relation to this larger political history.

State of Exception?

It is possible to consider that, for some, the Cultural Revolution may have been experienced as a time of liberation and opportunity, especially in the absence, or overthrow, of authority. Destroying the monuments of the past or burning revered books may possibly lend a degree of carnivalesque inversion to events (whether the Cultural Revolution or indeed, any revolution), much as one may expect of the state of exception. Such consideration, however, is speculative, and beyond the bounds of a discrete work such as this. Even so, what we can say for certain is that *Though I am Gone* emphasises events which took place at the time which suggest parallels with the carnivalesque. The school janitor, Lin Mang, an eyewitness to events, testifies that Bian and others targeted by the Red Guard suffered insults and humiliations, including having their faces painted with ink, being forced to carry large baskets of earth, to parade publicly whilst self-denunciating (striking an iron dustpan), and having to clean toilets. Tellingly, Lin observes that after the beating of Bian, including being trampled underfoot by the military boots of the girls, the Red Guards partook of ice cream.

During the Cultural Revolution, public spectacles of humiliation, torture, and even execution were at times given a terrifying carnivalesque dimension. Anarchical societal inversion is demonstrated by such practices as the humiliation of party officials paraded publicly in dunces' caps (Bailey 2001, 181). The Red Guard, their intention to 'turn the world upside down' (182), not only 'bombarded the headquarters', as per the infamous slogan, but also invaded the homes and lives of Chinese citizens (the practice of *Chao jia*), committing acts of vandalism and burning books. This Wang testifies to in *Though I am Gone*, showing his photos of the invasion of his home by the Red Guard. This included the posting of numerous accusatory and threatening big character posters on walls and doors, caricaturing Bian and comparing her to a pig. Public beatings like that of Bian led to several deaths. Hu's documentary notes that 1770 were killed in Beijing in August 1966 alone. More broadly, Paul J. Bailey observes how the Cultural Revolution

> quickly degenerated into random and arbitrary violence (often the result of frustrations and resentments caused by official party policies in the 1950s), with thousands of party and government bureaucrats, teachers, intellectuals and artists being publicly humiliated, beaten and even killed. (2001: 7)

Hence, whilst the extent to which the Cultural Revolution was (brutally) carnivalesque is arguable, the suspension of the rule of law, which enabled numerous unlawful killings, does indicate that a state of exception took place. Yet, how else this moment might be understood to be exceptional rewards further investigation. After all, for Agamben, in its origins the state of exception emerges from the 'democratic-revolutionary tradition and not the absolutist one' (5), making any claim for the Cultural Revolution as a state of exception seem universalising. A more Chinese-focused investigation is necessary.

Various scholars consider the Cultural Revolution in a manner suggestive of historical *continuity*, rather than exception. For example, Richard Curt Kraus considers the Cultural Revolution 'the last and perhaps final push in a century-long trajectory of Chinese revolution' (2012: 1). There had already been several campaigns of purges previously, during the 1950s especially (Bailey 2001: 187), and there were marked similarities between those and the Cultural Revolution.[5] Nevertheless, and in spite of such continuities, Lynn T. White III observes that the Cultural Revolution was exceptional in being 'so widespread' and 'directed at so many kinds of victims at so many levels of society' (1991: 84). This was due to, for White, the ossified status quo which emerged prior to the Cultural Revolution – a convergence of widespread social anxiety (cultivated by the CCP), the use of labels to categorise people into status groups, and the power of local party bosses in determining social advancement (87–91). Kraus similarly considers the Cultural Revolution to be an exceptional event amidst China's twentieth century of 'revolutionary waves' (5), not least because 'it was directed against the Communist-Party state itself' (14). Determining the 'norm' which was inverted during the Cultural Revolution, then, is not a simple matter, which begins to point towards the intricacies of political history which require greater nuance of Deleuze's cinematic ethics.

The complexities surrounding the political history which the film illuminates come into sharp focus around the death of Bian. As noted, some of the girls at the school were related to members of the Standing Committee of the CCP. Wang calls it a 'royal school'. The Cultural Revolution, then, was not exactly a situation which elevated the lowest to the position of kings, as per the carnival or charivari as state of exception. Rather, it gave license to the children of high-ranking party officials to kill their teachers. After all, Mao's sixteen-point programme defining the Cultural Revolution in August 1966 was declared in the wake of his criticism of Liu Shaoqi and Deng Xiaoping for 'dampening down the student movement on Beijing University campuses' (Bailey 2001: 180). For White, the actions of more radical elements of the Red Guards can be interpreted as demonstrating a revolutionary zeal indicative of a desire for *personal advancement* against an establishment which could only be overthrown violently (94–6). The death of Bian might thus be considered an attack on an established position per se, during a state of exception, perpetrated in part by those destined to inherit power in the future.

With the complexities and contestations of this political history in sharper focus, the challenges this creates for claiming a cinematic ethics around the cinematic maintenance of obscured histories can be explored in more depth. Hu's documentary, in fact, shows the contingency of the intertwined personal and political histories that comes to the fore during the state of exception. It illustrates that what was attacked during the Cultural Revolution was effectively the right of some individuals to tell their *own story of their place in official history.*

The Yanan Way Revisited

Some of the most lingering images of *Though I am Gone* are photographs of the inside of the flat where Wang, Bian and their children lived, after Red Guard rebels vandalised it. Wang recounts how he maintained the big character posters in place for two to three years after Bian's death. At the core of the film, then, is a familial space from the past, in which a violent event occurred that indicates the entwinement of personal and political histories. Initially maintained as though a personal museum of memory, during a period when this domestic space was forcibly opened to the outside due to the state of exception (the flat was invaded by the Red Guard), this space now only exists in that form in photographs (a return visit to the front door simply demonstrating its physical unavailability in the present). It has become a *virtual*, personal museum of memory.

Wang's grievance is thus represented as not only due to the injustice of his wife's death, but, more precisely, at the injustice of his wife's death at the hands of rebels, in a context in which both he and she had been loyal party members since the Sino-Japanese War. Here again, time is the theme used to indicate this. During the film's emotive last minutes, when Hu opens the suitcase containing the personal effects of his deceased wife, he removes a wristwatch. Its hands stopped, we are led to infer, during Bian's violent beating. Almost immediately afterwards an old-fashioned fob watch is produced from the suitcase, which Bian inherited from her stepmother. This watch, Wang informs us, was used in 1947 during the Civil War, by the Xinhua News Agency and Shanbei Radio Station. This was then based in the Taihang Mountain region, after the Communist withdrawal from Yanan. This fob watch enabled the time to be announced to the Communist troops over the radio. In the same climactic section of the film, Wang shows the camera Bian's Battlefield Service Group badge. Wang also, when prompted by Hu, notes Bian's love of certain songs, popular from the Sino-Japanese War, such as 'Ode to the Yellow River' and 'On the Taihang Mountain.' As he recounts how Bian sang the latter song in 1945, in the Taihang Mountain region, the music is heard on the soundtrack.

The violence unleashed by the Cultural Revolution against such loyal party members, for Wang, 'stopped the clock' on the history of their service to the party, de-legitimising their personal narrative of political history. The film thus recreates this narrative, virtually, using the images of the time, along with Wang's personal recollections. Wang describes how, during the Sino-Japanese War, he and Bian organised a revolutionary group. In 1944, Wang programmed a photo exhibition at the American News Agency in Chengdu: pro-democracy, anti-fascism, anti-Goumingdang. He photographed the end of the Sino-Japanese War, some of which we are shown from his personal archive. As these images appear, after those of the devastation caused to his family by the Cultural Revolution, Wang's past as a photographer documenting the victory of the Communists in the war in the 1940s, and again in the 1960s the murder of his wife, creates the impression of an interrupted continuum. A certain path through history – that of long-serving, loyal party members – stopped with Bian's death. This is a particular political history of China whose legacy was de-legitimised during the Cultural Revolution. As Wang unpacks the suitcase of his deceased wife's effects, with the music from 'On the Taihang Mountain' playing on the soundtrack, the film intersperses the physical evidence of Bian's murder with photos of her as a patriotic revolutionary, with child, in the 1940s. By thus juxtaposing the photographs of the past, *Though I am Gone* exhibits the injustice of Bian's death as that of a previously valorised national history that was brutally 'packed away' within official history, hidden out of sight, by the Cultural Revolution.

The history under attack during the Cultural Revolution, then, was not just that of the monuments or books of national heritage. Large sections of the population whose recent biographical pasts intertwined with the past of the CCP's revolutionary struggle and ascension to power also came under scrutiny. Attacking the party faithful meant that a certain history of the CCP was also under attack. It is this 'truth of history', personal but also standing in for a collective disenfranchised, which Wang seemed 'determined to record' with his camera. Bailey, drawing on Roderick MacFarquhar, argues of the Central Committee plenum held in August 1966 at which the aims of the Cultural Revolution were defined, that it 'finally shattered the "Yanan Round Table" – the tightly knit party group that had been together since the days of the Sino-Japanese war' (Bailey 2001: 181). The destruction of monuments, and the elimination of many who were considered in line with the 'capitalist road', or the 'four "olds"' (Kraus 2012: 44–9), including figures at the top such as Deng and Liu, were undertaken in a way which had the effect of reconsidering the path taken since the war with the Japanese. The Yanan period of 1937–45 was at once an era influential in establishing the direction towards revolution and also the time when Mao consolidated his power. Significantly, it was during the Yanan period, as the CCP conducted its guerrilla war against the Japanese during the late 1930s, that Mao's personality cult was fostered. This ultimately propelled the adoption of Mao's thought as dogma during the Cultural Revolution (Bailey 2001: 5–7). It is this history, then, of loyal party members serving since the Japanese War but 'betrayed' by rebels during the Cultural Revolution, which *Though I am Gone* foregrounds.

For this reason, Bian is associated, through Wang's testimony, with the Yellow River songs composed in Yanan in 1939, and her personal effects are unveiled to the soundtrack of a patriotic song of the Sino-Japanese War. Noticeably, Bian's stopped watch (apparently marking the moment of her beating) is placed alongside Bian's badges and other artefacts of loyal service. These include the fob watch which helped the Communist radio keep time during the Civil War. Together the two watches symbolise the interrupted historical narrative of the revolutionary movement – that which had maintained itself through the Sino-Japanese and Civil Wars due to the dedication of loyal party members like Bian (the fob watch), but which was suddenly interrupted by the Cultural Revolution (the 'stopped' watch).

This is not to argue that *Though I am Gone* considers there to have been a rosy hued pre-Cultural Revolution originary moment that was betrayed during the state of exception. Rather, it shows that in the Cultural Revolution, as was the case during the Yanan period, a struggle took place as to whose revolution it was (only this time with a much stronger consolidation of power for Mao [see also Kraus 2012: 21–2]). *In this way the contingency of history which is highlighted during the state of exception comes to the fore.* The history which was attacked during the Cultural Revolution, now memorialised only in the private lives of family members of deceased victims (and banned films about them like *Though I am Gone*), was that of another possible road, or roads, for the revolution that also stemmed from the Yanan period.

A Reason to Believe in this World's History?

To begin to conclude, *Though I am Gone*'s emphasis on bringing to the surface a 'lost' past seems to neatly align with a Deleuzian cinematic ethics. Certainly Wang's lifelong quest for justice for Bian would seem to evidence a mode of existence which supports the belief that human actions can influence the world, even in the most 'intolerable' of circumstances. The additional nuance which I would immediately add to this is that, in fact, what Wang's personal preservation of history shows is a belief that our actions can keep alive the possibility that other, '*not-necessarily true pasts*' can potentially relativise the official version of history. As much a reason to believe in this world, then, as a reason to believe in this world's history.

Even so, there is more to consider. How much can the viewer *grasp* of the complexities surrounding the intertwined personal and political histories which underpin what is seen? This surely influences what can be claimed of a cinematic ethics in relation to such a film. Ultimately, *Though I am Gone* leaves us with several questions. Not least of which is why Wang pursued Yuan Shue, legally, for falsely discrediting Bian, rather than the Red Guards who actually beat Bian causing her death. Is it because, as he claims (although this is not addressed in the film), he believes the young students were incited to commit acts of violence (Zhang and Wright 2018: 81)? Or, is it perhaps because he did not feel he could succeed in prosecuting daughters of high-ranking officials? Was the target of his legal proceedings, in fact, shaped politically? Moreover, the documentary does not reveal much of Wang's experiences preceding the Cultural Revolution. We are not informed as to why he bought a camera, but we are led to infer that, from his own experiences, Wang knew the history of his wife's life might well be rewritten in an Orwellian manner by the party he himself served. At the opening of the film, Wang's photographs of his happy, smiling family are suddenly juxtaposed by the insertion of a picture of four men apparently about to be executed by Communist forces. This is a photograph Wang took in the countryside whilst participating in the 'Four Cleanups Movement' after his graduation from the Central Party School in 1965. Wang describes his young self as wanting to be a professional revolutionary. Was he involved in executions similar to the killing of his wife? It is hard to tell from the film itself. Perhaps all we can say is that Wang knew enough from experience to create an archive with which to seek justice in a time yet-to-come, during which its images would contrast with the propaganda-like images of the era. In this particular documentary, to return to Jelin, 'memory against memory' indicates specifically the intertwined nature of the private past with the official story of the public past. The film does not, then, create a memory to counter state silence over the past, so much as it does a memory to contrast the official history: one which retains the legitimate place of the obscured personal story within the official story. The question which remains, then, is how much can be appreciated of such nuance in the encounter with such a film, especially considering the immensity of world history represented in a world of cinemas?

For those familiar with the historical incident, as may be the case for many Chinese viewers, much in *Though I am Gone* does not seem to need to be stated explicitly. For example, the documentary includes footage of a famous scene at the Tiananmen Square rally in which a young Red Guard, Song Binbin, put a Red Guard armband on Mao. He, also famously, enquired after her name, and remarked that it would be better were it 'Want Arms'.[6] This was interpreted by many as a legitimising call to violence which propelled the murderous excesses which would follow (Zhang and Wright 2018: 47). In the documentary this is presented, to the uninitiated, as contextualising 'evidence' of Mao's role in inciting violence. For those with some knowledge of the events themselves, there is a much more direct link evident. At the centre of the controversy surrounding who killed Bian is Song Binbin, who was a leading Red Guard at the girls' school (Zhang and Wright 2018: 40–1 and 49–74). Song was the daughter of Song Renqiong, then first secretary of the party's North East region, later of the Politburo (MacFarquhar and Schoenhals 2006: 517). The incident with the armband occurred twelve days after the death of Bian (Edwards 2015: 89), the two events becoming linked by the presence of Song and the increased violence which soon followed. The insertion of this footage may be intended – for viewers aware of this granular history – to imply that the Cultural Revolution cleared a path for the social advancement of the elite's children at the expense of loyal party members. Noticeably the controversy surrounding Song Binbin's possible direct involvement in Bian's death continued even many years after the film (52–3). But, amidst the vast maelstrom of films from a world of cinemas, how many potential viewers will know of this specific controversy – whether viewers in China or elsewhere? For many, depending on their existing knowledge of China, the documentary may be all they can know of this history, and even that will be patchily understood without more in-depth research.

Thus the initial impression left by the film – of its encouraging of an ethical re-engagement with the world via the recovery of a tragic, emotionally affective obscured familial past – ultimately appears to reflect more upon the *difficulties of realising* the complexities of the many lost or censored (world) histories which re-emerge in the time-images of modern political cinema. This distinction is crucial because, if the re-emergence of a submerged history is the ethical potential of such cinemas, then the way in which this story of a submerged history is told and understood (the politics of this history), will directly influence its ethical potential to rejuvenate (or not) a belief in this world and its history. A cinematic ethics, then, may not always be solely about reviving our belief in this world in the manner Deleuze outlined. With a world of cinemas in mind it is necessary to consider that grasping the immensity or understanding the nuance of world history encountered in such films may be impossible.[7] Depending on the viewer, an encounter with a film like *Though I am Gone* may actually challenge our ability to know what precisely to believe in in this world, which for the ethical life of Wang revolves around a sense of justice, granted, but with a particular political inflection revealing of *the competing or contested nature of history itself* (memory against memory, or perhaps, memories against memories). In terms of Deleuze's cinematic ethics and the time-image, the experience of viewing *Though I am Gone* may, for some, indicate the challenges surrounding how a film can ever really represent, or a viewer grasp, the complexity of the world (and its histories) in a way which might unproblematically rejuvenate a belief in it.

Even so, hope may not be lost. What the encounter with *Though I am Gone* also shows, is the *ability of cinema to indicate, even if tacitly, its inability* in this respect, and, correspondingly, the *ability this gives the viewer to realise their inability* to fully know the history (rather, histories) upon which a renewed belief in the world might be founded. Put another way, what the time-image provides in terms of a cinematic ethics is still akin to the belief which Deleuze felt it offered – it is, in short, a reason to at least *engage* with this world, even if (to add the necessary nuance) this is undertaken in the knowledge that how its history is (rather, how its histories are) constructed and reconstructed in the present is a process which they are (imperfectly) involved in even as they watch. This ethical prompt to continue to engage in spite of what can only be partially understood may be of great importance in our contemporary world, in which the state of exception continues to be normalised under neoliberalism with all the attendant ramifications this has for how history is recorded and preserved. These are precisely the ramifications we are reminded of by their re-emergence from 'out of the past' in the encounter with *Though I am Gone*. Thus the relationship between a cinematic ethics and the representation of history may be more complex than Deleuze's formulation perhaps originally envisaged, but there remains an important relationship and in the current moment its ethical function remains extremely vital.

Thanks to Heather Inwood, Victor Fan, William Brown, Lucy Bolton and Robert Sinnerbrink for insights which greatly strengthened the work. Especially to those who offered invaluable feedback on an early draft.

Notes

1. Modern political cinemas, in the second half of the twentieth century, often emerged from contexts which sought to challenge their marginalised place in the world, to reconsider their relation to the formerly colonial, Eurocentric, Enlightenment view of world history which remains in the Westocentrism of neoliberal globalisation. Even so, more recently Chinese cinema has also been explored in terms of its creation of modern political cinema. For example, Matthew Holtmeier explores how director Jia Zhangke films the aimlessness of the 'birth control generation' whose lives encounter the 'intolerable features' of 'rapid economic growth and urbanization in China' (2019: 114). This, in a contemporary China which David Harvey famously described in terms of its development of 'neoliberalism "with Chinese characteristics"', as the economic reforms which followed the Cultural Revolution (under Deng Xiaoping in the late 1970s) constructed 'a particular kind of market economy that increasingly incorporates neoliberal elements interdigitated with authoritarian centralized control' (Harvey 2005: 120).
2. For the purposes of this discussion I leave to one side the – at time of writing – ongoing reconsideration of this idea which has been prompted by Agamben's own publications in reaction to the global pandemic of 2020.
3. On platforms like YouTube, *Though I am Gone* sometimes goes by alternative English translations such as *Although I am Gone*, or *Though I was Dead*. The film's proposed mainland premiere at the Yunnan Multi Culture Visual Festival (Yunfest) is commonly held to be the reason for the festival's interruption in 2007.
4. See further on Deleuze and Chinese cinemas in Martin-Jones and Fleming 2014; Brown 2014; Holtmeier 2019.
5. Indicative of this continuity, class labels were attached to people persecuted in the wake of the Civil War, a process often at odds with reality which was enacted in an intensified manner during the Cultural Revolution (188). Further evidence of continuity is offered in relation to the broader economic policy of the Third Front which shaped the nation militarily and industrially from 1964 to 1971. In this context, the Cultural Revolution's mass mobilisation of youth can be understood as preparing the populace for war with either the USA or the USSR (Joseph et al. 1991: 2–3). Economically, moreover, Cultural Revolution policies around health and education, laid the ground upon which Deng Xiaoping's economic reforms were built (75–83, 98).
6. This is sometimes otherwise translated as 'Be Violent'.
7. See further on this in an article published after the completion of this work on *Though I am Gone*, but before its publication (Stone and Freijo 2021).

References

Agamben, Giorgio (2003), *State of Exception*, translated by K. Attell, 2005, Chicago: University of Chicago Press.
Bailey, Paul J. (2001), *China in the Twentieth Century*, Oxford: Blackwell.
Berry, Chris and Lisa Rofel (2010), 'Alternative archive', in Chris Berry, Lu Xinyu and Lisa Rofel (eds), *The New Chinese Documentary Film Movement*, Hong Kong: Hong Kong University Press, pp. 135–54.

Brown, William (2014), 'Bringing the past into the present', *Cinema: Journal of Philosophy and the Moving Image*, 6: 73–93.
Deleuze, Gilles (1985), *Cinema 2*, translated by H. Tomlinson and R. Galeta, 2005, London: Continuum.
Edwards, Dan (2015), *Independent Chinese Documentary*, Cambridge: Cambridge University Press.
Harvey, David (2005), *A Brief History of Neoliberalism*, Oxford: Oxford University Press.
Holtmeier, Matthew (2019), *Contemporary Political Cinema*, Edinburgh: Edinburgh University Press.
Jelin, Elizabeth (2003), *State Repression and the Struggles for Memory*, London: Latin American Bureau.
Joseph, William A., Christine P. W. Wong and David Zweig (1991), 'Introduction', in William A. Joseph, Christine P.W. Wong and David Zweig, *New Perspectives on the Cultural Revolution*, Cambridge, MA: Council on East Asian Studies/Harvard University Press, pp. 1–18.
Kraus, Richard Curt (2012), *The Cultural Revolution*, Oxford: Oxford University Press.
Li, Jie (2009), 'Virtual museums of forbidden memories', *Public Culture*, 21: 3, 539–49.
Macfarquhar, Roderick and Michael Schoenhals (2006), *Mao's Last Revolution*, Cambridge, MA: Belknap Press.
Martin-Jones, David (2018), *Cinema Against Doublethink*. London: Routledge.
Martin-Jones, David and David Fleming (eds) (2014), 'Special Issue: Deleuze and Chinese Cinemas', *Journal of Chinese Cinemas*, 8: 2.
Rodowick, D. N. (2010), 'The world, time', in D. N. Rodowick (ed.), *Afterimages of Gilles Deleuze's Film Philosophy*, Minneapolis: University of Minnesota Press, pp. 97–114.
Sinnerbrink, Robert (2015), *Cinematic Ethics*, London: Routledge.
Stone, Rob and Luis Freijo (2021), 'World Cinema between the rock of the unknowable and the hard place of the as yet unknown', *Transnational Screens*, 12: 1, 1–22.
Sutton, Damian (2009), *Photography, Cinema, Memory*, Minneapolis: Minnesota University Press.
Tatlow, Didi Kirsten (2016), 'Fate catches up to a cultural revolution museum in China', *The New York Times*, 2 October, <https://www.google.co.uk/amp/s/www.nytimes.com/2016/10/03/world/asia/china-cultural-revolution-shantou-museum.amp.html> (accessed 13 August 2019).
Wang, Hui (2009), *The End of the Revolution*, London: Verso.
White, Lynn T. III (1991), 'The Cultural Revolution as an unintended result of administrative policies', in William A. Joseph, Christine P. W. Wong and David Zweig, *New Perspectives on the Cultural Revolution*, Cambridge, MA: Council on East Asian Studies/Harvard University Press, pp. 83–104.
Zhang, Joshua and James D. Wright (2018), *Violence, Periodization and Definition of the Cultural Revolution*, Leiden: Brill.

3. MEMORY, WITNESSING AND RE-ENACTMENT: *THE LOOK OF SILENCE*, *S21: THE KHMER ROUGE KILLING MACHINE* AND CINEMATIC ETHICS

Robert Sinnerbrink

Contemporary cinema is rife with films dealing with ethical issues, moral problems or cultural-political concerns. This is evident in the rise of new ethically and politically engaged cinema, particularly within diverse cultural traditions and social contexts, amidst the dissemination of what is loosely called 'world cinemas' (see Nagib 2011; Chaudhuri 2014; Martin-Jones 2011, 2019). Contemporary documentary, moreover, is where many socially charged ethical problems and cultural-moral debates today are vigorously examined and creatively explored. It is where cultures across the globe can find cinematic ways to address, reflect upon, question, and explore some of the most important moral-ethical and cultural-political issues of our times. Most discussion of the ethical dimensions of documentary, however, has focused on the question of truth and objectivity in relation to documentary presentation (the ethics of representation), or on the question of ethical practices of informed consent and transparent communication in the treatment of documentary subjects (the ethics of production). What of the ethical dimensions of spectatorial experience, the way documentary film can evoke emotional engagement, critical reflection, even social action? How might the medium of documentary be used to solicit ethical experiences in viewers as part of making arguments, presenting claims, or exposing problems? As I explore in what follows, such questions raise the question of documentary cinema's ethical potential, a question I propose to address via the notion of a *cinematic ethics*: the idea of cinema as a medium of ethical experience (see Sinnerbrink 2016: 3–24).

The idea of cinema as medium of ethical experience offers a way of understanding what cinema can do: its transformative potential to sharpen our moral perception, challenge our beliefs through experiential means, and thus enhance our understanding of moral-social complexity. It can also provoke philosophical thinking through morally confronting or provocative forms of ethical experience conveyed and evoked through film. In this way it can bring together the three important aspects of the cinema-ethics relationship: ethical content in narrative cinema; the ethics of cinematic representation (from filmmaker and spectator perspectives); and the ethics of cinema as symptomatic of broader cultural, social and ideological concerns. To these three dimensions we can add a fourth: the *aesthetic dimension* of cinema – the role of aesthetic form in intensifying our experience, refining and focusing our attention, and thus of conveying complexity of meaning – as a way of *evoking ethical experience* and thereby inviting critical reflection. It is important to understand how the aesthetic elements and features of a film are articulated with each other, and how these together serve to communicate ethical meaning via aesthetic means.

The possibilities of cinema understood as a medium of ethical experience are richly evident in documentary, one of the most innovative areas in global cinema. Recent documentary theory, for example, has highlighted the importance of ethics, subjectivity, reflexivity, fictional and aesthetic techniques in the production and reception of non-fictional film (see Winston 2000; Renov 2004; Bruzzi 2006; Cooper 2006; Saxton 2008; Hongisto 2015; Nichols 2016). Others have emphasised the role of emotional engagement, subjectivity, and narrative form in persuading viewers through argument and rhetoric (see Plantinga 1997; Renov 2004; Bondebjerg 2014). Far from assuming a transparent or veridical relationship between cinematic image and documentary evidence, contemporary filmmakers – such as Werner Herzog, Michael Moore and Errol Morris – have explored the possibilities of non-fiction film to include fictional elements, to question the 'constructed' nature of images, and to explore the dialectic of complicity between filmmaker, subject and spectator (see Williams 1993; Renov 2004). What remains, however, is to explore how documentary can also serve as a medium of ethical experience, a way of eliciting and expressing experiences of moral-social complexity, political violence and ethical responsiveness.

In what follows I begin to address this challenge by examining two of the most confronting and original non-fiction film of recent years, *The Act of Killing* (2012) and *The Look of Silence* (2014), directed by Joshua Oppenheimer, Christine Cynn and an Indonesian filmmaker (Anonymous).[1] Emerging from an earlier collaborative film project dealing with the violent oppression of one of Indonesia's plantation unions, both *The Act of Killing* and its companion piece, *The Look of Silence* (2014), explore the ongoing legacy of Indonesia's state-sanctioned death squads, who were responsible for killing over a million alleged 'communists' following the Indonesian military coup of 1965 (see Cribb 2001;

McGregor 2009). A disturbing fusion of reflexive 'perpetrator documentary' and cinematic investigation of the traumatic effects of political violence, *The Act of Killing* focuses on the perspectives of several 'gangster killers' involved in the 1965–6 massacres.[2] Not only are these men treated as heroes by their community, freely boasting about their past, they are filmed making their own fictional movie re-enactments of their crimes. Such a documentary project is ethically and politically risky, so it is not surprising that *The Act of Killing* attracted criticism from some film scholars concerned that it violated ground rules of ethical film-making practice (see Cribb 2014; Heryanto 2014; Winston et al. 2017). This is no doubt due to the challenges facing documentary films that deal with political violence and historical trauma; above all, the problem of how to acknowledge and adequately represent violent experiences of trauma that resist psychological assimilation and defy conventional forms of representation (see Saxton 2008; Douglass and Vogler 2003; Walker 2005; Cooper 2006; Daniels-Yeoman 2017; Mroz 2020). My claim here, however, is that this confronting exploration of the traumatic intersection of cinema, violence and politics is precisely what makes Oppenheimer's documentaries a challenging case study in cinematic ethics.[3]

The Look of Silence (2014), Oppenheimer's companion piece to *The Act of Killing* (2012), is a film that addresses many of the issues raised by, and criticisms made of, its controversial counterpart (Cribb 2014; Heryanto 2014; Winston et al. 2017). Indeed, the two films compose a documentary diptych, *The Look of Silence* providing the absent victim/survivor perspective and reckoning with historical responsibility that were lacking in *The Act of Killing*'s focus on the perpetrators of the massacres following Suharto's military coup. In what follows, I explore *The Look of Silence* as an observational study of 'ethical witnessing' in which the brother of a victim questions and confronts his sibling's killers, showing the complexities of witness/perpetrator testimony as a survivor demands recognition of shared suffering and an acknowledgment of historical injustice. I focus on the difficulties of narrating traumatic memories and the need for recognition of historical and political violence, exploring how we can approach the encounters between survivor/witness and perpetrator as cases of 'ethical witnessing' (see Douglass and Vogler 2003; Cooper 2006; Saxton 2008). *The Look of Silence* explores the ethical force of the survivor's gaze, and the power of ethical questioning to seek acknowledgment of injustice. It enacts a demand for recognition of past suffering, while demonstrating the challenges in attempting to document witness testimonials that acknowledge, rather than perpetuate, social and political violence.

I contrast this film with Rithy Panh's powerful perpetrator/witness documentary *S21: The Khmer Rouge Killing Machine* (2003), which focuses on the genocide/crimes against humanity perpetrated by the Pol Pot regime in Cambodia (1975–9). The latter combines perpetrator re-enactment with witness testimonial as well as the ethical questioning of perpetrators by one of the few remaining survivors of the notorious Tuol Sleng or S21 (Security Prison 21), a former Phnom Penh high school that was converted into a prison and interrogation centre.[4] I focus on how traumatic violence, which dissociates memory and blocks speech, is released in two ways within this film: (1) visual representations (former prisoner/survivor Vann Nath's paintings of prison scenes, and the prison collection of photographs of political enemies/victims taken prior to their deaths); and (2) bodily or 'somatic memory' (elicited via the perpetrators' physical re-enactments of their daily routines of disciplining and brutalising the prisoners).[5] In sum, I aim to show how each film uses a different strategy to both elicit and depict memories of violence and trauma, and how each engages in different kinds of ethical witnessing and political memorialising of the past. In *The Look of Silence,* it is via ethical witnessing or an ethics of solidarity in which direct questioning of perpetrators is accompanied by a witnessing of past suffering that offers an expression of solidarity with the survivors' perspective, creating an ambivalent space of recognition in which the traumatic work of reconciliation might begin. In *S21*, it is via physical re-enactment as a performative means of releasing bodily memory dealing with traumatic violence. In both films, the affective and emotional dimensions of performative re-enactment open a space where the representation of experiences of political violence can facilitate the recognition of this violence as a first step towards both memorialising the past and making possible the creation of a democratic future.

The Look of Silence

Released in 2014 (although shot before *The Act of Killing* was released in 2012), *The Look of Silence* differs sharply in style, focus and mood from its predecessor. If *The Act of Killing* was a disturbing 'fever dream', a 'documentary of the imagination' (as Oppenheimer put it), *The Look of Silence* enacts a confrontation with that imagination, an expression of ethical solidarity with the survivor's gaze in confronting perpetrators about their past. It adopts a more sober, observational mode of presentation, highlighting the survivor's acts of ethical witnessing, while revealing the ambiguity of the perpetrator testimony that it presents. It also shows how historical trauma renders the possibility of truth (about the past) and reconciliation (with the perpetrators and their institutional supporters) exceedingly difficult.

The film's compositional style is poetic and contemplative. It frames what is to come using a close-up of an elderly man's face, his eyes framed by red plastic frames fitted with test lenses (a phoropter) as he stares silently into the camera. The film's title – *The Look of Silence* – appears over an image of jumping bean moth pupae, randomly moving across a shiny table, against a background drone of insect sounds. We see a man, staring off-screen, watching video footage of another man narrating how he killed someone; the killer on television laughs as he tells the story of the man's death, explaining how he choked his victim (Ali Sumiton), then ripped him open, spilling his intestines. The man watching this footage is Adi Rukun, whose older brother Ramli was brutally murdered during the massacres; his arresting face offers an eloquent symbol of the film's title, an expression of Stoicism in response to historical trauma.

This sequence is followed by a long shot of trucks wending their way along a rough dirt road, lights flaring. Against this melancholy background appears an introductory text:

> In 1965, the Indonesian government was overthrown by the military. Anybody opposed to the military dictatorship could be accused of being a communist: union members, landless farmers, intellectuals. In less than a year, over one million 'communists' were murdered – and the perpetrators still hold power throughout the country.

The framing of this introductory text within contemporary Indonesia – a country emerging from decades of dictatorship and struggling to build a democratic culture – situates what we are about to see within an historical and political perspective: how does the experience of political violence and historical trauma continue to affect its citizens and community in the present? How does it block attempts to build a democracy when the historical violence of the past remains unacknowledged or when its victims and their descendants are still oppressed? Such are the questions that both *The Act of Killing* and *The Look of Silence* seek to address, using the medium of (documentary) cinema itself to both stage and express, elicit and expose, complex varieties of ethical and historical experience.

The film's central metaphor, correcting moral blindness through ethical witnessing, is introduced in the next sequence, which shows Adi – an optometrist – testing an older woman's eyes and asking about the past. In this sequence, we see Adi's unorthodox method of gathering witness testimony, patiently questioning an elderly woman, and later, perpetrators themselves, about their memories of the past, in a direct but respectful manner. He does so while testing their eyes, checking both their visual and moral perception, their historical recollection and ethical recognition. As with other witnesses, the old woman both does and does not remember, denying then admitting the slaughter. This simultaneous acknowledgment and denial mark all the encounters between survivor and perpetrator, complicating the veracity of any witness testimony.

Adi's quest to establish how his brother Ramli died is embedded in a global history of political violence, ideological mystification and economic exploitation. This complex nexus is deftly evoked by two related vignettes. In the first,

MEMORY, WITNESSING AND RE-ENACTMENT

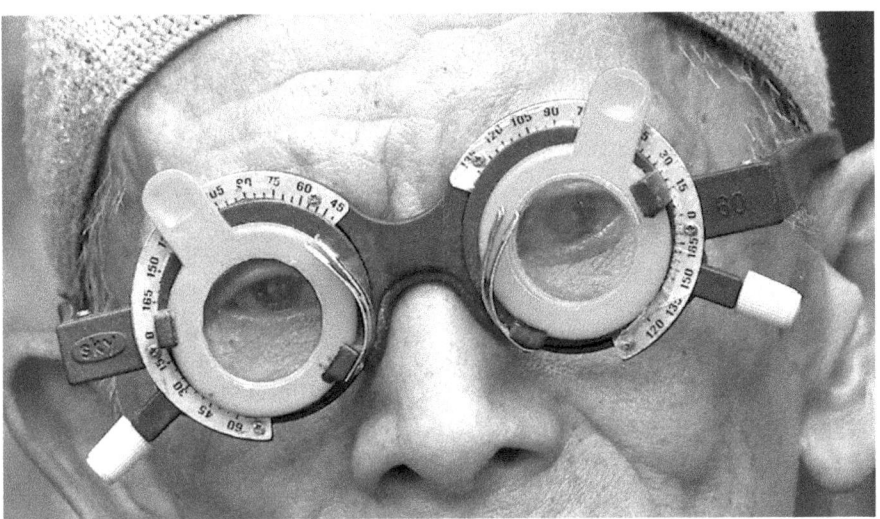

Figure 3.1 Moral blindness and ethical witnessing.

Adi is shown watching a 1967 American NBC news report on the 'successful' slaughter of communists in Indonesia. One scene features an Indonesian interviewee boasting that 'Bali becomes even more beautiful without communists', and that some of the communists even 'wanted to be killed'. These extraordinary comments go unquestioned by the reporter, who remarks on the potential wealth and resources available in Indonesia. This background of Western interests supporting the slaughter of 'communists' with an eye to political and economic advantage is encapsulated in one shot, an image of a Goodyear tyre factory, followed by a shot of surviving 'communists' as plantation slave labour being marched at gunpoint. A fledgling union organised by rubber plantation workers is decimated, the 'communist' members killed by local citizens, an event that provided the core of Oppenheimer's original project, *The Globalisation Tapes* (2003). Here again the link is made between the cold-war economic and political interests of Western powers supporting the Suharto regime, and the latter's anti-communist stance being used to justify exploitation, corruption, oppression and violence.

The second vignette emphasises the continuity in the ideological discourse concerning the 'communist threat' to Indonesian society and politics. A schoolteacher in a present-day classroom is delivering a history lesson: 'Communists are cruel. Communists don't believe in God. To change the political system, the communists kidnapped six army generals, sliced their faces with razor blades, ripped out their eyes, and killed them.' The teacher asks the wide-eyed children whether they would like their eyes ripped out – eyes and vision,

Figure 3.2 Adi Rukun: the look of silence.

historical and moral blindness, visual and ideological perception coming into focus once again. 'Communists were cruel, so the government had to repress them, put them in prison.' This officially sanctioned version of the failed 30 September 'Kidnapping of the Generals' coup is well-known from the movie *Treachery of the G30S/PKI* (Arifin C. Noer, 1984), which until Suharto's resignation in 1998 had been mandatory viewing for schoolchildren every year on the anniversary of that event. The teacher explains to the children that distrust of the communists remains in force: their descendants are not allowed to work for the government, join the army or the police force. The lesson is clear: 'If you rebel against the state, you go to jail. So, let's thank the heroes who struggled to make our country . . . A democracy!' Later, in conversation with his son, Adi explains that what the teacher said about the communists was false: 'It's all lies'. Did your teacher tell you about the people killed at Snake River? Or the million innocent people who were murdered?' This moment of generational reckoning, Adi challenging the state propaganda and insisting on historical truth, encapsulates the film's ethical project: to articulate the survivors' silence against that of the perpetrators, to foster acknowledgment of their crimes, and to find a voice demanding recognition of historical injustice and the legacies of political violence in the present.

The Look of Silence is a documentary work that engages in an ethics of witnessing or ethics of solidarity: a witnessing of past suffering and expression of solidarity with the survivors' perspective, one that allows them to speak on their own behalf across historical and political divides. Throughout the film, the camera is unobtrusive and observant, providing long takes of Adi watching footage of perpetrators describing their crimes, of Adi conversing with his mother, then examining the eyes of perpetrators, questioning them about their memories of the past. The dialogue between past and present, perpetrator and survivor, is conducted via the medium of cinema: through Oppenheimer's footage of the perpetrators demonstrating how they killed 'communists' like Ramli, footage that is shown to a killer's wife and sons (who falsely deny any knowledge of their father's actions). Adi watches footage of the killers boasting about their actions, then is shown testing their eyes and questioning them about their past. The camera documents the exchange, capturing nuances of expression – or Adi's suppression of such expression – drawing out a brazen candour from the perpetrator that is rendered suspect and opaque. The footage both underlines and attempts to bridge the gulf between the historical past and the political present, prompting an ethical space of engagement within which recognition of historical injustice and ethico-political reconciliation might be possible.

In one of the most confronting sequences in the film, Adi interviews Amir Siahaan, commander of the Snake River death squads, who is introduced via television footage, which Adi watches, showing Siahaan recounting the gruesome killings: 'We exterminated communists for three months, day and night. We took them two miles from here, dug holes, and buried them alive.' He explains how they received hundreds of prisoners from Snake River and is proud of the approval he received for his role in their slaughter: 'We should be rewarded with a trip to America, by airplane or cruise. We deserve it! We did this because America taught us to hate communists.'

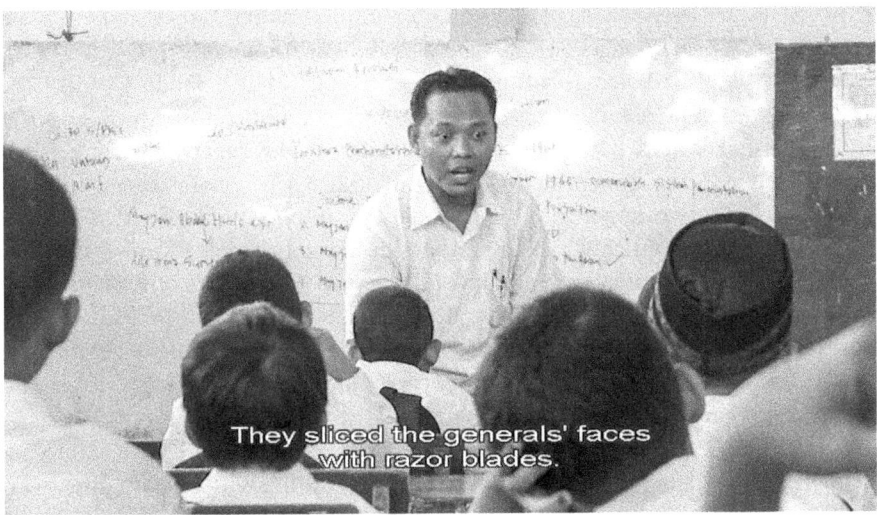

Figure 3.3   Historical trauma and political propaganda.

This shocking footage, linking the death squads with the Indonesian government and US political support, frames Adi's interview with the elderly death squad leader. Adi asks him whether he acquired his wealth from what he did. 'If you do good, you are rewarded,' Siahaan replies, boastfully. Adi takes up the challenge by asking whether he was responsible for the killings here, and whether locals are aware of his past – an exchange of gazes, the look of silence confronting the look of violence. To make his point clear, Adi explains: 'My elder brother, he was killed. Because you commanded the killings . . .'. What follows is an extraordinary exchange, Siahaan denying responsibility, claiming that there were many Komando Aksi groups and other commanders above him. He takes refuge behind the regime, who sanctioned the violence: 'we were protected by the government. So, you can't say that I was responsible.' Siahaan appears visibly upset at this point, even on the verge of tears.

Adi observes that none of the killers he meets feels responsible; they don't even feel regret. In a direct challenge to their (moral and legal) impunity, Adi accuses him of avoiding his moral responsibility; he stares directly into Siahaan's face, another moment of witnessing. Siahaan changes tack and wants to know where Ramli (who remains unnamed) was killed, which village and district, almost ordering Adi to supply this information, which he refuses to do. 'I must hide my identity because the killers are still in power and still consider themselves heroes.' The standoff between them intensifies, marked by menacing silence and threatening stares. Amir then exercises his intimidatory social power, as the other killers do in response to the moral pressure of Adi's questioning. We see him in profile, sporting a red-orange camouflage shirt with the *Pemuda Pancasila* (Pancasila Youth) insignia, as he warns Adi: 'These days subversives are everywhere. The known communists aren't dangerous; it's the secret ones who are dangerous. Maybe what you are doing now is a secret communist activity!' Adi remains unperturbed, asking what Siahaan would have done he had come asking such questions during the dictatorship. 'You can't imagine what would have happened,' Siahaan warns darkly, clearly regarding himself still as a government-sanctioned killer. Adi remains silent, looking away, his moral courage crumbling under the implicit violence of Siahaan's gaze. It is clear from this exchange that the effects of political violence and threat of social intimidation remain in force; the killers' acts still reverberate today as they continue to enjoy impunity. Adi embodies the 'look of silence' maintained by the descendants of the victims to force a reckoning with the past; but he, along with others in his situation, remains vulnerable to the power and impunity of the perpetrators, even today.

The ambiguous hope for reconciliation comes to the fore in a troubling sequence. Adi visits the home of an elderly killer sitting with his daughter, who tells how she was proud of her father for having exterminated so many communists. 'My father is famous around here; people respect him.' This accolade rouses the ageing father to tell an anecdote about how he once brought a woman's severed head into a Chinese coffee shop to frighten the patrons. His daughter is shocked, repeating that she knew nothing about her father's bloodthirsty actions ('I never knew this; it's terrifying, sadistic'). When Adi reveals that his own brother was killed, showing real emotion, the reactions are startling: the father shifts uncomfortably, acts distracted, and wants the conversation to end; the daughter is shocked, offering an apology on her father's behalf, embracing Adi and inviting him into their family. Whether this gesture is to offer reconciliation for the past or just to end the uncomfortable interrogation is hard to say. 'It's not your fault that your father is a murderer,' Adi remarks, opening an ambiguous intergenerational ethical space of communication between him and the daughter: they embrace, and Adi even shakes the father's hand, who remains unmoved. A fleeting moment of recognition opens – at least across generational divides – but quickly closes again. An exhausted Adi takes his leave, in a distressed state, suggesting how far the community remains from any truth and reconciliation process, and leaving unclear whether survivors will be genuinely acknowledged or just placated into silence.

There remains a clear asymmetry in the relationship between (descendants of) perpetrators and victims. The latter cannot speak on their own behalf and must be spoken for by others; either by their descendants, who risk their own safety in doing so, or by the perpetrators, who minimise their own responsibility and continue to intimidate the survivors. The perpetrators retain the power to give or refuse recognition, controlling the terms on which such recognition is granted, demanding a diminution of personal culpability by appealing to excuses. These follow a familiar script: political necessity, chain of command, elapsed time, historical amnesia, lack of choice, frailty of the perpetrators ('he's an old man now'), or mandatory social harmony ('why don't we all just get along, like the dictatorship taught us', as the son of one of the killers says). Indeed, what Leshu Torchin calls the 'veracity gap' – the gap between perpetrators' testimony and historical reality – becomes evident in the perpetrator testimony offered in the film, a testimony tainted by the unreliability of perpetrator/witnesses, their self-deception coupled with self-justification.[6] This testimony is not only difficult to obtain, given the perpetrators' impunity and power; it requires a moral courage to bear witness to past injustices by questioning those still in power whose past actions remain unpunished. The survivor's gaze encompasses the ineradicable memory of past violence, of unimaginable suffering, and its traumatic effects on survivors; but it also remains stymied by the effects of this trauma, a silence that does not cease.

The emotional dynamics of the exchanges between perpetrator and victim are telling: Adi's emotional imperturbability and self-control, evident during his questioning of perpetrators, is broken only by his intimidating encounter with Siahaan, the Komando Aksi leader. We see his ageing mother's anger at the brutal

Figure 3.4 Amir Siahaan: denying responsibility and threatening Rukun.

murder of her son, Ramli, and melancholy grieving for her son's loss; there is the perpetrators' exuberant boasting and display of (moral and political) impunity, coupled with their ambiguous testimony, mixing acknowledgement with refusal, moral guilt with self-serving rationalisations. The film highlights the pathos and suffering of the victims' surviving descendants, still traumatised by the unacknowledged injustice that they suffered. In contrast with *The Act of Killing*, the mood of the film is contemplative, melancholy, sorrowful; respectfully distant yet intimately involved in Adi's quest to seek justice and acknowledgement from his brother's killers. It is a documentary of the effects of political trauma and historical injustice on the present generation, who are finding the moral courage and political impetus to confront the perpetrators and force social and historical recognition of their experience. *The Look of Silence* thereby seeks to open a dialogue between this surviving generation and the perpetrators, to create a space of shared memory for the experience of recognition – an acknowledgement of the ongoing effects of historical trauma – without which the survivors will be unable to create a meaningful future.

S21: The Khmer Rouge Killing Machine (2003)

The question of memory – especially the memory of traumatic political violence that haunts a nation – is also at the centre of Cambodian filmmaker Rithy Panh's *S21: The Khmer Rouge Killing Machine* (2003). Perhaps his best-known film, *S21* bears close comparison with both *The Act of Killing* and *The*

Look of Silence for combining perpetrator re-enactments of violence with survivor testimony and moral questioning of the perpetrators. As survivors of the Pol Pot regime's oppressive violence, Rithy Panh's family was deported from Phnom Penh to a rural village, where only Rithy survived, the rest of his family succumbing to 'starvation, physical and psychological exhaustion, or disease' (Boyle 2009: 95). At age eleven, he was put into a forced labour camp, escaping when he was fourteen, spent time in a refugee camp in Thailand and eventually reached France, where he studied film at the prestigious IDHEC (l'Institut des Hautes Études Cinématographiques) (Boyle 2009: 95). He has made both documentaries and narrative works, focusing on the Cambodian genocide, experiences of refugees, and life in post-Khmer Rouge Cambodia. He has also ventured into fictional and experimental works.[7] *The Missing Picture* (2013), for example, combines found footage with clay animation to recreate – and to reimagine visually, finding the 'missing image' of what was not represented – the experiences and atrocities defining life under the Khmer Rouge regime.

Like *The Look of Silence*, S21 commences with an establishing shot of contemporary Phnom Penh, followed by found propaganda footage from the Vietnam War and Khmer Rouge periods, the images accompanied by a contextualising introductory text concerning the historical and political context of the film:

> Before the war, Cambodia was an independent, neutral country with a population of 7.7 million. 1970: Coup d'Etat against Prince Sihanouk. Extension of the Vietnam War. American bombardments. Civil War. 600 000 dead. 17 April, 1975. Victory of the Khmers Rouges. Displaced populations. Town-dwellers driven out, schools closed, currency abolished, religions banned, forced labour camps, surveillance, famine, terror, executions. A genocide: 2 million dead.

The shots of contemporary Phnom Penh and the introductory text are accompanied by sounds of gunshots and muffled voices. Black and white propaganda footage is accompanied by martial political songs, followed by gunshots and ominous sounds. Another revolutionary song commences. The lyrics are displayed on screen and are chilling in their glorification of blood as the source of revolutionary nationhood: 'Bright red blood/ that covers cities and plains of Kampuchea, our motherland/ Sublime blood of workers and peasants/ Sublime blood of revolutionary fighting men and women/ The blood, changing into unrepentant hatred/ and resolute struggle.'

The song fades to a contemporary scene, a family working in the rice paddies, planting seedlings under a hot sun. As they work, the song concludes: 'On 17 April, under the flag of revolution/ Frees us from slavery . . .'. We are introduced to a family, a man and his wife with a small baby and child; we cut to a shot of the man (whom we soon learn is former guard, Him Houy) with his mother, who appear to be watching something off-screen. She wishes that a ceremony could wipe away images of the past, that her son could become a new man as of today; they are discussing his past, that it would have been better to go to the front during the war (than serve as an S21 prison guard), and that he must tell the truth about what happened. We then see his father who agrees that the truth must be told about how many people were killed, and that there should be a ceremony so that the dead can rest in peace. As his parents discuss the terrible events, the man looks troubled and wants the discussion to stop ('I'm sick all day long. I can't eat a thing'). The woman exclaims that she cannot understand how her son did what he did, that he was good but was indoctrinated, 'turned into a thug who killed people'. She laments the brutality of the Khmer Rouge, who killed people with terrible cruelty. The grandfather reiterates the 'blood' theme; the Khmer used to say, 'The bones cry out, the flesh calls for blood'. The son is asked for his opinion; he explains that freely killing people of one's own free will is evil, but since he was given orders, terrorised at gunpoint, it was 'the leaders who gave the orders' who are morally responsible. Like other perpetrators, he absolves himself of moral responsibility by stressing the institutionalised character of the killing. Despite his war crimes, he has tried to live a good life but fears he will be punished for what he did – echoing the sentiments of fellow perpetrators in *The Look of Silence*. This framing sequence contextualises historically and psychologically what we are about to see – a combined witness testimony and perpetrator confrontation set at the site of unnameable atrocities, the S21 prison and execution centre.

S21, the code name for Tuon Sleng, is one of nearly one hundred and fifty imprisonment and interrogation centres that existed across Democratic Kampuchea during the Khmer Rouge years (1975–9). Panh brings together Vann Nath and Chum Mey, two of the only remaining survivors of the S21 prison, who struggle to deal with the traumatic memories solicited by this terrible place.[8] They stand in front of the former high school turned prison and torture centre, Mey in tears, unable to find the words to express the pain and suffering he witnessed and experienced there nearly thirty years earlier. Nath remains a calming voice and presence, comforting him, and gently talking him through the pain, trying to recall the details of the unspeakable acts that were committed there – as a painter, he was able to make images to represent what could not be assimilated to memory, to depict visually that which defied verbal description and personal recollection. At the same time, his ability to paint found him favour with the notorious commander of S21 – nicknamed Duch – who personally authorised that Nath be spared as 'useful' since he liked his paintings. His haunting prison paintings, which in one scene Nath continues to paint as he narrates the story of his arrest, interrogation and torture, provide a nonverbal means of articulating memories and experiences that would otherwise have remained buried, too traumatic to recall or repeat.

The film also focuses on the perpetrators – Him Houy, deputy head of prison security, former guards, interrogators, a clerk-typist, a photographer, and a 'doctor' – who return to the prison and are asked to describe but also to show what they did and try to explain why (Boyle 2009: 98). As with Oppenheimer and his collaborators in *The Act of Killing*, Panh took years to gain the trust of the perpetrators, persuading them to visit the site, and to re-enact their daily routines, all to create a space of acknowledgement where they could find a way to 'restore their humanity' (Oppenheimer and Panh 2012: 248–9). They are questioned by Nath, former prisoner and painter, about their role in the Khmer Rouge killing machine; he calmly asks how they felt about what they were doing, how they could justify it to themselves. The responses follow the same pattern evident in *The Look of Silence* (we were following orders, doing out duty; they would have killed us too). In one disturbing sequence, Nath asks the former guards whether they regard themselves as victims too, which they apparently do ('we were secondary victims', 'many guards also died'), to which Nath replies, 'If you were victims, then what does that make us?' (Alkan 2020: 274). The importance of maintaining a clear distinction between perpetrators and victims, holding firm to their moral accountability despite contextual circumstances, no matter how institutionalised the violence or 'banal' the evil meted out by the regime, remains one of the central arguments of the film.

The prison was not designed to kill the inmates – their fate had already been decided before they arrived – but to extract 'confessions' of false crimes, proofs of 'treason', membership of the fictitious Kampuchean Workers' Party, and acts of sabotage against the state (Boyle 2009: 97). Having extracted a 'confession' through torture, and another list of 'collaborators', the prisoners were then executed. When asked by Nath how they could have acted so cruelly, without thinking, they reply that they were following orders, that the Party never erred in who it arrested, and that their task was simply to extract confessions from Party enemies and act 'decisively' towards them. It is remarkable how readily these otherwise ordinary family men revert to familiar ideological justifications, using them as psychological shields against feelings of guilt or responsibility. The banality of their evil was carefully documented in neatly written records, which perpetrators and victims consult as providing both evidence and falsification of the past.

Indeed, Panh's goal in this documentary, as Boyle observes, was to retrieve the truth buried within the 'voluminous written records of interrogations', thereby 'restoring the memory of the thousands who died as well as the memories of what happened to them from those who tortured and killed them' (Boyle 2009: 97). By bringing together perpetrators and victims, opening a space of moral questioning, of reckoning with the past, *S21* aims to 'summon traumatic memory by exposing both perpetrators and victims to the site of trauma' (Boyle 2009: 97). Indeed, Panh's work on the Cambodian genocide more generally is concerned with recording and memorialising political violence in the face of political suppression or historical oblivion (Alkan 2020: 273).[9] S21 is a haunting site that reveals the spaces of suffering, confinement, and torture, yet also conceals the traumatic violence that happened there. Panh's film strives to make this manifest in a manner sharing common ethical ground with *The Look of Silence*'s emphasis on confronting the perpetrators and working through historical trauma.

Indeed, the film shows two ways in which traumatic memory might be accessed. The first is *visual representation* as a mediated way of memorialising traumatic experiences that resist verbal description (Nath reflecting on his paintings of prison scenes and on the photographic images of the murdered prisoners). The second is by *physical re-enactment* as a way of retrieving somatic or bodily memory (former guard Khieu Ches transforming himself into the guard he was at S21, pacing up and down the corridors, marching into cells, shouting at the inmates, while narrating his actions blankly but forcefully). When we first encounter Ches, one of the small group of perpetrators participating in the documentary, he is inarticulate and withdrawn about his role in the prison. It is only when he undertakes to act out his physical routines – using the very space where he served as a guard, repeating the daily routines of imprisonment – that we see him transform before our eyes, becoming the guard that he was nearly thirty years before. As Panh remarks in an interview, by re-enacting his daily guard routine, 'his gestures, the memory of his body, came flooding back. Because someone trained him to do this. And the memory of the body never lies' (Camhi 2004: 24; quoted in Boyle 2009: 98). His physical actions thereby reveal the past as an embodiment of "traumatic memory" (Boyle 2009: 98). The prison cells were emptied of furniture (beds, and so on), which the guard treated as imaginatively present, but there were also props made available that he could use (a rusted out 'can' used for toileting, for example, that Ches uses in one sequence enacting his harsh treatment of prisoners sharing a cell). In addition, Panh added to the soundtrack martial revolutionary songs that were played during these routines, which lends a memorial and rhythmic dimension to the somatic memory and motor activity (Oppenheimer and Panh 2012: 244–5). Ches's gestures and comportment strip away the layers of affective and emotional resistance to recalling the past, his body repeating the routines of prison life, while his voice manifests the affectively flat, resolute and emotionally cold demeanour of the guard disciplining, berating and surveilling the vulnerable prisoners.

The other way traumatic memory is retrieved, this time from the victim/survivor perspective, is via visual representations (paintings and photographs). We are shown Nath while he adds some colour detail to the figure of a prisoner being marched with others, pulled by a rope tied around each prisoner's neck, as he narrates details of his experiences of interrogation and torture while in S21. We see paintings of cells with inmates in beds packed head to toe in tiny cells, including children, and hear about the daily brutalities meted out by the guards, the torture and the killings. The act of painting – and continuing to paint – provides a space of representation and recollection, one that allows Nath to both externalise his experiences and then narrate them in a more distanced manner. Indeed, he believes he owes his survival – one of only seven surviving prisoners from S21, where about 17,000 Cambodians were interrogated and tortured before being executed – due to his paintings, which Duch (head of S21, whose portrait Nath painted) and other guards evidently liked (Alkan 2020: 273).[10] Nath also peruses the voluminous photographic records kept at S21, where inmates would be photographed and assigned a number before being tortured or killed. These small headshots – famous from various exhibitions on the Khmer Rouge death camps seen internationally – include people Nath and Mey knew personally; but they also serve, in their institutionalised anonymity and visual simplicity, to open a space in which traumatic memories of these people – who they were and what they experienced – could be rescued from this site. They are images that indirectly document and implicitly express the enormity of the traumatic violence inflicted by the Khmer Rouge regime – one given fuller expression thanks to this documentary intervention.

Like *The Look of Silence*, the mood of the film is melancholy, poignant and reflective. On the one hand, it documents directly witness testimony from two of the remaining survivors of S21, creating a space where they can narrate their experiences and question their torturers. On the other, it uses the two indirect means just mentioned of opening a space to narrate and represent past trauma of the past, mediating devices that create distance while also bringing such experience into focus. As often noted, traumatic experiences remain operative in the present, never fully processed or worked through but also submerged or suppressed; they can be evoked, however, through absence, ellipsis, or poetic suggestion, creating a space in which experiences of pain and suffering or 'world-collapse' that resist literal representation can nonetheless be articulated and expressed (Scarry 1985). The empty space of S21 prison hall, with nothing but dust and piles of detritus from the past accumulating in corners, offers a recurring image of absence that evokes the trauma of the past. In one sequence, a former guard paces up and down the empty hall, furnished with a single desk and chair, piles of rags or rubbish heaped in a corner, as he mechanically recites while performing his daily routine of checking the locks and bars on the beds, checks on the prisoners, yells at those failing to comply, coldly meting out disciplinary cruelty. The bodily re-enactment of his routines, conjured up in the desolate empty hall, enables the narration of traumatic forms of institutionalised violence that are otherwise difficult to imagine.

In this respect, we can speak of the role of (documentary) cinema as a means of accessing memory, confronting trauma, creating a space for the staging of (fictional/non-fictional) re-enactments as means of recollecting traumatic pasts. Both films explore this possibility as a way of retrieving traumatic memory and creating a space in which historical-political violence might be confronted and acknowledged by a society still reckoning with its past. These films do so, however, in different ways. *The Look of Silence* focuses on an ethics of witnessing/ethics of solidarity, emphasising the power of the ethical gaze of the survivor confronting and questioning the perpetrators of political violence. Using cinema as a means of recording but also prompting moral acknowledgement and critical dialogue (as well as the evasion and refusal of the same), *The Look of Silence* enacts an ethics of solidarity with the perspectives of survivor/victims, thereby allowing the latter to speak the truth to power. Adi questions perpetrators about their past, pressing them for acknowledgement of moral and political responsibility, while also seeking ways to create a space in which the traumatic effects of political violence are not only recognised but conditions are put in place for the difficult societal and ethical task of 'working-through' this historical trauma.

S21, by contrast, eschews cinematic/fictional mediation in favour of direct physical re-enactment within the actual site of traumatic violence. Bodily or somatic memory, rather than recollective narration, serves as a means of unlocking the past (for the perpetrators) and retrieving memories that otherwise resist recollection. Alternatively, for the victims, visual representation (painting or photography) depicting individuals imprisoned, beaten or killed, offers a space for reflection, an indirect way of retrieving traumatic memories and of creating space for the recognition of past injustices within the present – a present ever haunted by the suppressed memories of the past. *The Look of Silence* also deploys direct questioning of perpetrators by victims but does so in 'neutral' everyday contexts (Adi examining the eyes of perpetrators at their homes; interviewing a perpetrator, in military uniform, in a domestic space; meeting a perpetrator and his daughter at their home). *S21* does so, however, at the site of trauma itself, now converted into a museum documenting the genocide/crimes against humanity. This leaves the perpetrators more exposed than rehearsing within a studio setting or being interviewed in their homes (given the impunity they still enjoy); but it also enabled them to engage in physical re-enactments that revealed their attitudes as part of the Khmer Rouge 'killing machine' far more than ordinary testimony or direct questioning would have done.

In both cases, however, extracting acknowledgement of past atrocities and recognition of the suffering inflicted remains difficult: the traumatic power dynamic between perpetrator and victim/survivor still holds sway, preventing reciprocal historical and social recognition of the injustices of the past. Mey asks Nath what he thinks of talk of reconciliation, overcoming past resentments, and so on, to which Nath replies, they can do what they want, pointing out that no-one has properly acknowledged what was done at S21 – 'that two million dead among the Khmer people was wrong. Has anyone begged for forgiveness?' His criticism of calls for reconciliation in the absence of leaders and perpetrators taking responsibility and acknowledging the atrocities they committed is telling – all we hear from the perpetrators state in the film is that they were following orders, had no choice, were indoctrinated, and so were victims too. Without acknowledgement of guilt and responsibility, calls to 'forget the past' only further exacerbate historical trauma, making it impossible to reconcile the damaged community and rebuild democratic society in the present.

I have focused on *The Look of Silence* and *S21* as cases of cinematic ethics: both films aim to confront the viewer with experiences of political violence, provoking experiences of ethical reflection on the legacy of historical trauma and its ongoing effects in the everyday. Both films use the medium of documentary cinema to both elicit and express ethical experience. They do so through ethical witnessing, giving testimony concerning historical violence and questioning perpetrators in the hope of soliciting a recognition of historical injustice and a taking responsibility for political violence; or through physical re-enactment, as an indirect means of accessing traumatic memory and opening a space for dialogue and recognition of historical responsibility for political violence. Both films, moreover, also show the limits of such a project, the inherent asymmetry between perpetrators and survivors, whose demands for recognition ultimately rest on confronting perpetrators with evidence and testimony of their wrongdoing. They intervene in concrete historico-political situations with the aim of exposing the memory of traumatic violence and thereby demanding recognition of historical injustice exercised through the force of moral-ethical witnessing and critical questioning of the past. As these films show, documentary can stage an ambiguous space of ethical encounter between perpetrators and survivors, however psychologically difficult and morally complex, in which a reckoning with political violence and historical trauma might finally begin.

Notes

1. See Sinnerbrink (2016: 165–84) for a discussion of *The Act of Killing* as a case of cinematic ethics.
2. On 'perpetrator documentaries', see Morag 2012.
3. See Sinnerbrink 2017 and 2021. The present chapter offers an expanded and revised discussion of these films drawing on material from these earlier pieces.
4. See the United States Holocaust Memorial Museum entry on S-21, Tuol Sleng, <https://www.ushmm.org/genocide-prevention/countries/cambodia/case-study/violence/s-21>.
5. Oppenheimer and Panh (2012) discuss the role of 'bodily memory' in re-enactment as a means of eliciting traumatic memory. See also Boyle 2009 for a good discussion of trauma and bodily memory, drawing on psychoanalytic theory.

6. As Torchin asks (2015: 27), how can testimony, understood as the 'truthful narration of a past occurrence for the purposes of transformation and social justice', function under conditions 'flooded by fantasy, amnesia, and intimidation?'.
7. See, for example, *Site 2* (1989), *The People of the Rice Field* (1994), *Bophana: A Cambodian Tragedy* (1996), *The Burnt Theatre* (2005), *Duch: Master of the Forges of Hell* (2012), *Graves without a Name* (2018) and *Irradiated* (2020).
8. See the entry on S-21, Tuol Sleng in the United States Holocaust Memorial Museum: <https://www.ushmm.org/genocide-prevention/countries/cambodia/case-study/violence/s-21> (accessed October 5, 2021).
9. As Panh remarks, 'I concentrated on the shooting on S21 for one reason: the Khmer Rouge continued to say that S21 did not exist. And maybe in 25 years somebody will be able to say that the genocide did not exist' (Oppenheimer and Panh 2012: 253).
10. Duch, the nickname of Kaing Guek Eav, supervisor of torture procedures in S-21 and currently serving a thirty-five-year prison sentence for crimes against humanity, is the central subject of Panh's later documentary, *Duch: Master of the Forges of Hell* (2012), widely regarded as a sequel to *S21: The Khmer Rouge Killing Machine*.

References

Alkan, Didem (2020), 'Refiguring the perpetrator in Rithy Panh's documentary films: *S-21: The Khmer Rouge Killing Machine* and *Duch, Master of the Forges of Hell*', *Continuum: Journal of Media and Cultural Studies*, 34: 2, 271–85.

Behlil, Melis (2015), '*The Look of Silence*: an interview with Joshua Oppenheimer and Adi Rukun', *Cineaste*, 40: 3, 26–31.

Bondebjerg, Ib (2014), 'Documentary and cognitive theory: narrative, emotion and memory', *Media and Communication* 2: 1, 13–22.

Boyle, Deidre (2009), 'Shattering silence: traumatic memory and reenactment in Rithy Panh's *S-21: The Khmer Rouge Killing Machine*', *Framework: The Journal of Cinema and Media*, 50: 1 and 2 (Spring and Fall), 95–106.

Bruzzi, Stella (2006), *New Documentary: A Critical Introduction*, 2nd edn, London and New York: Routledge.

Camhi, Leslie (2004), 'FILM; The Banal Faces of Khmer Rouge Evil', *New York* Times, 16 May, <https://www.nytimes.com/2004/05/16/movies/film-the-banal-faces-of-khmer-rouge-evil.html> (accessed 15 July 2021).

Chaudhuri, Shohini (2014), *Cinema of the Dark Side: Atrocity and the Ethics of Spectatorship*, Edinburgh: Edinburgh University Press.

Cooper, Sarah (2006), *Selfless Cinema? Ethics and French Documentary*, Oxford: Legenda.

Cribb, Robert (2001), 'Genocide in Indonesia, 1965–1966', *Journal of Genocide Research*, 3: 2, 219–39.

Cribb, Robert (2014), '"The Act of Killing"', *Critical Asian Studies*, 46: 1, 147–49.

Daniels-Yeoman, Finn (2017), 'Trauma, affect and the documentary image: towards a nonrepresentational approach', *Studies in Documentary Film*, 11: 2, 85–103.

Douglass, Ana and Thomas A. Vogler (2003), 'Introduction', in Ana Douglass and Thomas. A. Vogler (eds), *Witness and Memory: The Discourse of Trauma*, New York: Routledge, pp. 1–53.

Heryanto, Ariel (2014), 'Great and misplaced expectations,' *Critical Asian Studies*, 46: 1, 162–6.
Honigsto, Ilona (2015), *Soul of the Documentary: Framing, Expression, Ethics*, Amsterdam: Amsterdam University Press.
McGregor, Katherine E. (2009), 'The Indonesian killings of 1965–66', *SciencePo*, 4 August, <https://www.sciencespo.fr/mass-violence-war-massacre-resistance/fr/document/indonesian-killings-1965-1966.html> (accessed 10 August 2021).
Martin-Jones, D. (2011), *Deleuze and World Cinemas*, London and New York: Continuum.
Martin-Jones, D. (2019), *Cinema against Doublethink: Ethical Encounters with the Lost Pasts of World History*, London and New York: Routledge.
Morag, Raya (2012), *Waltzing with Bashir: Perpetrator Trauma and Cinema*, London: I. B. Tauris.
Mroz, Matilda (2020), *Framing the Holocaust in Polish Aftermath Cinema: Posthumous Materiality and Unwanted Knowledge*, London: Palgrave Macmillan.
Nagib, Lúcia (2011), *World Cinema and the Ethics of Realism*, New York and London: Continuum.
Nichols, Bill (2016), *Speaking Truths with Film: Documentary: Evidence, Ethics, Politics*, San Diego: University of California Press.
Oppenheimer, Joshua (2013), The Act of Killing *Press Notes*, Berlin: Wolf. <http://ff.hrw.org/sites/default/files/THE%20ACT%20OF%20KILLING%20press%20notes.pdf> (accessed 10 August 2021).
Oppenheimer, Joshua and Rithy Panh (2012), 'Perpetrators' testimony and the restoration of humanity', in Joram Ten Brink and Joshua Oppenheimer (eds), *Killer Images: Documentary Film, Memory, and the Performance of Violence*, New York: Columbia University Press, pp. 243–55.
Plantinga, Carl R. (1997), *Rhetoric and Representation in Non-Fiction Film*, New York: Cambridge University Press.
Renov, Michael (2004), *The Subject of Documentary*, Minneapolis: University of Minnesota Press.
Saxton, Libby (2008), *Haunted Images: Film, Testimony, Ethics, and the Holocaust*, London: Wallflower Press.
Scarry, Elizabeth (1985), *The Body in Pain: The Making and Unmaking of the World*, New York: Oxford University Press.
Sinnerbrink, Robert (2016), *Cinematic Ethics: Exploring Ethical Experience through Film*, London and New York: Routledge.
Sinnerbrink, Robert (2017), 'The act of witnessing: cinematic ethics in *The Look of Silence*', *Post-Script: Essays in Film and the Humanities*, Special Issue on Documentary Ethics, ed. Dan Geva and Yvonne Kozlovsky-Golan, 36: 2 and 3, 30–44.
Sinnerbrink, Robert (2021), 'Re-enactment and traumatic memory: cinematic ethics in *The Act of Killing* and *S21: Khmer Rouge Killing Machine*', *Emotions, History, Culture, Society* 5: 1, 124–42.
Torchin, Leshu (2015), 'Chronicle of a quest: silence after killing', *Film Quarterly*, 69: 2, 25–35.
Walker, Janet (1997), 'The traumatic paradox: documentary films, historical fictions, and cataclysmic past Events,' *Signs*, 22: 4, 803–25.

Walker, Janet (2005), *Trauma Cinema: Documenting Incest and the Holocaust*, Berkeley: University of California Press.
Williams, Linda (1993), 'Mirrors without memories: truth, history, and the new documentary', *Film Quarterly* 46: 2, 9–21.
Winston, Brian (2000), *Lies, Damn Lies and Documentary*, London: BFI Books.
Winston, Brian, Gail Vanstone and Wang Chi (2017), *The Act of Documenting: Documentary Film in the 21st Century*, London: Bloomsbury Academic.

PART TWO

BODIES AND IDENTITIES

4. BECOMING BEYONCÉ: DISIDENTIFICATION AND RACIAL IMAGINARIES

Tina Chanter

Besides, women among themselves begin by laughing. To escape from a pure and simple reversal of the masculine position means in any case not to forget to laugh.

(Irigaray, 'Questions', *This Sex*, 163)

There is, in an initial phase, perhaps only one 'path,' the one historically assigned to the feminine: that of *mimicry*. One must assume the feminine role deliberately. Which means already to convert a form of subordination into an affirmation, and thus to begin to thwart it.

(Irigaray, 'The Power of Discourse', *This Sex*, 76)

In this chapter I hold in tension with one another two identificatory scenarios, the first of which shores up and recapitulates racial stereotypes, while the second, I suggest, stages an ethico-political intervention in the circulation of such stereotypes by offering a divergent racial imaginary. The first scenario is that which fuelled, informed and was crystallised in a cartoon depicting African-American tennis star Serena Williams and mixed-race tennis champion Naomi Osaka after the controversy that marked the final of a tennis grand slam event. The second scenario is humorously and poignantly explored and celebrated in Luisa Omielan's comedic performance *What would Beyoncé Do?*, originally performed at the Edinburgh Fringe Festival and subsequently filmed by the BBC, and available on YouTube.[1]

After Serena Williams's loss to Naomi Osaka in the US Open Final women's tennis match in September 2018, which was marked by a controversy between the umpire and Williams, Mark Knight's cartoon appeared in *The Herald Sun*.[2] Rachel Withers (2018) describes the cartoon as a 'bigoted caricature of Serena Williams' and goes on to say that

> Knight's degrading cartoon depicts Williams with an exaggeratedly large face and body, her face screwed up in rage and her coiled black hair flying as she stomps on her smashed racket. Many have pointed out that it draws on anti-black, Jim Crow-era tropes.

Withers adds that 'mixed-race champion Naomi Osaka . . . is whitewashed into a faceless blonde being asked to let Williams win'.

Cartoons, as Mara Ahmed (2018) puts it, 'create certain visual codes and a certain shorthand for an idea or a concept and a particular racist language which can shape the political and social landscape in a very powerful way'. In the light of defences of Knight's cartoon in the name of satire, the reflections on Serena Williams by poet, playwright and essayist Claudia Rankine in *Citizen: An American Lyric* constitute essential reading.[3] Rankine recalls a series of misjudged line calls that were made in a 2004 US Open tennis match between Serena Williams and Jennifer Capriati. In her semi-final against Kim Clijsters in the 2009 US Open, Williams received a foot-fault call on her second serve when she was match point down.[4]

Reflecting on these episodes, Rankine focuses upon the relationship between anger and insanity, suggesting that what might be understood as an explosion of craziness from one perspective, seen from another perspective is the release of pressure built up as a result of what Rankine identifies as the 'low flame', the 'constant drip' that constitutes the 'quotidian struggles against [the] dehumanization of racism' (2014, 17, 15).

Prior to the publication of *Citizen*, in an open letter to the poet Tony Hoagland, Rankine (2011) raised the question of whether Hoagland's poem *The Change* was racist. The poem includes a thinly veiled reference to Venus Williams, and explores questions of racial identification in the context of a tennis match with a white opponent. Hoagland responded to Rankine's 'Open Letter', maintaining that the poem is not racist, but 'racially complex', and distancing himself from the presumption that a poem is 'in the voice of the author'. Rankine's consideration of Serena Williams (sister of Venus Williams) in *Citizen*, in which she takes up and reworks a passage from her open letter to Hoagland, elaborates her response to *The Change*.[5]

The wider strategy that Rankine employs in *Citizen* explores questions of voice, experimenting with the first, second and third person throughout the text, thus cutting across obvious lines of racial identification, creating zones of discomfort for her readers, sometimes placing readers into identificatory positions to which they might be unaccustomed. Having addressed her reader in the second person for much of the book, but in such a way as to invoke herself, as in 'For so long you thought the ambition of racist language was to denigrate and erase you as a person . . . [but] you begin to understand yourself as hypervisible' (Rankine 2014: 22), toward the end of the text she rapidly glides through subject positions: 'And yes, I want to interrupt to tell him her us you me I don't know how to end what doesn't have an ending' (2014: 57). In effect, Rankine is blurring the lines that hold subjects distinct from one another and sets races against one another, while also asking her readers to inhabit racial identifications they do not usually inhabit.

Omielan's playfully evocative homage to Beyoncé can be juxtaposed to cartoons such as Knight's, which renders Williams hypervisible as the quintessential angry black woman. Instead of trading in Jim Crow-era stereotypes, and defending them as satire, Omielan's humour trades in celebratory positivity, holding up Beyoncé, and in particular the lyrics and dance moves in the video *Survivor*, as a site of iconic identification for herself, and for her audience.

What gaze might be operative in the comedic performance of Omielan's *What would Beyoncé Do?* Not only is there a constitutive instability in all identificatory practices, but as Sara Ahmed makes clear this instability is exacerbated by the regimes that legitimate some subjects in relation to their race and gender while de-legitimating others (1997). The success of calling a subject into being as raced or gendered will depend on how that subject is recognised according to what imaginary regime, on who is hailed by whom, on how that interpellation is underwritten by what symbolic authority, and in what ways a subject identifies or disidentifies with the subject position under which it is hailed.

While feminist film theory has mobilised psychoanalytic theory to help direct attention to the ways in which cultural scripts are driven by unconscious imaginaries, despite some notable exceptions, film theory has tended to take its bearings from (usually white) psychoanalytic theory (see hooks 1996). Focusing on the question of disidentification, I take my inspiration not from mainstream psychoanalytic theory, but from rather different sources: Kalpana Sheshadri-Crooks (2000) and José Esteban Muñoz (1999). Sheshadri-Crooks elaborates the need for white subjects to traverse the fantasy of whiteness that feminist philosophers and psychoanalytic thinkers tend to assume, while Muñoz provides me with a lexicon with which to take heed of the importance Irigaray attributes to laughter and mimesis (as signalled in the epigraphs to this chapter), while at the same time refusing to 'sanitize' the white, Western, imperialist and colonialist implications of the subject of feminism that Irigaray's interventions tend to assume (see Muñoz 1999: 9). I take my cue from Muñoz's interpretation of performance artists as not only culture makers but also producers of theory.

I offer Omielan, then, as a performance artist who also produces theory, a theory that contests the privilege of high theory, using mimesis not as a distancing strategy of interrogation to bring into question the authority and dogmatism of a string of white, Western male philosophers who have traditionally claimed the prerogative to ethical theory, but rather to celebrate a female mixed-race American pop singer from humble origins, named as music's most powerful woman by the BBC's Woman's Hour (BBC 2018). Neither Beyoncé nor Omielan offers seamlessly politically correct views of the world. One could easily take a critical distance on Beyoncé's lyric 'put a ring on it' as failing to put into question what some would argue is the archaic institution of marriage. Equally, one could cite Omielan's thumbing her nose at 'feminists' in embracing the idea that she wants to get married and take her husband's name. Yet what Omielan offers is a strong, hilarious performance by a woman whose beauty does not conform to the anorexic standards to which the fashion industry still, by and large, adheres, one that touches a nerve, and reaches an audience that neither film theory nor ethical theory is likely to reach. At the same time, I want to take the risk of suggesting that there is something transgressive in Omielan's tongue-in-cheek but also totally celebratory admiration for Beyoncé.

The success of Omielan's performance relies, in part, on the fact that the audience of *What would Beyoncé Do?* is intimately familiar not only with the lyrics of Beyoncé's songs but also with her dance moves, which the audience performs, along with Omielan, in group renditions at key points of the show. The extensive circulation of Beyoncé's videos serves as the precondition for this familiarity. The official video of *Survivor*, one of the songs that provides the soundtrack to Omielan's show, had 161,753,438 views on YouTube at the time this essay was prepared. Omielan becomes a conduit, channelling Beyoncé for her audience, and facilitating their identification with Beyoncé through her own starstruck dentification with her idol. Omielan (2018) announces 'In this show I am Beyoncé, okay' and goes on to remark upon her similarity to Beyoncé at the same time as undercutting it: 'very often people confuse us. Like, only the other day someone stopped me in the street and said: oh my god, are you mixed race? Thanks babe.' At once self-deprecating and self-aggrandising, Omielan's comedic idolisation of Beyoncé, I want to suggest, provides white members of her audience with an opportunity to begin to traverse the fantasy of whiteness.

To interrogate the ease of identifications that make up invisibly white normative mainstream feminist subjectivities would mean to open up the possibility of traversing the fantasy of whiteness in its role as a grounding narrative of Western feminist subjectivity, to be willing to work through that fantasy bit by bit, to unpick the authority of the symbolic that underpins it piece by piece, to try to contribute, however hesitantly and inadequately, to a rearticulation of its symbolic meaning. As Seshadri-Crooks suggests, 'One must traverse the fundamental fantasy of singular humanity upon which racial identity is founded. It is a question of resituating oneself in relation to the raced signifier' (2000: 159). Such a commitment of unlearning might well take a lifetime, and still not be done, but you've got to start somewhere, and Omielan's playful and passionate homage to Beyoncé is a good place to start – or else a step along the way.

In Lacan's psychoanalytic consideration of identification, there is a distinction between the ideal ego and the ego ideal, the imaginary and the symbolic registers of identification. At the imaginary level of identification I posit my ideal ego, which I would like to resemble, an ideal to which I aspire.[6] Yet insofar as this imaginary ideal of resemblance is a function determined in advance by the symbolic, those who function as imaginary ideas will be made available by the governing socio-symbolic norms of any given regime.[7] If a symbolic regime of identification is governed by the 'Name-of-the-father' (Žižek 1992: 108), then the superegoic agency by which I judge myself – find myself wanting – will be the paternal gaze.

As Slavoj Žižek puts it, 'The interplay of imaginary and symbolic identification under the domination of symbolic identification constitutes the mechanism by means of which the subject is integrated into a given socio-symbolic field – the way he/she assumes certain "mandates"' (1992: 110). Yet, there is always a remainder, always something 'leftover', a 'gap' between symbolic and imaginary identification (see Žižek 1992: 111). It is in such a gap that race is located, as the 'Real' that resists symbolisation, for a subject that fails to problematise the whiteness of the symbolic in relation to which it positions itself, even as it problematises masculine prerogative.

When the subject 'resists interpellation', when there is a 'failed interpellation', this might be explained in traditional psychoanalytic terms, as when Žižek accounts for it by the hysterical 'incapacity of the subject to fulfil the symbolic identification, to assume fully and without restraint the symbolic mandate' (1992: 113). Or it might rather be accounted for by, as Judith Butler says, an 'affirmation of that slippage', where a 'failure of identification is itself the point of departure for a more democratizing affirmation of . . . difference' (1993: 219). Or again, it might be that a subject resists interpellation in one regard, by interrogating the masculinist assumptions that constitute hysteria for psychoanalysis, while at the same time consolidating the racialised imaginary that is allowed to remain intact in the effort to forge a new female symbolic and imaginary. It is at this level that Irigaray's intervention might be situated, as disidentification of the psychoanalytic paradigm, insofar as it interrogates the authority of the name of the father, the normativity of the castration complex, and the universality of the Oedipal scenario, yet affirms the master signifier of whiteness.

By disidentifying with its masculinist assumptions, Irigaray messes with the machinery of psychoanalysis. She intervenes in the meta-theoretical vocabulary of the symbolic, imaginary, and the real. The intervention is rendered complex since the masculine symbolic world that Irigaray's thought interrogates is not the universal, neutral body of thought it takes itself to be, but as Irigaray interprets it, is itself imaginary, the product of a masculinist, philosophical imaginary that grants itself socio-symbolic authority (see Whitford 1991: 90). If the imaginary is an effect of a symbolic that itself is the product of a masculinist fantasy, then the psychoanalytic imaginary is structured by a symbolic grounded in this masculinist fantasy. If an imaginary cannot exist without symbolisation, and the only available symbolisation is based on a masculinist fantasy, far from evacuating the need for imaginary, identificatory and institutional supports for women, Irigaray calls for them. At the same time, she speaks to the need to elaborate a female symbolic to underpin a female imaginary (Whitford 1991: 91). Assuming the viability of such a project, the question remains as to its desirability. What would be the status of a female symbolic and imaginary? Would these in turn purport to be universal? If so, would their universality cover over a hidden appeal to whiteness as a master signifier?

If, as Seshadri-Crooks suggests, 'Whiteness' is a 'master signifier' that operates in the symbolic register (see 2000: 32), what would it mean for those of us who have assumed whiteness as an unthought '"ground"' (46) to 'trouble' the stability of that ground? If blackness is not immediately given, but has 'to be learned' (35), then what would it mean to unlearn the privilege of whiteness, to make visible that privilege, to make it available for interrogation? Perhaps it would be to dislodge, rework and transform the production of the 'racial body' as a 'phobic object' that sustains the white 'body image' (37). What might such a reworking and transfiguring look like, or consist of? Seshadri-Crooks suggests that '[i]t would confound racial signification by stressing the continuity, the point of doubt among the so-called races, to the extent that each and every one of us mistrust the knowledge or our racial belonging' (159).

By way of contributing to such a project, I explore Omielan's comedic performance and celebration of Beyoncé as aligned with Irigaray's critical engagement of the Western tradition of philosophy through her strategy of mimesis, while at the same time moving beyond Irigaray's terms of reference, which tend to perpetuate the privilege of white, Western imperialist, feminist subjects. Let me frame my consideration of Omielan with a brief acknowledgment of the discourse of intersectionality as refracted through June Jordan's navigation of its issues, before going on to elaborate Muñoz's notion of disidentification, which I will adapt for my own purposes.

As is by now well known, the term intersectionality was originally introduced in the context of US labour discrimination. Kimberlé Crenshaw (1991) showed that even a law that was hailed as progressive in so much as it provided a rubric for individuals to establish grounds for racial or sexual discrimination in the workplace, provided no conceptual tools to address the specificity of black women's oppression. The law required black women to identify either as black or as women. Crenshaw used the term intersectional to capture how gender and race intersected in the experience of black women, in a way that was inadequately reflected by the legal categories available in order to claim discrimination in the sphere of labour. Initially developed in order to problematise the 'monocausal protocols' that are 'established through the reproduction of normative accounts of woman that always imply a white feminist subject' and the 'equally normativizing accounts of blackness that assume maleness' (Muñoz 1999: 8), the term intersectionality has widened considerably beyond its original application; it has come to refer to the relationship that pertains between multiple identity markers, not only gender and race but also sexuality, dis/ability, age, nation, ethnicity, religion and so on.

Although it does not utilise the language of intersectionality, a short story by Caribbean-American poet, playwright and essayist June Jordan, entitled 'Report from the Bahamas', explores in a literary manner the tensions that structure her daily life in a way that speaks precisely to the conundrums of intersectionality (2002). We might say that Jordan's narrative, which predates *Crenshaw's* intervention, performs intersectionality by interrogating and reflecting upon her experiences while on holiday in the Bahamas. Jordan describes the ways in which her own black skin fails to unite her with Olive, the maid who cleans her hotel room, with the woman who serves her salad in a café, or with the man who, having waded into the sea fully clothed, is pictured with his feet immersed in water, bearing aloft a tray of banana daiquiris for the delectation of bathing tourists who hail from countries such as America. Jordan suggests that we need to go beyond using concepts such as gender and race as 'automatic concepts of connection' (2002: 219), by resisting the idea that our race or gender will automatically unite us with others who might share our race or gender, but whose experience is riven with structures of class, nationality and colonialism that render us worlds apart.

Another narrative unfolds against the background of Jordan's exploration of the discomfort she experiences in her various encounters with those who, she feels sure, construe her as a rich American tourist. The narrative concerns an encounter she recalls between two students she teaches at a US state university, an Irish woman and a South African woman. The students are brought together when one of them seeks refuge from a husband who is physically abusive and an alcoholic, and the other reaches out to her, drawing on her own experience in order to support her. Jordan comments, 'It is not only who you are . . . but what we can do for each other that will determine the connection' (2002: 219). By creatively engaging with what is at stake in the concept of intersectionality, Jordan's essayistic short story might be said to perform it in a literary mode. I want to further refract intersectionality through the constellations of ideas Muñoz brings together under the heading of disidentification.

Muñoz's investigation is firmly centred around the politics of performance; he is interested in those 'cultural workers' (1999: xiv) whose performances promise to change the world, promising the possibility of a new world. By 'disidentification' Muñoz means to describe 'the survival strategies the minority subject practices in order to negotiate a phobic majoritarian public sphere that continuously elides or punishes the existence of subjects who do not conform to the phantasm of normative citizenship' (1999: 4). To illustrate this, let me briefly recap Muñoz's example of a moment in Cuban and Puerto Rican-American performance artist Marga Gomez's 1992 performance *Marga Gomez in Pretty, Witty, and Gay*. It is a moment in which Gomez 'reminisces about her first interaction with lesbians in the public sphere at the age of eleven' which Muñoz understands as a 'disidentification with mainstream representations of lesbians in the media' (1999: 3). Having already developed what she calls '"homosexual hearing"', Gomez recounts how her eleven-year-old self 'catches the voice of David Susskind explaining that he will be interviewing "lady homosexuals"' (1999: 3) on the television programme *Open End*. Quoting Gomez, Muñoz writes:

> [I] sat next to my mother on the sofa. I made sure to put that homophobic expression on my face. So my mother wouldn't think I was mesmerized by the lady homosexuals and riveted to every word that fell from their lips ... There were three of them. All disguised in raincoats, dark glasses, wigs. It was the wigs that made me want to be one. (1999: 3)

Muñoz goes on to report how in her performance Gomez 'channels the lesbian panelists ... luxuriat[ing] in the seemingly homophobic image of truck-driving closeted diesel dykes' (1999: 3):

> Mr. Susskind, I want to thank you for having the courage to present Cherene and Millie and me on your program. Cherene and Millie and me, those aren't our real names. She's not Cherene, she's not Millie and I'm not me. These are just our, you know, synonyms. We must cloak ourselves in a veil of secrecy or risk losing our employment as truck drivers. (1999: 3)

Gomez parodies these 'pre-Stonewall stereotypes of lesbians' as, to quote Muñoz again, she

> performs her disidentificatory desire for this once toxic representation. The phobic object, through a campy over-the-top performance, is reconfigured as sexy and glamorous, and not as the pathetic and abject spectacle that it appears to be in the dominant eyes of heteronormative culture. (1999: 3)

Understanding Gomez's performance as the site of a transformative recycling, Muñoz observes: 'Marga's disidentification with these damaged stereotypes recycled them as powerful and seductive sites of self-creation. It was, after all, the wigs that made her want to be one' (1999: 4). Making good on his gloss on Foucault to the effect that 'disidentification' is a strategy that 'resists a conception of power as being a fixed discourse' (1999: 19), Muñoz locates the power of interpellation in Gomez's rendering of her ability to 'hear the lesbian's call' (1999: 4) when one of Susskind's guests 'flicks her tongue at Marga on the screen' (1999: 3). He reads this 'lasciviou[s] flic[k]' of the tongue' at the young Gomez as a moment of interpellation that reworks a more unilateral understanding of Althusser's 'Hey you There!' (1999: 33). Rather than seeing queers as those 'who have failed to turn around' in response to the heteronormative call, Muñoz cites Gomez's 'willful disidentification with this call' and points to Gomez's fabrication as 'a remade and queered televisual hailing' (1999: 33), reminding us that '[n]o one knows better than queers' that 'we are continuously . . . being hailed as "straight" by various institutions' (1999: 33).

Quoting Eve Kosofsky Sedgwick, *The Epistemology of the Closet*, Muñoz says identification

> always includes multiple processes of identifying with. It also involves identifications as against; but even if it did not, the relations implicit in identifying with are, as psychoanalysis suggests, in themselves quite sufficiently fraught with intensities of incorporation, diminishment, inflation, threat, loss, reparation, and disavowal. (1999: 8)[8]

The conflicted nature of identification comes to the fore in Muñoz's analysis of an example of disidentification that he describes as 'crisscrossed' or as 'cross-identification' (1999: 15), an example he draws from James Baldwin's *The Devil Finds Work*. Growing up under the shadow of his father's 'physical and verbal abuse', Baldwin, Muñoz tells us, finds 'refuge in a powerful identification with a white starlet' (1999: 15). Quoting Baldwin, Muñoz goes on:

> So here, now, was Bette Davis . . . in close-up, over a champagne glass, pop-eyes popping. I was astounded. I had caught my father not in a lie, but in an infirmity. For here, before me, after all, was a movie star: white: and if she was white and a movie star, she was rich: and she was ugly . . . Out of bewilderment, out of loyalty to my mother, probably, and also because I sensed something menacing and unhealthy (for me, certainly) in the face on the screen, I gave Davis's skin the dead white greenish cast of something crawling under a rock, but I was held, just the same, by the tense intelligence of the forehead, the disaster of the lips: and when she moved, she moved just like a [N-word]. (1999: 15)[9]

What Muñoz finds suggestive about the 'mediated and vexed identification' Baldwin describes is that 'Davis signifies something both liberatory and horrible' (1999: 18). Muñoz continues:

> The example of Baldwin's relationship with Davis is a disidentification insofar as the African-American writer transforms the raw material of identification (the linear march that leads toward interpellation) while simultaneously positioning himself within and outside the image of the movie star. For Baldwin, disidentification is more than simply an interpretive turn or a psychic maneuver; it is, most crucially, a survival strategy. (1999: 18)

As is clear from the above, which is itself a brief recitation of various disidentificatory strands running through Muñoz's work, he mobilises the term in diverse directions, in keeping with his aim to 'push against reified understanding of theory' (1999: 32), understanding artists as both 'culture makers' and 'theory producers' (1999: 33).

It is when he is reflecting upon Frantz Fanon that Muñoz is perhaps most directly relevant for my purposes here. Recalling those moments in the work of Fanon in which Fanon allows himself to be besieged by an unreflective indulgence in homophobia and sexism, as when Fanon 'dismisses . . . queerness' as if it were '"a white thing"' (1999: 9). Muñoz asks the following question, '[w]hat process can keep an identification with Fanon' for 'the queer revolutionary from the Antilles, perhaps a young woman who has . . . been burned in Fanon's text by his writing on the colonized woman' (1999: 9)? His answer, in a word, is: disidentification.

'Disidentification' says Muñoz,

> offers a Fanon, for that queer and lesbian reader, who would not be sanitized; instead his homophobia and misogyny would be interrogated while his anticolonial discourse was engaged as a *still* valuable yet mediated identification. This maneuver resists an unproductive turn toward good dog/bad dog criticism and instead leads to an identification that is both mediated and immediate, a disidentification that enables politics. (1999: 9)

Mobilising the vocabulary of disidentification, I would like here, then, to offer a reading of Omielan's invocation of Beyoncé that is indebted to the mimetic strategy of Irigaray – an Irigaray who would not be sanitised, whose imperialism and colonialism would be interrogated, while her anti-sexist discourse is engaged as a still valuable yet mediated identification. I want to resist a disciplinary rapping of Irigaray over her ideological knuckles, by merely reprimanding her in what risks falling into an unproductive engagement of the type that Muñoz calls 'good dog/bad dog criticism'. Instead I want to take up her strategy of mimesis, by applying it to a scenario which can breathe new life into it, in an approach that is indebted to a reworked version of Muñoz's understanding of disidentification.

Drawing on the post-Althusserian work of Michel Pêcheux, Muñoz distinguishes the 'identification' of a 'Good Subject' from the counteridentification of a 'Bad Subject'. In the first approach, the good subject 'chooses the path of identification with discursive and ideological forms' (1999: 11). To be a good Irigarayan, then, would be to be a loyal, devoted, and faithful follower, to be thoroughly and uncritically assimilated into an Irigarayan paradigm. Were I to merely reprimand Irigaray, calling her out for her lack of attention to women of colour, I might stand accused of being a bad subject, a wayward Irigarayan, who has strayed from the path of discipleship, where I 'resist and attempt to reject the images and identificatory sites offered by dominant [in this case Irigarayan] ideology' and proceed to rebel, to '"counteridentify" and turn against [her] symbolic system' (Muñoz 1999: 11). To dismiss or refuse to engage with the thought of Irigaray at all is to run the risk of either evacuating the significance of her insights altogether – which are, after all, already counteridentificatory in their own way – in a manner that would either reaffirm the sexism that her work seeks to dislodge, or leave in place a feminist paradigm that does not speak to women of colour.

In contrast to uncritical identification and counteridentification, the latter of which risks reinstalling the dominant ideology it seeks to put in question, disidentification, as Muñoz understands it, is a 'third mode of dealing with dominant ideology' (1999: 11). What then, might it mean to work on and against Irigarayan ideology, to excavate it in a way that 'tries to transform' its 'logic from within' (1999: 11)? Inspired by Sheshadri-Crooks, who calls for a traversal of the fantasy of whiteness, and by Muñoz, for whom, 'the making of theory only transpires *after* the artists' performance of counterpublicity' (1999: 5), in order to work on and against Irigaray, I return to Omielan's *What would Beyoncé Do?*

If Irigaray's mimetic strategy vis-à-vis the Western philosophical tradition adopts a disidentificatory stance towards its male-centred bias, Omielan disidentifies with the normativity of the implicit male spectator of stand-up comedy, by addressing herself to issues and questions that appeal to women. In this respect, Omielan's approach might be compared to Irigaray's insofar as she is rendering visible what usually passes as invisible, namely the fact that the male dominated world of comedians addresses itself to male concerns, yet these go unmarked as such, passing instead as universal concerns. As a rule, women are expected to laugh at jokes that are not usually told from their perspective, but rather, often, at their expense. Yet Omielan puts female subjectivity and woman to woman identification centre stage, although she maintains that her performances should not be viewed as women's comedy. After all, mainstream comedy is not viewed as men's comedy.

While she displaces the normative masculine subject from the centre, rather than perpetuating the normativity of the white feminist subject, Omielan rejects the normative whiteness of feminist subjectivity. The framing narrative and meta-structure of Omielan's performance, as its title clearly indicates, is what Beyoncé would do. Appealing to the pertinence of Beyoncé's lyrics and relying on the familiarity of Beyoncé's dance moves, perhaps most powerfully at the culmination of the show, where she performs a rendition of 'Survivor', Omielan identifies with and celebrates Beyoncé, even as she disidentifies with her in a complex and humorous choreography. From the beginning of the show, Omielan has the audience singing along with her, dancing in their seats, and in one or two cases, performing alongside her onstage. As we have seen, she relates to the audience, tongue in cheek, how she often gets mistaken for Beyoncé, proudly recounting how someone in the street mistook her olive, tanned skin for 'mixed race'. Omielan aspires to be Beyoncé, she claims to become Beyoncé, even as she comedically figures herself as falling short of Beyoncé. It is not an implicitly white female subject who furnishes a role model, it is Beyoncé.

If Omielan identifies with Beyoncé, she does so in a way that leaves her audience to unpick the problematic illusions that fuel her identifications. In this way she provides an opening for her audience to begin to do the work of traversing the fantasy of race. The audience is confronted with the suggestion that Omielan gets mistaken for Beyoncé because of her olive skin tone. People stop her in the street, mistaking her as mixed race. The leap from her being mistaken for mixed race to being mistaken for Beyoncé is, of course, untenable in everyone but Omielan's comedic mind – part of her illusory disidentification. Yet it also serves as a reminder of an uncomfortable truth, namely the elision that occurs too often when white imaginaries elide the difference between dark-skinned individuals.

Omielan's disidentification with Beyoncé is at once celebratory and joyful, providing her with succour and psychological strength, and riven with illusion. In this respect, it is like the illusory identification of Lacan's mirror stage. Yet, unlike film theorists, Omielan does not set out to demystify for her audience the symbolic, ideological code implicitly informing the imaginary fantasy she plays out.[10] She is not a theorist of the gaze, she is a comedian. She elicits laughter, not at her, but with her, through (dis)identification. In this laughter the audience confronts the real of race.

At the same time as proclaiming her independence, speaking to a generation plagued by unemployment, Omielan also confesses that she has moved back home and that she doesn't pay rent. Her self-deprecating humour about how she knows the doorman at the unemployment centre well enough to high-five him also functions as a critique of the high rates of unemployment. Her account of the Christmas that her little brother took an overdose, which is as moving as it is hilarious, and how her desperate call to her estranged father merely elicited the response that her brother should call him once he is home, functions as a critique of fathers who fail to live up to their parental and emotional responsibilities. At the same time, it allows her to make the case that depression should be taken as seriously as physical illnesses, while affording her the opportunity of lampooning herself, as she wonders whether her boyfriend issues could be related to her issues with her father, and concludes with heavy irony, that no, they couldn't possibly be.

If Marga Gomez retrieves the lost phobic object of Susskind's lesbian trio, and reinvests it with the enticing, libidinous appeal of a mysterious object of desire, Omielan retrieves the lost phobic object that blackness becomes not merely through the neglect to which Irigaray abandons it, but as the unthought of an entire Western tradition, which returns to haunt a white imaginary that sees nothing wrong with Knight's cartoon of Williams. By identifying with Beyoncé at the level of the imaginary, by saying, in effect, if only I were more like Beyoncé I would be likeable, Omielan makes a counter symbolic intervention. She does so not by drawing excessive attention to race, but rather by assuming the legitimacy and appropriateness as a prop for her imaginary identification, and in so doing, to return to the words of Seshadri-Crooks, 'confound[ing] racial signification by stressing the continuity . . . to the extent that each and every one of us must mistrust the knowledge of our racial belonging' (2000, 159). I say this not because I believe that race is a category that can be dispensed with, but because I think that Omielan's playfully self-conscious self-parody, into which she invites her audience, points toward a future in which it might be dispensable, because it invites a working through of the fantasy of whiteness.

Drawing on the music video *Survivor*, Omielan takes up the image of a boat as an extended metaphor for her erstwhile relationship in which she finds herself abandoned by her boyfriend. Re-enacting how she felt, Omielan crawls on her belly, childlike, sobbing and broken. Reaching for the question, what would Beyoncé do? she slowly recovers herself, recycling and transfiguring the image and lyrics of Beyoncé's music video *Survivor*. Beyoncé rises like a phoenix from her shipwrecked state, replete with all its resonances of the middle passage that played such a crucial role in the history of the US, as a 'former slave economy' (Muñoz 1999: 43), a history that informs the way in which the US 'still counts on and factors in the exploitation and colonization of nonwhite labor' (1999: 43). As she overcomes her emotionally shipwrecked state, with the lyrics 'I'm a survivor' as her soundtrack, Omielan honours Beyoncé's success.[11]

In a complex negotiation of her (dis)identificatory relationship to Beyoncé, Omielan navigates her disidentification with the pop star icon in various registers, while firmly installing her in a position of symbolic authority at the same time as invoking her as the figure she fantasises resembling. We have seen how in her playful navigation of variously positing herself in relation to Beyoncé's symbolic power and imaginary pull, Omielan humorously declares herself to be Beyoncé, and continually invites her audience to play at being Beyoncé too. Omielan's savvy, punchy, politically and emotionally astute, nuanced performance uses humour to effect her disidentification. In celebrating Beyoncé's music videos, Omielan recuperates the 'often effaced presence of black production' (Muñoz 1999: 44) thereby making a symbolic intervention that destabilises whiteness as a master signifier. In doing so she disidentifies white feminist subjectivity from an unproblematic relationship to the privilege of whiteness, placing Beyoncé at the centre of her identificatory narrative. If Irigaray enacts a parodic mimesis, showing how women's bodies and thought have constituted the excluded ground of the Western canon and culture, Omielan answers to her call to produce positive imaginary and symbolic interventions, by supplementing Irigaray's focus on sexual difference through a transformation of mimesis into a joyful celebration of Beyoncé that not only challenges whiteness as a master signifier but also stages the importance of cultural performances that playfully interrogate norms, rather than relying on rapping theorists we ourselves have elevated to icons for not thinking through everything at once.

In these reflections I have interrogated the relationship between identification, and gendered and racial imaginaries. We are embedded in worlds that are constituted through invisible regimes that inculcate in us habitual and often unconscious assumptions. Such assumptions foster and facilitate normative identifications around whiteness and gender. Through her comedic disidentification with Beyoncé, Omielan might be understood to disrupt and rework the normative invisible assumptions that dictate default racial identifications. By tapping into the impact of Beyoncé's music videos, which have a global reach, such comedic interventions have the potential to mobilise identificatory regimes that could help move us beyond the kind of racialised impasses that Claudia Rankine explores in *Citizen: An American Lyric*. Rankine's nuanced investigation of identificatory regimes, as we have seen, includes her consideration of scenes that lead to the appearance of cartoons such as Knight's depiction of Serena Williams. The impasses that Rankine explores proceed from microaggressions that occur unbidden and can go unseen by those who have the luxury of not having to see them, but they help to make up the fabric of racism, on which Knight's cartoon capitalises. I have offered a reading of Omielan's complex configuration of Beyoncé as one in which her disidentification functions more positively, not by unpicking the illusions that fuel it, but by rendering them visible, and eliciting joyful laughter that plays on our recognition and misrecognitions, while also leaving room for us to begin recognise the failures of recognition.

The ethico-political reconfiguration of racial and gendered imaginaries is required in order for a shift to take place in our habitual attitudes, which are generated in ways that transcend individual intentions and consciousness. Music videos play a part in cultivating socio-cultural imaginaries; in capitalising on the familiarity of *Survivor* and other hits by Destiny's Child and Beyoncé, Omielan's *What would Beyoncé Do?* has the capacity to contribute to a rethinking of and a reworking of habitual acquiescence to pernicious racial stereotypes. Omielan does not do the work for us; she invites us to laugh at ourselves with her, and in that laughter, lays bare knots of the indecipherable, redistributing sites of indecipherability for us to acknowledge and work through – or not.

NOTES

1. Luisa Omielan, *What would Beyoncé Do?*, <https://youtu.be/Y4BLN-Gh88I>.
2. The cartoon, which choose not to reproduce here, can be seen in an editorial piece by Michelle Garcia in the *Huntsville Tribune*, <https://huntsvilletribune.com/a-new-editorial-cartoon-shows-yet-another-racist-depiction-of-serena-williams/>.
3. See Rankine (2014: 23–36).
4. Both episodes can be viewed on YouTube in highlight videos. See Serena Williams vs Jennifer Capriati 2004 US Open QF Highlights, <https://youtu.be/gyECzEKShz0> and Kim Clijsters VS Serena Williams Highlight 2009 SF, <https://youtu.be/GTc-gv8tNWQ>.
5. Hoagland's poem can be found at <https://poets.org/poem/change>.
6. As Slavoj Žižek says, 'imaginary identification is identification with the image in which we appear likeable to ourselves, with the image representing "what we would like to be", and symbolic identification, identification with the very place *from where* we are being observed, *from where* we look at ourselves so that we appear to ourselves likeable, worthy of love' (1992: 105).
7. As Žižek puts it, the ideal ego, symbolised by Lacan as 'i{o}', is 'always already subordinated to I(O) [the ego ideal]; it is the symbolic identification . . . which dominates and determines the image, the imaginary forms in which we appear to ourselves likeable' (1992: 108).
8. The quote is from Eve Kosofsky Sedgwick (1990), *The Epistemology of the Closet*, Berkeley: University of California Press.
9. The quote is from James Baldwin (1976), *The Devil Finds Work*, New York: Dial Press, p. 7. The editors have removed the original word used by Baldwin and substituted [N-word].
10. As Todd McGowan sees it, for earlier film theorists the task of the film theorist was to destroy the imaginary pleasure created by (Hollywood, mainstream) film, whereas in his own view we need to theorise desire not in terms of the Hegelian desire, which 'aims at obtaining the Other's recognition' but rather in terms of the 'the recognition of recognition's necessary failure' (2013: 311). As McGowan says, for early theorists of the gaze in the context of cinema such as Mulvey, 'The

pleasure we derive from the filmic experience is . . . a deceptive pleasure, for it situates viewers within ideology and mutes any efforts at questioning the truths that ideology proffers. The only political alternative then becomes the destruction of this imaginary pleasure – a task Mulvey foregrounds in "Visual Pleasure and Narrative Cinema"' (2013: 39). Yet, for McGowan, this 'critique of fantasy' is based on a 'misconception of the gaze', focusing only on the relationship between fantasy and ideology (fantasy and the symbolic) rather than on the relationship between fantasy and the gaze, fantasy and the Real' (39). By locating desire not at the level of the signifier/symbolic – which for McGowan reduces it to the (illusory) demand for recognition – but rather in relation to the 'gap in the Other, that absence . . . or piece of nothing' that Lacan names the '*objet petit a*' (2013: 313), McGowan argues we have the possibility of moving beyond the demands of ideology. For McGowan, film can expose spectators to the desire of the other as 'indecipherable' (2003: 37). I am suggesting that Omielan's comedic performance *What would Beyoncé do?* exposes her audience to the indecipherable.

11. It might be seen as a bit of a stretch to connect Beyoncé's video to the middle passage. I am suggesting this resonance is part of the cultural reservoir of associations that play into the iconography Beyoncé mobilises, and as such could be operating at some level, a suggestion that is not as leftfield as it might seem, given Beyoncé's overt political engagement. This might be seen as a risky move – indeed the entire enterprise of this paper takes something of a risk, but one that I wager might be worth taking.

References

Ahmed, Mara (2018), <https://www.maraahmedstudio.com/2018/09/12/connections-discussing-satire-and-the-controversy-surrounding-the-cartoon-of-serena-williams/>.

Ahmed, Sara (1997) '"It's a Sun-tan isn't it?": auto-biography as an identificatory practice', in Heidi Safia Mirza (ed.), *Black British Feminism: A Reader*, London: Routledge, pp. 153–67.

Butler, Judith (1993), *Bodies that Matter: On the Discursive Limits of 'Sex'*, London: Routledge.

Crenshaw, Kimberlé (1991), 'Demarginalizing the intersection of race and sex: a black feminist critique of antidiscrimination doctrine, feminist theory and anti-racist politics', in Katharine T. Bartlett and Rosanne Kennedy (eds), *Feminist Legal Theory*, London: Routledge, pp. 57–80.

Destiny's Child, *Survivor*, <https://www.youtube.com/watch?v=Wmc8bQoL-J0>.

Garcia, Michelle (2018), 'A new editorial cartoon shows yet another racist depiction of Serena Williams', *Huntsville Tribune*, <https://huntsvilletribune.com/a-new-editorial-cartoon-shows-yet-another-racist-depiction-of-serena-williams/>.

hooks, bell (1996), *Reel to Real: Race, Sex and Class at the Movies*, New York: Routledge.

Irigaray, Luce (1985) *This Sex Which is Not One*, translated by Gillian C. Gill, Ithaca, NY: Cornell University Press.

Jordan, June (2002), 'Report from the Bahamas', in *Some of Us did Not Die: New and Selected Essays of June Jordan*, New York: Basic/Civitas Books, pp. 211–22.

McGowan, Todd (2003), 'Looking for the gaze: Lacanian film theory and its vicissitudes', *Cinema Journal*, 42: 3 (Spring), 27–47.

McGowan, Todd (2013), 'The singularity of the cinematic object', *Continental Philosophy Review*, 46: 311–25.

Muñoz, José Esteban (1999), *Disidentifications: Queer of Colour and the Performance of Politics*, Minneapolis: University of Minnesota Press.

Omielan, Luisa (2018), *What would Beyoncé Do?*, <https://youtu.be/Y4BLN-Gh88I>.

Rankine, Claudia (2011), 'Open letter to Tony Hoagland', with a response, <https://www.poets.org/text/open-letter-dialogue-race-and-poetry>.

Rankine, Claudia (2014), *Citizen: An American Lyric*, London: Penguin.

Rankine, Claudia (2015), 'The meaning of Serena Williams: on tennis and black excellence', *The New York Times Magazine*, 25 August.

Savage, Mark (2018), 'Beyoncé named music's most powerful woman by BBC's Woman's Hour power list', BBC News, September 28: https://www.bbc.com/news/entertainment-arts-45639433

Seshadri-Crooks, Kalpana (2000), *Desiring Whiteness: A Lacanian Analysis of Race*, London: Routledge.

Whitford, Margaret (1991), *Luce Irigaray: Philosophy in the Feminine*, London: Routledge.

Withers, Rachel (2018), <https://slate.com/news-and-politics/2018/09/mark-knight-australian-cartoon-serena-williams-sexist-racist.html>.

US Open QF Highlights (2004), YouTube, Serena Williams vs Jennifer Capriati, <https://youtu.be/gyECzEKShz0>.

US Open SF Highlights (2009), Kim Clijsters vs Serena Williams, <https://youtu.be/GTc-gv8tNWQ>.

Žižek, Slavoj (1992), *The Sublime Object of Ideology*, London: Verso.

5. RACE, BODIES AND ALTERED IDENTITIES IN *SLEIGHT* AND *US*

Mary K. Bloodsworth-Lugo

The movies *Sleight* (2016), directed by J. D. Dillard, and *Us* (2019), directed by Jordan Peele, were released in the United States during a political moment heavily influenced by the Trump presidency (since January 2017) and the post-9/11 era (since September 2001). While it is beyond the scope of this chapter to lay out how the Trump presidency logically extends, rather than ruptures, the US landscape since the events of 11 September 2001, I nonetheless take this idea as a point of departure and backdrop here. In the main, Americans, during the past twenty years, have been positioned to fear, be anxious about, and show heightened concern for 'foreigners' and 'enemy others'. This posture has not fundamentally changed during the last several years and actually appears to have strengthened (Norman 2016). As a simultaneous phenomenon, the categories of perceived threat(s) to American citizens and the United States as a nation have undergone stark expansion. Presidential or state discourse has marked a primary mechanism for propelling and bolstering these conceptions (Bloodsworth-Lugo and Lugo-Lugo 2010).

The last several years have also witnessed a number of films released by black directors, including but not limited to Dillard and Peele, that have featured black actors. Such films as *Get Out* (Peele 2017) and *Black Panther* (Coogler 2018), along with *BlacKkKlansman* (Lee 2018), *The Equalizer 2* (Fuqua 2018), and *Creed II* (Caple 2018) offer examples of these box office and critical successes. Brian Welk notes that 'Black filmmakers had a record year at the box office in 2018, earning $1.5 billion at the domestic box office from 16 films' (2019). And Trey Williams adds, 'while it wasn't so long ago that Hollywood studios and producers argued that a star like [Denzel] Washington couldn't open a movie abroad because he's black, *Equalizer 2* grossed nearly half of its $190.4 million in ticket sales from theaters overseas' (2019).

I have suggested elsewhere (Bloodsworth-Lugo 2019) that philosophers of film are well-served to consider lessons contained in recent films directed by black filmmakers, especially as these lessons are situated against a backdrop of lived (racial) realities within the contemporary United States and its particular political dimensions. In this regard, I maintain that it is not accidental that these films have been released during a period of increased racial antagonism within the United States and the perception of many Americans that race relations are in fact deteriorating (Horowitz et al. 2019). This perception emerged early in the Trump presidency and was revealed in a public opinion poll conducted by Reuters following the president's first 100 days in office. According to the poll, in which Americans were asked to 'rate the danger of racism and bigotry in America,' approximately 36 per cent of respondents 'gave it the worst rating possible, saying they considered racism and bigotry an "imminent threat" to the country' (Whitesides 2017). A majority of Americans also reported that 'they have recently sensed an unsettling rise in racial hostility – or at least a greater willingness by some Americans to express it' (Whitesides 2017).

As an additional point of departure for this chapter, I note that both Dillard and Peele have remarked that *Sleight* and *Us* are not explicitly about race. Dillard states that his protagonist in *Sleight*, Bo, could be swapped out with someone of any race, and the story would still make sense' (Robinson 2017). Dillard continues, 'We really do want to tell stories with different faces. It doesn't always need to be about "the black experience"' (Robinson 2017). Regarding *Us*, Peele has similarly commented: 'Scores of people will walk into this movie waiting for the racial commentary, and when it doesn't come in the form they're looking for, they'll be forced to ask themselves: "Why did I think a movie with black people had to be about blackness?"' (Obenson 2019). In what follows, I would like to consider some of the ethical and political dimensions of films such as *Sleight* and *Us* – films by black writers and directors featuring black actors – given real and perceived racial hostilities within the United States and given that the expressed intent of the films is not to be about race.

BLACK BODIES AND *SLEIGHT*

Sleight appeared in theatres in the United States in April 2017. As broader context for the film, we can note that, according to statistics from Mapping Police Violence, despite the fact that there are 160 million more whites than blacks in the United States (62 per cent versus 13 per cent of the population), black Americans are three times more likely than white Americans to be shot and killed by police (Mapping Police Violence 2018). In other words, while the white population is nearly five times larger than the black population, black Americans are still three times more likely than white Americans to be shot and killed by police (Mapping Police Violence 2018). While black men comprise only 6% of the US population, they represented 40% of all unarmed people shot and killed by police in 2015 (Mapping Police Violence 2018). As a *Washington Post* article clearly states, 'The only thing that was significant in predicting whether someone shot and killed by police was unarmed was whether or not they were black' (Lowery 2016). Moreover, FBI statistics cited 990 fatal police shootings reported in 2015, while prior to this year, no more than 460 fatal police shootings had been reported in any given year (Lowery 2016).

The main character in *Sleight*, Bo (played by Jacob Latimore), is a young black man living in Los Angeles. He is a street magician by day and a somewhat reluctant drug dealer by night. His engagement with illegal activities was necessitated in the wake of his mother's death and the responsibility of caring for his younger sister, Tina (played by Storm Reid). The siblings are both orphaned, as their father has also died earlier in their lives. Pivotal to the plot of *Sleight* is the fact that Bo wants to extricate himself from dealing drugs and the man who employs him, Angelo (played by Dulé Hill), after the environment turns increasingly dangerous and violent. As such, the film plays off the idea of 'sleight of hand' and improving one's lot in life with the tagline, 'You can change the cards you're dealt.'

As Dillard points out in an interview about the film, there is 'a natural relationship between the skill sets of street magic and crime. Both require a certain level of deception' (Robinson 2017). He conveys, 'Part of the goal in centering ourselves in that world was to find a different, empathetic way into a trope that's maybe a little too familiar' (Robinson 2017). Dillard continues, 'By centering it on this kid who is brilliant and artistic and has a scholarship going for him, we're showing that a fall into this world really could happen to anyone' (Robinson 2017). In this sense, *Sleight* differs from the film *Dope* (Famuyiwa 2015), which was released at Sundance a year earlier. Peter Debruge states in his review of *Sleight*, *Dope* 'similarly dealt with the idea that inner-city kids can't necessarily steer clear of crime in their climb out of poverty but brought so much detail and specificity to that conflict, the movie felt like a genuine revelation' (2017).

Debruge's remark positions *Dope* as a better film than *Sleight*, but part of the 'detail and specificity' that Debruge references can be linked to a certain racial and contextual positioning of the lead character, Dom (played by A$AP Rocky), that Dillard rejects for Bo. Soraya Nadia McDonald states that '*Sleight* suffers from the lack of specifics that turn an intriguing idea into a film with a protagonist with whom we could [otherwise] become heavily emotionally invested' (2017). And in his review of *Sleight*, Sam C. Mac maintains, 'It can't be discounted that Dillard, and about 90% of the film's cast, are black – and that *Sleight* is taking a traditionally white genre and diversifying it' (2017). Mac continues, 'Unfortunately, unlike Jordan Peele's superior *Get Out*, *Sleight* never shows much interest in exploring how blackness can inform a genre's tropes, or even the realities of its characters' (2017).

Sleight's lead character is a sympathetic figure – young, caring, intelligent and resourceful. And like Dom in *Dope*, Bo is a sort of 'geek', having been awarded a university scholarship for his sharpness in science. Bo turned down the scholarship precisely because he needed to care for his sister – a fact that is likely to garner even more admiration from viewers. Moreover, Bo's science talent is central to the plot in other ways, as he uses his knowledge to supplement his street magic; namely, he implants a battery-driven device into his arm that allows objects to be secretly moved and levitated during his magic tricks. The device ultimately provides Bo with the necessary tool for protecting and removing himself from Angelo, as well. Thus, it is through scientific knowledge, technological skill and bodily modification that Bo gains the power to press beyond his current circumstances.

In my view, it is not unimportant to the story or for viewers that Bo, as a black man, modifies his own body in this way. As broader context, we can consider the historical legacy of the United States as it relates to black bodies. This legacy dates to the transport and enslavement of black bodies through the formal institution of slavery and continues today through various forms of policing, surveilling and containing black bodies. As the statistics opening this section suggest, the disproportionate and negative effects of US policies and programmes on racially marked black or brown men (and often women) mean that these bodies have often been the very targets (or points of origin) for the policies and programmes themselves and not 'merely' the recipients of their impacts. We can note an intersection, for instance, between the long-standing 'War on Drugs' and the US-led 'War on Terror', since in both cases black and brown bodies have been both construed as threats to US society/the American people and marked as demanding action (see Bloodsworth-Lugo 2019).

Given this backdrop, the fact that Bo modifies his body to improve his magic and his circumstances is significant. And its significance is not unrelated to race, for Bo manipulates his own body for his own purposes. This stands in contrast to the situation for Chris, Peele's lead character in *Get Out*, where the horror of the film lies in its takeover of Chris's body – and by extension other black bodies – in a way that mirrors black experience(s) in the United States. And while the takeover or theft that *Get Out* signals is most markedly represented by the institution of slavery, it also recalls myriad other scenarios taking place within the United States: medical experiments and studies conducted on black bodies for the ultimate benefit of whites, ways that black bodies have been positioned to perform and entertain for the pleasure of whites, and ways that black bodies have been commodified or appropriated by whites (see Bloodsworth-Lugo 2019).

Interestingly, this feature of *Sleight* – Bo's bodily manipulation – along with other aspects of his backstory, have led many film critics and reviewers to see *Sleight* as a low-key superhero origin story. Some commentators even consider this angle on the film to provide its most generous reading (see Dowd 2017). A. A. Dowd notes that *Sleight* is 'self-contained, goes easy on the special effects, and stars a young black actor instead of some blond dude . . . If this is a superhero movie, it's a welcome deviation from formula' (2017). Even *Sleight*'s director, Dillard, who maintains that the lead character could be switched with an actor of any race, also states that Bo 'is pulled from my own childhood because I was the Black nerd that was building computers and tearing apart televisions to create things' (Tinubu 2017). Dillard notes that such figures are important 'especially for young Black people who are still desperate to see representations of themselves on screen' (Tinubu 2017). But Dillard conveys that he did not intend *Sleight* to offer a superhero origin story, stating that a 'superhero origin story was not necessarily part of the DNA when we started' the project (Couch 2017).

In some respects, the fact that a superhero origin story was not initially intended by the writer/director makes the fact that so many critics and commentators interpreted the film in this way even more meaningful. It is important to remember that *Sleight* appeared in US theatres nearly a year prior to the release of *Black Panther* (February 2018). And while *Sleight*'s release was relatively small and limited, especially compared to the worldwide impact of *Black Panther*, its positive portrayal of a young, black man in the United States – a hero/superhero, either as a person and black man or an emerging character with superpowers – should be contextualised by the statistics that frame this section and the continuing perception of black men as dangerous. As a contributor to *Black Hollywood Live* maintains, *Sleight* 'builds a movie around a young black man with superpowers' in a way that 'feels like a rebuke of demonizing' (NERDSoul 2017).

Having made this point, a certain ambiguity around the racial dimensions of the film makes it most provocative. Bo is both a drug dealer and a hero. He is implicated in a circumstance he seeks to escape. The story conveys how black men must navigate the US social/political landscape. It also suggests that anyone, given a certain set of circumstances, could find themselves in a precarious and fallen situation. In an environment of increased racial hostility in the United States, the film evokes compassion. This is no small aim or achievement given the Trump presidency and its promotions and displays of ethnic and racial antagonism. And the film does this with black characters at the centre of the story, but the story itself is not about blackness per se.

American Anxieties and *Us*

In an article for *The New York Times*, in the wake of the 2016 presidential election, Eduardo Porter claimed, 'tens of millions of Americans voted for a policy platform that included profiling Muslims, expelling millions of unauthorized immigrants, walling off the nation's third-largest trading partner, and starting a trade war with the world's next superpower' (2016). Porter continues,

> Racism is hardly new in America. It lies behind the United States' knottiest paradox: Millions of white Americans who would benefit from a more robust government are steadfastly against it, at least partly out of a belief that minorities would gain at their expense. (2016)

Eric Kaufmann, in an opinion piece for *The New York Times*, adds to Porter's position, maintaining that 'since 2012, white liberals have moved considerably left on questions related to race' and that 'people of color are not the driving force behind most of today's forms of racial liberalism' (2019). This point is significant for a film, such as *Us* (discussed below), that claims not to be straightforwardly about race or 'the black experience' and in which the central (black) family is also middle-class.

In addition, in a piece for *The Atlantic*, Vann Newkirk II conveys, 'Contra Barack Obama, there is a white America and a black America' (2019). A PRRI/Atlantic poll revealed 'major differences among racial groups on some of the basic questions about what makes America America, and what makes Americans so' (Newkirk 2019). Overall, 'the data indicate that white, black, and Hispanic voters have markedly divergent ideas on what exactly makes the American identity' and 'show competing visions of America . . . separated by race and region' (Newkirk 2019). Newkirk indicates that 'other polls show black voters increasingly concerned about racism' (2019).

Jordan Peele, in the film *Us*, uses the metaphor of the 'tethered' to highlight a variety of social divisions currently in force within the United States. These divisions include but are not limited to the categories of social identity, 'race' and 'class', particularly as differential access to resources has become the societal norm (resources such as health care, employment, education, food and clean water). At its most basic level, Emily Yoshida points out, 'Ideas about a hidden or bifurcated America abound in *Us*' (2019). And Peele portrays this bifurcation through the tethered, who live below the Earth's surface, unseen and neglected. Their invisibility to those above ground represents the reality of people living at society's margins today.

In a comment that frames the film, viewers of *Us* are told that there are thousands of miles of forgotten tunnels below the surface of the United States. *Us* posits that the forgotten tethered might be residing inside these underground tunnels, poised to surface and strike a sort of revenge towards people living above ground who exist in a state of unaware privilege. While these tunnels have a metaphorical significance in the film as well, we can consider for a moment their factual reality in the actual world. In his recent book, *Underground: A Human History of the Worlds Beneath Our Feet*, Will Hunt conveys, 'There are way more tunnels underground wherever you are in the United States than you would imagine', including 'active or abandoned transportation tunnels, sewer lines, aqueducts or even military or government infrastructure' (Shorey 2019). Mirroring the idea of the tethered residing underground but being forgotten, Hunt notes that there is 'something under your feet that people don't think about'; for instance, under the surface of New York City, 'you find mole people ... these marginalized, forgotten people who are living completely out of sight in essentially a separate reality' (Shorey 2019). Within the film *Us* itself, the idea of humans or human-like beings living below or underneath one's feet, with its horrifying implications, can be seen in allusions to two other horror films: *C.H.U.D.* (Cheek, 1984) and *The People Under the Stairs* (Craven, 1991).

Keeping with the message of *Us*, Hunt remarks in an interview that these underground populations

> can be understood as a metonym for national identity. The underground has always been the unconscious. When we're talking about the unconscious of a culture, of the United States, a good place to explore those forces is beneath the surface. (Shorey 2019)

If we situate *Us*'s tale of underground tunnels politically, we can recall a major US news story from January 2019. The story concerned 376 people, including 179 children, who had entered the United States from Mexico via seven different tunnels dug under an existing border wall. An *ABC NEWS* headline read, 'Largest single group of migrants ever tunnels under border wall in Arizona' (Gutman 2019). This particular story dovetailed the discovery of 'several tunnels originating in a Mexican border town and ending in various locations within the United States' (Phillips 2019). Ironically, the discovery of these tunnels occurred as President Trump pressed to build more walls at the United States–Mexico border. In his words, 'building barriers would stave off illegal immigration and drug trafficking into the United States' (Phillips 2019). News of tunnels between Mexico and the United States clearly revealed the folly of building more walls.

As the plot of *Us* unfolds, the family on which the film centres, the Wilsons, see their exact doubles standing, hand in hand, in the driveway of their vacation home at night. The father and husband, Gabe (played by Winston Duke), provokes the doubles with a baseball bat, and the doubles attack the family. Viewers experience the scariness of being attacked by a slightly distorted version of themselves. Within the current political environment, Emily Yoshida claims the doubles provide 'the perfect conduit for contemporary anxieties about foreign threats', as well as various modern-day dissociations (2019). Peele remarks, concerning his overall message in *Us*:

> We are our own worst enemy, not just as individuals but more importantly as a group, as a family, as a society, as a country, as a world. We are afraid of the shadowy, mysterious 'other' that's gonna come and kill us and take our jobs and do whatever. (Rose 2019)

He continues, 'But what we're really afraid of is the thing we're suppressing: our sin, our guilt, our contribution to our own demise. No one's owning up, blaming ourselves for our part in the problems of the world' (Rose 2019).

In this respect, the doubles in the film are not so separate or distinct from the people they duplicate; rather, the relationship between them is one of 'tethering'. David Edelstein comments that *Us* is intended to make viewers consider 'their own capabilities for harm, and their own culpabilities in what goes on in America' (2019). This point makes the Wilsons' middle-class background an important element in the film, for Gabe, in particular, is focused on 'keeping up' with his (white) friends, the Tylers. Following the lead of the Tylers, the Wilsons own a beach house, Gabe buys a boat, and Gabe claims that Josh Tyler (played by Tim Heidecker) bought a new car 'just to fuck with me'. Thus, the Wilsons are caught in a web of privilege and middle-class desire. They aim to advance on the social ladder without acknowledging those who attempt to survive beneath them. When the doubles arrive at the Wilsons' home, Gabe initially asks, 'Hi, can I help you?' But he quickly escalates, 'I need y'all to get off my property'. When the doubles do not budge, Gabe goes inside and returns with the baseball bat. It is at this point that the doubles attack, suggesting that this show of force instigates their acts of retaliation and revenge.

Dualities in *Us* and *Sleight*

Importantly, as noted by Tasha Robinson, 'Peele makes the point that while the doubles may look and act like monsters, especially to the victims, they still have an unacknowledged humanity that brings them a kind of horrible pathos' (2019a). And 'by giving the tethers names, Peele is also giving them the humanity that the country does not afford them' (Miller 2019). According to Peele, 'The movie's about maybe the monster in you. It's about us, looking at ourselves as individuals and as a group', and it tackles the question 'what is good and what is evil' (Cummings 2019). Joelle Monique notes, 'There are no monsters in *Us*. Peele holds a reflective mirror to American society. Pop culture shapes and defines how America looks at itself' (2019).

While Gabe plays a central role in the film, it is the mother of the Wilson family, Adelaide (played by Lupita Nyong'o), who is its lead character. Viewers learn that Adelaide's double is Red (also played by Lupita Nyong'o), and in a significant twist, that Red has actually maintained the position of Adelaide for the entire film. In choosing this direction for *Us*, Peele states that he wanted viewers to wonder whether the construct 'good or evil' is even viable. He indicates, 'Both characters are lovable and terrifying, based on the lives they'd led they've just sort of inverted paths' (Cummings 2019). Peele continues, 'I wanted to suggest that maybe the monster we really need to look at has a face. Maybe the evil [if there is evil], it's us' (Robinson 2019a). Regardless, 'It is less clear-cut who to root for when the heroes and villains are essentially the same people' (Rose 2019).

This feature of *Us*, I think, echoes Dillard's intention in crafting the character Bo in *Sleight*. That is to say, Bo's character hits close to home and is relatable given that anyone could lose parents to unforeseen circumstances and have the course of their lives altered. In the wake of such events, many directions and outcomes are possible depending on resources, choices, positionality, environment, etc. Aisha Harris comments that *Us* reimagines a classic trope in which 'the protagonist [is] forced to reckon with another version of him or herself . . .' (2019). A. A. Dowd remarks that *Sleight* offers 'a human-scale origin story' (2017). This is underscored in the film's final scene where Bo's girlfriend, Holly (played by Seychelle Gabriel), opens the door to a room as Bo seems to have perfected his body-technology. Viewers do not see Bo and are only offered Holly's surprised expression, as a bright glow emanates from the space. Viewers are left to wonder what happens, exactly; what does Holly witness, precisely? If Bo has perfected and advanced his powers, how will he use them? Will he use them to help others, or will he enact some sort of revenge?

Soraya Nadia McDonald relays, 'Peele has been explicit that *Us* is not a film about race, and yet it pulls off something that feels transcendent' – creating 'a role that is a worthy showcase of Nyong'o's talent' and building 'on a tradition of black horror as social commentary and pushback against stereotypes of blackness' (2019). Writing for *Afropunk*, Kyle AB interprets Red's suffering in tandem with Adelaide's success as pointing to 'the film's concern with repressed identity' and 'the horror of double consciousness' (2019). Melina Abdullah agrees, stating,

> To many Black moviegoers, the dichotomy of two 'selves' is at the movie's core. Connected through a single form but opposed in perspective . . . In a sense, the double meaning of *Us* – one apparent to white American masses and the other accessible to Black people – itself illustrates Black American twoness. (Abdullah 2019)

As such, instead of considering Peele's *Get Out* and *Us* as two very different films, AB maintains that they come together via their 'central fear of being replaced by imposters' (2019). In other words, both films cast light on the historical theft of black bodies within the US context and ways that black bodies continue to suffer. Further, using Peele's image of a pair of scissors, AB recalls, 'For DuBois, Black consciousness is both haunted and hunted, on the one blade, by what white people think of us and, on the other blade, by what we think of ourselves' (2019). He continues:

> But, whereas the Armitages [in *Get Out*] attempt to submerge Chris' identity in their basement, Adelaide's repressed identity emerges from the depths. In this sense, Peele's attempt to frame *Us* as 'not about race' is not so much a distancing from *Get Out*, as it is a positioning across from *Get Out*. These are the shears of double consciousness, where Black folks sit between the sharp edges of losing who we are (*Get Out*) or our suppressed, traumatized selves breaking free (*Us*). (2019)

Shreyan Jain extends 'double consciousness' to the nation, saying that Peele stands the notion 'on its head and implicates all of us, demanding the audience to confront the shadow selves we have forgotten and neglected' (2019). In this respect, Jain continues, 'The *Us* of the film is double, just like the film's doubles; it refers both to the "us" of the Wilson family, and to the broader "U.S."' (2019).

Conclusion

During the summer of 2019, several months after the release of *Us*, high-profile news stories in the United States began to report the fact that migrant children, who were being detained after crossing the southern border into the United States, were going without soap, toothbrushes and sleep. The Trump administration faced charges for the treatment of detainees dating back to the Obama presidency, and representatives went before a federal court 'to argue that it shouldn't be required to give detained migrant children toothbrushes, soap, towels, showers or even half a night's sleep inside Border Patrol facilities' (Flynn 2019). According to an article published by *The Washington Post*, 'the government was in court to appeal a 2017 finding that child migrants and their parents were detained in dirty, crowded, bitingly cold conditions inside U.S. Customs and Border Protection facilities along the Southern border' (Flynn 2019).

Regarding *Us*, Jain remarks, '*Us* is nothing less than an allegorical documentary of Trump's America, an investigation of the rifts, divides, and walls that separate us from the people who are just like us' (2019). Incorporating the film's tagline, 'We are our own worst enemy', Bill Bria suggests that *Us* 'is a film about entire nations and cultures being self-destructive' (2019). Viewers can note this idea illustrated many times in the film, with the television images from the 1986 Hands Across America charity event, opening the film, and the scenes of doubles standing hand in hand, in the present day, being graphic examples. As with the duality of scissors, the hand in hand images are able to evoke either a friendly togetherness or an ominous presence, depending upon one's point of reference.

Given the current reality and divisions in the United States, it is striking that the 1986 television clip promoting Hands Across America shows the Golden Gate Bridge in San Francisco, on the west coast, and the World Trade Center towers in New York City, on the east coast. While the charity event was promoted as raising money for hunger and homelessness in the United States, its lasting failure and shallowness is underscored by extreme present-day homelessness in San Francisco (up 30 per cent between 2017 and 2019 alone). And in New York City, the destruction of the Twin Towers and deaths of nearly 3,000 people with the 11 September 2001 attacks served to justify wars in Iraq and Afghanistan and the US-led 'War on Terror'. Calls for securing US borders, being vigilant of 'enemy others', and viewing 'brown' and 'black' populations as threats to national security ensued. These appeals and policy platforms only intensified with the Trump presidency, with many Americans in the general population following along.

Briefly returning to the specific issue of blackness in *Us*, Robinson posits:

> *Us* doesn't ignore race, but it doesn't make it the central focus. The power in *Us* when it comes to centering the Black experience, is that Blackness is on proud display throughout the film, but is done not in the vein of 'otherness', as though the viewer is looking at something different from themselves, but rather that the terror the Wilson family experiences is universal. (2019b)

Placing a black woman in the film's central role (Nyong'o in the role of Adelaide) means that 'white isn't used as the default portrayal of the human condition [but] allows Black people to be fully realized characters outside of overused tropes' (Robinson 2019b). I would add that it also allows *black women* to be placed at the centre in the human condition narrative. And this point about gender is not a small one, for if 'white man' is the well-worn default human universal, then Nyong'o's place in *Us* is vast. Peele describes Adelaide as 'the emotional center' of the film, and she is, importantly, 'conflicted and isolated' (Rose 2019). Her conflict and isolation, in turn, remind all of us of our own discomfort and dissociation. At the same time, they cast a reflection on the political stakes of 'race' within the recent and current United States.

J. Stokes suggests that since Adelaide is leader and protector of the family and largely acts on her own throughout the film, 'one could argue that the path Adelaide takes throughout *Us* mirrors that of many Black women in the US today' (2019). Thus, Peele might be 'suggesting that the Black community look inward as a way to alleviate the burden placed on Black women to protect their families largely on their own' (2019). There is a similar point to make about Bo, in *Sleight*, given that he is a black man raising his sister alone. This aspect of the story works to counter stereotypes and familiar media representations of black men. Moreover, Bo is presented in a role of 'universal human', given Dillard's commentary about blackness and the film. And it is this ambiguity about race that highlights the conflicted and even untenable situations in which the characters find themselves. The characters are implicated within the structures that act to marginalise them, pointing to an ethical tension left unresolved by both films.

This tension and disorientation also reflects sentiment within the United States. A 2016 study by the Chicago Council on Global Affairs, released in close proximity to the release of these films, noted that while the US economy [was] 'booming', Americans [did] not feel optimistic. The study explains,

> A big reason for this disconnect is that many Americans feel insecure. They may be doing well at the moment, but they fear that, however high they are on the economic ladder, a single bad step or bad event could cause them to slip. (Smeltz et al. 2016)

Recognising this uncertainty, Dave Anderson writes, in a piece for *The Baltimore Sun*, 'The majority of Americans are not extremists when it comes to politics. It's best to recognise the state of mind many of them have about policy issues . . . namely: uncertainty' (2018). Anderson continues, 'The majority of Americans do not believe that they know with certainty how to address' a variety of social issues. 'They do not have the cognitive state of mind of certainty. Nor do they feel comfortable in their beliefs' (2018). It is this lack of certainty, perhaps, that grounds the films discussed here. While the films centralise black characters and offer racial lessons, they are also positioned to exploit a broader human experience. This experience, for Americans, includes the path we are on as a nation – and how we all are ultimately and intimately implicated in that very path.

References

AB, Kyle (2019), 'Jordan Peele's "Us" is a Commentary on Double Consciousness', *Afropunk*, 25 March, <https://afropunk.com/2019/03/jordan-peeles-us-review/> (accessed 26 July), p. 201.

Abdullah, Melina (2019), 'Jordan Peele's "Us" depicts black double consciousness', *The Northstar*, 13 April, <https://thenorthstar.com/articles/jordan-peeles-us-depicts-black-double-consciousness-spoilers> (accessed 26 July 2019).

Anderson, Dave (2018), 'The majority is uncertain; let them lead', *The Baltimore Sun*, 15 May, <https://www.baltimoresun.com/opinion/op-ed/bs-ed-op-0517-uncertain-americans-20180516-story.html> (accessed 28 July 2019).

Black Panther, film, directed by Ryan Coogler, USA: Marvel Studios and Walt Disney Pictures.

BlacKkKlansman, film, directed by Spike Lee, USA: Focus Features.

Bloodsworth-Lugo, Mary K. (2019), 'Race, bodies, and lived realities in *Get Out* and *Black Panther*', in Christina Rawls, Diana Neiva and Steven S. Gouveia (eds), *Philosophy and Film: Bridging Divides*, New York: Routledge, pp. 281–97.

Bloodsworth-Lugo, Mary K. and Carmen R. Lugo-Lugo (2010), *Containing (Un)American Bodies: Race, Sexuality, and Post-9/11 Constructions of Citizenship*, New York: Brill/Rodopi.

Bria, Bill (2019), 'Jordan Peele's sleight of hand: marketing us', *Crooked Marque*, 1 April, <https://crookedmarquee.com/jordan-peeles-sleight-of-hand-marketing-us/> (accessed 21 July 2019).

Couch, Aaron (2017), '"Sleight" director on how "Star Wars" led to his own superhero origin story', *The Hollywood Reporter*, 28 April, <https://www.hollywoodreporter.com/heat-vision/sleight-director-how-star-wars-led-his-own-superhero-origin-story-998146> (accessed 21 July 2019).

Creed II, film, directed by Steven Caple, Jr, USA: MGM and Warner Brothers.

Cummings, Moriba (2019), 'Jordan Peele finally explains the twisted ending of "Us"', *BET*, 2 April, <https://www.bet.com/celebrities/news/2019/04/02/jordan-peele-explains-ending-us.html> (accessed 22 July 2019).

Debruge, Peter (2017), 'Film review: "Sleight"', *Variety*, 28 April, <https://variety.com/2017/film/reviews/sleight-review-1202402594/> (accessed 18 July 2019).

Dope, film, directed by Rick Famuyiwa, USA: I am OTHER and Forest Whitaker's Significant Productions.

Dowd, A. A. (2017), '*Sleight* only looks fresh when compared to your average overblown superhero story', *AV/FILM*, 28 April, <https://film.avclub.com/sleight-only-looks-fresh-when-compared-to-your-average-1798191154> (accessed 18 July 2019).

Edelstein, David (2019), 'Us doesn't live up to Get Out, but it shows the promise of Jordan Peele', *Vulture*, 22 March, <https://www.vulture.com/2019/03/jordan-peeles-us-movie-review.html> (accessed 22 July 2019).

Equalizer II, The, film, directed by Antoine Fuqua, USA: Columbia Pictures.

Flynn, Meagan (2019), 'Detained migrant children got no toothbrush, no soap, no sleep. It's no problem, government argues', *The Washington Post*, 21 June 2019, <https://www.washingtonpost.com/nation/2019/06/21/detained-migrant-children-no-toothbrush-soap-sleep/?noredirect=on&utm_term=.a4b8a14530d3> (accessed 23 June 2019).

Get Out, film, directed by Jordan Peele, USA: Blumhouse Productions.

Gutman, Matt (2019), 'Largest single group of migrants ever tunnels under border wall in Arizona, says border protection', *ABC News*, 18 January, <https://abcnews.go.com/US/largest-single-group-migrants-tunnels-border-wall-arizona/story?id=60462672> (accessed 23 June 2019).

Harris, Aisha (2019), '"Us" reflects a mirror image of "The Twilight Zone"', *The New York Times*, 28 March, <https://www.nytimes.com/2019/03/28/arts/television/us-twilight-zone-mirror-image.html> (accessed 26 July 2019).

Horowitz, Juliana, Anna Brown and Kiana Cox (2019), 'Race in America 2019', *Pew Research Center*, 9 April, <https://www.pewsocialtrends.org/2019/04/09/race-in-america-2019/?fbclid=IwAR2GYP--7iYwwnfUd5VGtcxF1HtmuFV_gkeJEH89A5Bkx Sfef2uU12obSvw> (accessed 2 June 2019).

Hunt, Will (2019), *Underground: A Human History of the Worlds Beneath Our Feet*, New York: Spiegel and Grau.

Jain, Shreyan (2019), '"Us" and the double consciousness of a nation', *The Tech*, 4 April, <https://thetech.com/2019/04/04/us-movie-review> (accessed 4 April 2019).

Kaufmann, Eric (2019), 'Americans are divided by their views on race, not race itself', *The New York Times*, 18 March, <https://www.nytimes.com/2019/03/18/opinion/race-america-trump.html> (accessed 2 June 2019).

Lowery, Wesley (2016), 'Analysis | Aren't more white people than black people killed by police? Yes, but no', *The Washington Post*, 11 July, <www.washingtonpost.com/news/post-nation/wp/2016/07/11/arent-more-white-people-than-black-people-killed-by-police-yes-but-no/?noredirect=on> (accessed 18 July 2019).

Mac, Sam C. (2017), 'Review: Sleight', *Slant*, 24 April, <https://www.slantmagazine.com/film/ sleight/> (accessed 21 July 2019).

McDonald, Soraya Nadia (2017), 'Jordan Peele's "Us" has a message for those who can hear above the screams', *The Undefeated*, 22 March, <https://theundefeated.com/features/jordan-peeles-horror-movie-us-has-a-message-for-those-who-can-hear-below-the-screams/> (accessed 26 July 2019).

Mapping Police Violence (2018), 1 September, <https://mappingpoliceviolence.org/unarmed/> (accessed 18 July 2019).

Miller, Matt (2019), 'Us movie ending explained by Jordan Peele', *Esquire*, 3 April, <https://www.esquire.com/entertainment/movies/a27028615/twist-ending-explained-jordan-peele-interview/> (accessed 22 July 2019).

Monique, Joelle (2019), 'There are no true monsters in "Us"', *The Hollywood Reporter*, 22 March, <https://www.hollywoodreporter.com/heat-vision/us-was-movies-biggest-twist-hiding-plain-sight-1196584> (accessed 22 July 2019).

NERDSoul (2017), 'My top 5 reasons Sleight needs a sequel', *Black Hollywood Live*, 10 September, <https://www.youtube.com/watch?v=UC9YrzgBwCQ> (accessed 20 July 2019).

Newkirk II, Vann R. (2019), 'The racial divide is a political divide', *The Atlantic*, 21 February, <https://www.theatlantic.com/politics/archive/2019/02/racial-divisions-exist-among-whites-blacks-and-hispanics/583267/> (accessed 2 June 2019).

Norman, Jim (2016), 'Four nations top U.S.'s greatest enemy list', *Gallup*, 22 February, <https://news.gallup.com/poll/189503/four-nations-top-greatest-enemy-list.aspx> (accessed 2 June 2019).

Obenson, Tambay (2019), '"Us" makes a radical argument for black identity by ignoring it', *Indie Wire*, 22 March, <https://www.indiewire.com/2019/03/us-movie-jordan-peele-lupita-nyongo-1202051703/> (accessed 20 May 2019).

Phillips, Kristine (2019), 'As Trump pushes for a wall, authorities keep finding drug tunnels under the U.S.-Mexico border', *The Washington Post*, 15 January, <https://www.washingtonpost.com/world/2019/01/14/trump-pushes-wall-authorities-keep-finding-drug-tunnels-under-us-mexico-border/?noredirect=on&utm_term=.0a8e950e9233> (accessed 12 May 2019).

Porter, Eduardo (2016), 'After the election, a nation tinged with racial hostility', *The New York Times,* 8 November, <https://www.nytimes.com/2016/11/09/business/after-the-election-a-nation-tinged-with-racial-hostility.html> (accessed 22 May 2019).

Robinson, Chauncey K. (2019), 'Review: Jordan Peele's "Us": horror on duality of the human condition', *People's World,* 22 March, <https://www.peoplesworld.org/article/review-jordan-peeles-us-horror-on-duality-of-the-human-condition/> (accessed 22 July 2019).

Robinson, Tasha (2017), 'Sleight's writer-director on how his superhero origin story was "like making movies in high school"', *The Verge,* 21 April, <https://www.theverge.com/2017/4/21/15386632/sleight-movie-magic-jd-dillard-superhero-origin-story> (accessed 18 July 2019).

Robinson, Tasha (2019), 'Jordan Peele's Us turns a political statement into unnerving horror', *The Verge,* 22 March, <https://www.theverge.com/2019/3/9/18257721/us-review-jordan-peele-get-out-lupita-nyongo-winston-duke-elisabeth-moss-tim-heidecker-horror> (accessed 21 July 2019).

Rose, Steve (2019), 'Jordan Peele on Us: "This is a very different movie from Get Out"', *The Guardian,* 9 March, <https://www.theguardian.com/film/2019/mar/09/jordan-peele-on-us-this-is-a-very-different-movie-from-get-out> (accessed 20 May 2019).

Shorey, Eric (2019), 'Here's the truth about the unexplained tunnels in Jordan Peele's "Us"', *Oxygen,* 29 March, <https://www.oxygen.com/martinis-murder/us-movie-truth-about-america-underground-tunnels-network> (accessed 7 May 2019).

Sleight, film, directed by J. D. Dillard, USA: Diablo Entertainment.

Smeltz, D., I. H. Daalder, H. Friedhoff and C. Kafura (2016), 'America in the Age of Uncertainty', *The Chicago Council on Global Affairs,* 6 October, <https://www.thechicago council.org/publication/america-age-uncertainty/> (accessed 28 July 2019).

Stokes, J. (2019), 'Jordan Peele's "Us" – a social commentary on the black woman', *Medium,* 16 April, <https://medium.com/@j.stokes/jordan-peeles-us-a-social-commentary-on-the-black-woman-674335be228c> (accessed 27 July 2019).

Tinubu, Aramide (2017), '"Sleight" is the black superhero flick you have to see before "Black Panther"', *Jet,* 18 April, <https://www.jetmag.com/entertainment/sleight-black-superhero-flick-see-black-panther/> (accessed 21 July 2019).

Us, film, directed by Jordan Peele, USA: Monkeypaw Productions.

Welk, Brian (2019), 'Black filmmakers directed record number of top-grossing movies in 2018', *TheWrap,* 4 January, <https://www.thewrap.com/black-filmmakers-directed-record-number-of-top-grossing-movies-in-2018/> (accessed 4 May 2019).

Whitesides, John (2017), 'More Americans say race relations deteriorating: Reuters poll', *Reuters,* 28 April, <https://www.reuters.com/article/us-usa-trump-poll-race/more-americans-say-race-relations-deteriorating-reuters-poll-idUSKBN17U1JU> (accessed 22 May 2019).

Williams, Trey (2019), 'Inside black filmmakers record $1.5 billion year at the box office, from "Black Panther" to "First Purge"', *TheWrap,* 2 January, <https://www.thewrap.com/2018-black-filmmaker-record-box-office-black-panther-first-purge/> (accessed 4 May 2019).

Yoshida, Emily (2019), 'Jordan Peele's Us is a messy, chilling descent into the American nightmare', *Vulture,* 9 March, <https://www.vulture.com/2019/03/jordan-peele-us-movie-review.html> (accessed 7 May 2019).

PART THREE

LOVE AND BELONGING

6. A PLANETARY WHOLE FOR THE ALIENATED: JOHN AKOMFRAH'S *VERTIGO SEA* THROUGH JAMESON AND DELEUZE[1]

Jakob A. Nilsson

The ecological crisis calls for vast and rapid socioeconomic changes that seem less than imminent. The changes seem remote, rather, and outside our grasp. And for many reasons: most concretely, the current system of socioeconomic power is a colossal obstacle, which can inspire a sense of futility. The system also tends to bind our desires, channel our attentions and shape worldviews, which affects what we find worth pursuing, possible, and even thinkable. Additionally, as is often pointed out, the development of industrial capitalism came with an overly dualistic and anthropocentric separation between human history/society and natural history. This separation not only enabled the over-exploitation of nature, but also helped create modes of existence as alienation from nature. Certainly, the current crisis makes the two sides of the separation appear 'entangled for everyone to see' (Latour 2010: 484). But seeing does not seem to drive us towards thinking and acting in ways required by the situation. Perhaps we need visions that both capture our situation and stretch beyond our situation towards credible new modes of existence. Here art can play a role. This can even be posed as an ethical-artistic challenge: how to help foster a new sense of planetary belonging for alienated modern subjects, while remaining rooted in – rather than escaping from – historical-political realities of causes and obstacles?

This chapter explores John Akomfrah's *Vertigo Sea* (2015) as an intriguing response to such an ethical-artistic challenge.[2] *Vertigo Sea* is a video work projected on three large screens in a secluded dark room with cinematic sound that offers an 'immersive experience', as Nora Alter writes, comparable to 'the effect of Richard Serra's large-scale steel objects, or Olafur Eliasson's sublime installations' (2018: 3). It outlines a complex planetary whole, into which spectators tend to be gradually pulled.[3] What they are pulled into, I should first clarify, is neither an image of nature as organic unity and oneness, nor an idealised sphere to get back to, nor a utopian blueprint – i.e., wholes as unengaging clichés or general abstractions that tend to veil differences and socioeconomic and historic realities. Instead, *Vertigo Sea* charts a whole that is immersive, visionary and critically historical and in ways sensitive to a feeling of planetary alienation.

Vertigo Sea is also a vast and sprawling work of montage, in its temporal and spatial scope, in combining a large array of original and archival material, and in expressing a multitude of motifs and issues. The material includes BBC Nature footage of plants and animals, wild sceneries, and phenomena, original soundscapes and landscape tableau shots, readings of literary and philosophical texts, aural testimony, newsreels, film clips, and photos of slaves and political casualties. The motifs and issues, most explicitly, concern relations between man and sea with focus on industrial whaling and polar bear hunting, various associated lamentable historical and contemporary events, and memory relating to migration and postcolonial experience and identity. While these latter issues are well-known recurring themes in, and the focus in most scholarly work on Akomfrah,[4] in *Vertigo Sea* – and this also goes for its semi-sequel the six-screen video *Purple* (2017)[5] – they are woven into ethical-ecological concerns, and a creative charting of a planetary whole, which have not been duly acknowledged or investigated. In an exhibition catalogue text, T. J. Demos describes how in *Vertigo Sea* 'audiovisual matter unfolds to reveal a dizzying intersection of history, fiction and philosophy', through (referencing statements by Akomfrah himself) 'montage [that] possesses the power to elicit "unconscious relations between the subject and historical forces"' (2016b: 14). This chapter examines such relations and intersections, which are understood here as juxtapositions between histories of industrial, nature-ravaging, colonial capitalism, and outlines for a deepened sense of planetary belonging for ecologically alienated modern subjects.[6]

Along with exploring how this is expressed in the video,[7] I will engage a set of theories on how art can chart wholes in ways that are both creatively visionary and rooted in/revealing of sociohistorical reality. One is Fredric Jameson's notion of cognitive mapping: a speculative call for artistic maps that provide an experience of a ('late') global capitalist system that otherwise appears too decentred and intricate to be represented or experienced by individual subjects or groups, which in turn helps block their utopian desires and imaginations (Jameson 1988). I will also reference implicit extensions of Jameson's concerns in partly similar discussions of the Anthropocene/Capitalocene[8] (Morton 2013; Mirzoeff 2014). Cognitive mapping, however, will be fundamentally reimagined through the examination of *Vertigo Sea* and by utilising two aspects of

Deleuze: (1) his discussions of parts of the 'modern' cinema of the time-image in which there is an ethical struggle to formulate different logics of thought and links to the world when organic or traditionally totalising ones appear to have lost their sway; and (2) some of Deleuze's (and Guattari's) writings on art as means to outline new modes of existence on planetary or world scales. The chapter argues that these concerns coalesce in updating and developing ways in *Vertigo Sea*.

Planetary Cine-ethics Meets Alienation

Vertigo Sea is an unusually immense and (potentially) immersive example of what Anat Pick, in the context of ecological film studies, calls 'a multi-species conception of worldhood' (2013: 10, 28ff.), of films that David Martin-Jones says 'illustrate the intertwined nature of human and planetary history' (2016: 67; see also 2018: ch. 3), and of Asbjørn Grønstad's notions of film as 'ethical imagination' in the sense of a 'planetary ethics' (2016: 219–39). *Vertigo Sea* excels in expressing – checking most of the boxes for 'art in the Anthropocene' – co-existing temporalities (spanning the slow to the fast, the geological to the miniscule); humans, animals, plants, land and water as entangled with industrial capitalist practices; signs of vibrant matter; and so on. In addition to loosely charting a Capitalocene – including its starting points in colonialisms and the slave trade – *Vertigo Sea* can be said to trace what Haraway calls a 'Chthulucene', as this entails not only 'myriad temporalities and spatialities' but also 'webs of speculative fabulation' (2015: 160).

More subtly, however, *Vertigo Sea* also treats where we are in all this as (more or less) alienated modern subjects. It appears to try to meet us and open for us to be pulled from *there* towards a deepened sense of planetary belonging. Key here is a series of original tableaus, composed landscape shots, taken in the northern hemisphere, of which most have one or a couple of human figures positioned to variously echo the classical *Rückenfigur*. Not so much gazing in towards a scenery represented as appearing sublime to them, as in Caspar David Friedrich's prototypical paintings. Here, rather, the subjects are often somewhat turned away from the scenery – and many of the tableaus are variations of the same scene, taken from another angle, closer to the figure or with the figure in a different position – with semi-passive gazes and exuding a sense of not fully knowing how to look at or react to the scenery (in contrast to being stunned in the sense of sublimely moved by it). These figures function not only as 'an analogue of the viewer's own position watching the film', as Demos aptly suggests (2016b: 14f.). They also seem to stand in for the modern subject within the larger historical period of the Capitalocene. Many of the figures appear among scattered artefacts connected to a 'modern' period – ranging from the seventeenth to the twenty-first century – of colonisation, globalisation and industrialisation. Most are dressed

Figure 6.1 *Vertigo Sea*, 2015. © Smoking Dogs Films; Courtesy Smoking Dogs Films and Lisson Gallery.

Figure 6.2 *Vertigo Sea*, 2015.© Smoking Dogs Films; Courtesy Smoking Dogs Films and Lisson Gallery.

in historical clothing, eighteenth-, nineteenth- and twentieth century-, and a few in contemporary clothing (in tableaus resembling those in Akomfrah's *The Nine Muses* (2010)).

Almost all tableaus also contain water – oceans, lakes, or creeks – and many of the figures stand on or close to shores. Shores have often been interpreted as liminal spaces between sea and land (e.g. Naficy 2001: 243f.). In the thematic tapestry of *Vertigo Sea*, such liminality can be said to stand for many things: a liminality of movement/stillness, migration/home, forgetting/memory, non-human/human, (smooth/striated). But also alienation/immersion: on the one hand the modern subject standing in/in front of nature as a kind of removed picture and on the other hand a pulling of that subject – through montage with a host of other materials across three screens and a layered audio track – towards an open planetary complexity.

Vertigo Sea creates cracks in its images of alienation through a variety of subtle montage formations, which open for a kind of planetary flight. For instance, recurring black-and-white footage of a man with large 'Eyes heavy as anchors' (as an intertitle says, referencing a Derek Walcott poem), next to screens with colourful shots of flocks of birds that at times seem to emanate from his gaze.[9] The alienation does not thereby disappear, but through the cracks there is new movement. Below we will return to a closer look at such aspects of the montage. I should underline here, however, that this montage is not sadness as pre-existing alienation to which is added joyful positive entanglement. The montage results rather in an overall sense of melancholic wonder, a cautious, both sad and beautiful rediscovery of planetary multiplicity.[10]

Capitalocene Version of the Lost Link to the World

The 'modern' sense of a split between human cultures and an objectified (and mechanised) nature waiting to be exploited – a split ubiquitously critiqued in post-human and Anthropocene literature (a critique with roots going back through for instance previous ecological thought, Deleuze, Guattari, Adorno,

Figure 6.3 *Vertigo Sea*, 2015. © Smoking Dogs Films; Courtesy Smoking Dogs Films and Lisson Gallery.

German Romantics, to Spinoza) – is still quite ingrained in our societies and general sense of being in the world. The Capitalocene nevertheless makes the unsustainability of the split, and the entanglement of human and natural history, appear more obvious and unavoidable. This adds up to a situation, explored in *Vertigo Sea*, which is rife with remaining blockages and new possibilities simultaneously.

There are similarities here with passages in Deleuze's *Cinema 2* on modern subjects having lost a natural link to the world, which parts of 'modern' cinema aims to create new kinds of links to and belief in – belief, that is, as Deleuze later wrote, in the world's 'possibilities of movements and intensities, so as once again to give birth to new modes of existence, closer to animals and rocks' (Deleuze 2003b: 169–77, 220–1; 2003a: 205–15; Deleuze and Guattari 1994: 74f.). *Cinema 2*, however, is not directly referencing the longer story of a nature–culture split, but rather a post-war (later, if you will) state of nihilism in which a general 'we' have lost our belief in cultural-political wholes that used to integrate – also modern – subjects in organic, rational totalities of meaning that provided a natural link to the world, and which was expressed in the kind of pre-war cinema he called the classical movement-image.

The whole in movement-image cinema appeared through a 'logos which unifies the parts' and as that which 'can only be thought', and through a more subconscious and affective sense of a coherent totality (Deleuze 2003b: 158f.). While the whole itself is a whole of time with a 'fundamentally open character' this whole is only indirectly represented, and its force is bound up in a rational 'concept' which is 'presupposed'. And while the indirect representation is sometimes very dynamic – or even sublime – the expression is internalised and integrated in the concept-whole following 'the ideal of knowledge as harmonious totality' (210, 213, 161, 240). A totality of preconceived meaning, that is, such as a Mythic past/Universal History/Progress and/or ideas of organic Unity such as Spirit, the Subject, or the People, which entails a uniting 'sensory-motor relationship between world and man, nature and thought' (163).

When, for a variety of reasons, such wholes lost their ability to cohere and convince in the post-war period, a cinema of the time-image emerges on a broader front. In much of it there is a cine-ethical[11] struggle to create other *kinds* of connections to the world. Rather than merely wallowing in the debris of organic wholes, these films approached this state as also an opening for new modes of thought and existence. A differently and more openly thinking cinema appears, one that responds to a crisis in thought's ability to form a believable rational whole, with more non-linear forms of thinking. What is of particular interest to my concern here, is that this includes a 'transformation of the Whole' (Deleuze 2003b: 181). Below I will return to what such a transformed whole means in Deleuze and explore *Vertigo Sea* as an updated, developed, and partly altered version.

A Kind of Cognitive Mapping

For Deleuze the lost link to the world concerns lost belief in certain organic wholes bound by abstract concepts and/or mythic sentiments – a state of things that gives way to the banality and schizophrenia of post-war capitalist societies of cliché (Deleuze 2003a: 208; 2003b: 18, 21, 135, 182). Fredric Jameson argues for another (both different and interlinked) cause of disconnection: that we are unable to overview the factor that most determine our actual socioeconomic reality: the system of global capitalism. For Jameson this system has become large, intricate and abstract – starting under nineteenth-century imperialism and taking quantum leaps in recent decades – to the point of appearing impossible to mentally chart as a whole (Jameson 1988: 1991). The system can of course be intellectually abstracted through scientific concepts, but not really represented or experienced for individual subjects – and we should note here that the Capitalocene presents a similar (and intertwined) problem: while neither explicitly references Jameson's concept, Nicholas Mirzoeff (2014) describes the 'Anthropocene' as 'un-seeable' for humans and therefore in need of being 'visualized', and Timothy Morton (2013), even more to our point, describes global warming as a 'hyperobject' since too spatially and temporally vast and intricate for us to grasp.

For Jameson, as full consciousness of socioeconomic reality is thereby blocked – along with more obvious blocks such as ideology and material conditions – so is progressive political desire, utopian imagination and political agency. The point: if the current system cannot be envisioned, how could anything beyond it be envisioned. Jameson therefore calls for artistic maps – speculatively, as he cannot imagine what its aesthetic forms would be (previous Marxist thought also concerned with suitable aesthetic forms for revealing a socioeconomic whole no longer suffice) – that could organise the whole into a coherent subjective experience (that is, beyond the 'poor' mapping of uninformed conspiracy theories but also beyond art merely reflexively showing the limits of our knowing). The aim of such maps is to unblock a lost *precondition* – some orientation of the real terrain as a whole – for viewers' utopian desires and imaginations.

Vertigo Sea can be seen as a fundamental reimagination of this problem. It does not representatively boil down the concrete causal intricacies of the globalised system into a unified experience. Rather, it charts key intersections between planetary nature and the history and present of industrial, colonial/neo-colonial capitalism on a global scale, associatively, conceptually, poetically, and as aspects of a more visionary ethical venture. Furthermore, mapping real terrains is intertwined here with a theory-driven ethical imagination and cognition in the work *itself*. In Jameson, the map, however aesthetically inventive, implicitly has an instrumental role: it provides an overview of a terrain for the minds of viewers, which serves to unblock *their* utopian imaginations.[12] *Vertigo Sea* as itself containing utopian imagination is not to be confused with being programmatic (as Rancière might say). It means rather, as Deleuze and Guattari describe art, that it is 'independent of the viewer or hearer, who only experience it after' and only – regardless of the unpredictability and variety of their reactions – 'if they [so to speak] have the strength for it' [*s'ils en ont la force*] (1994: 164).

Planetary Countervisuality

Any real charting of our socioeconomic whole would mean a countervisualisation to capitalism's own images of a global whole – which functions as ideological skewers or veils of socioeconomic and ecological realities – including its visualisations of the so-called 'Anthropocene' (Mirzoeff 2014: 213, 217). But how far can such countervisualisation take us? From a more traditionally Marxist perspective, in Jameson and perhaps even more so in Toscano and Kinkle's more recent book on this concept, cognitive mapping should reveal what dominant visuality hides: negativity, contradictions, and seeds of capitalisms own demise (Toscano and Kinkle 2015: 4–8, 32, 93ff., 237). Similarly, Mirzoeff describes Anthropocene countervisualisation as a 'decolonial politics that claims the right to see what there is to be seen and name it as such: a planetary destabilization' (2014: 230). However, why would a map revealing such contradictions, negativity and destabilisation – while being a precondition – *suffice* to boost viewers' inner drives and imaginations for radical transformative action, as implied by Toscano and Kinkle, Mirzoeff, and Jameson?

In less traditionally Marxist terms, T. J. Demos analyses contemporary ecological art works that do something to this effect while also seeming to map other kinds of nodes in the terrain. These works, Demos writes, 'visualize environmental, technological, and economic process as a means to comprehend and critique', they show 'abstractions or unseen flows, networks, and conflicts on which both finance and global ecology depends'. But they are 'not simply mimetic' since they also show 'transformations and deformations of the[se] systems' (2016a: 119). It is a bit unclear, however, how these mappings, as discussed by Demos, themselves add to the transformations. They appear more concerned with documenting transformations seen in the terrain than with aiming to be transformative through their own ethical-aesthetical imagination. Can art be transformative in that sense and still be said to 'map'?

Sub-representational Cartography

While it is a – common – mistake to reduce Jameson's notion of cognitive mapping to authoritative truth, to factual information, and certainly to naïve realism (e.g. Demos 2013: 219), he does aim to reclaim the term representation. In contrast to understandings of the term 'as the synonym of some bad ideological and organic realism or mirage of realistic unification', Jameson defines representation as a 'synonym of "figuration" itself' including 'all forms of aesthetic production' (1988: 348). Yet, when he writes about 'poststructuralist discourses' that have 'stigmatized [. . .] anything that smacks of 'reality,' 'representation,' 'realism' [. . .]' (1991: 93f.), and thereby vaguely references something like Derridian deconstruction, Jameson mostly shoots past Deleuze, to which we will now return. Granted, Deleuze famously critiques representation in the sense of an identity-based logic of thought. But he does the opposite of stigmatising reality or realism. He does, however, alter the meaning of those terms.

Realism – in art and in philosophy – is for Deleuze not merely about styles producing a reality effect or even a truthful rendition of actual reality. Realism for Deleuze more essentially means charting sub-representational aspects of reality. The sub-representational is one name for the generative conditions for the actual aspects of the real, a register of virtual potential. In Deleuze's own writings on the contemporary social and political world such potentials appear increasingly as either blocked from having actual effect or as co-opted for the reproduction of dominant systems. But he also argues that it is the role of art and philosophy, besides charting the blockages, to bring out and develop/co-create through the potentials that still subsists in reality, however hindered from having immediate actual impact.

Charting such aspects of the real, in circumstances of blockage and strife, is what cartography primarily means in Deleuze. '[T]o write is to struggle and resist', he says in his book on Foucault, 'to write is to become; to write is to draw a map: "I am a cartographer"' (2006 [1986]: 44). John Rajchman describes Deleuze's own mappings as imaginatively 'indicat[ing] "zones of indistinction" from which becomings may arise, if they are not already imperceptibly in the making' (2000: 100). And for such cartographic thought to make new connections, it 'needs the sobriety of a certain realism' (2000: 8). Important to add here is that Deleuze talks about this in terms of also contributing to transformation. He will increasingly focus on how philosophy and art must co-create *with* the forces of potential – instead of merely (by going in the opposite direction from actualisation) revealing them. In his Francis Bacon book, Deleuze reiterates a notion of art as making invisible 'forces visible' and 'capturing forces' that are 'nongiven', but he also emphasises that this is not enough and that something must also take shape, 'emerge' from the 'diagram' of such forces.[13] A map along such lines, then, is on the one hand a realism of potentials for transformation that subsist within actual reality, and on the other hand an *active development* of such potentials, outlining new kinds of relations – always, however, firmly grounded in actual social-political circumstances.

Charting Planetary Wholes

Such mapping can – as in *Vertigo Sea* – concern global or planetary wholes. Deleuze conceives of global/planetary wholes in largely three – *interrelated* – ways:

1. A whole of (relatively deterritorialising) global capitalism, charted in parts of Deleuze's own work.[14]
2. An openly creative 'whole of Nature' that – with some similarities to what Jason Moore calls *the web of life* (2015) – spans human societies and everything else, 'the artificial and the natural'; a unified plane of multiplicity containing individuated multiplicities in 'an infinity of more or less interconnected relations', a whole that is open and inventive in and through itself, and which fits together in ways differential and non-linear, rather than as an organic unity with harmoniously connected parts (Deleuze and Guattari 1987: 254).
3. Social-cultural-political wholes to come: a concern with reconnecting modern subjects with the world in the sense of the above-described whole of nature/a unified plane. Deleuze and Guattari often return, as is well-known but worth underlining in this context, to the topic of art and philosophy as summing forth a new earth and a people that do not yet exist, which *What is Philosophy?* at one point refers to as a 'mass-people, world-people' (1994: 176). That is, for art or philosophy to let 'loose molecular populations in hopes that this will sow the seeds of, or even engender [. . .] a people to come, open a cosmos' (Deleuze and Guattari 1987: 345).

Vertigo Sea may be said to 'produc[e] utterances' that are 'like the seeds' of a planetary people to come (Deleuze 2003b: 221), while also charting blockages in the form of a history and present of colonial/neo-colonial, industrial capitalism and its corresponding modes of existence as alienation. Its simultaneous charting of capitalist reality, blockages, and new potentials, resonates also with further aspects of Deleuze's cine-ethics of the time-image. In *Cinema 2* many time-image films are shown as deeply explorative and expressive of (2) virtual time and potential, which is one of the conditions for the new for Deleuze. But they also appear mostly cut off from, or struggling to re-connect with, (3) actualising intensity, the other condition for the new, and as stuck within (1) socio-political situations that reproduces the same.[15]

The Place of a New Whole in Deleuze's Cine-ethics

In such situations the 'whole [*le tout*] undergoes a mutation', Deleuze tells us, 'it has ceased to be the One-Being [*l'Un-Etre*]', since the open whole of time is no longer indirectly represented through a type of montage that (however dynamically) makes it appear part of rational/organic totalities (2003b:

180, 187). In the time-image the whole instead 'passes into the interstice' – pre-eminently through the 'irrational' cut (including the relation between sound and image) – in which it can present itself directly as virtual force, as that which is 'the constitutive "and" of things' (180). Montage here 'takes on a new sense' and 'comes into its own' (181). The possibility of a different logic thereby appears, which is more capable of handling virtual multiplicity and potential, and which 'we should make our way of thinking [. . .] without claiming to be restoring an all-powerful thought' (167, 170).

Again, the whole is not thereby disappeared but 'transformed'. There is 'a new status of the Whole' in which the parts make up 'non-totalizable relation[s]' (179, 256). This is why some of the most thought-packed (and political) of time-image films in Deleuze's discussion – those of Straub-Huillet, Duras, Syberberg, Resnais, Kubrick – 'does not form a whole' while still creating a whole in the sense of an 'always re-created disjunction' in which thought forms constellations that are rigorous and coherent in more non-linear ways (255, 256, 206f.). In Deleuze's discussion of various time-images, however, few seem to go very far in the direction of a new kind of whole on a planetary level, with Kubrick's *2001: A Space Odyssey* as a kind of exception. Of course, Deleuze also claimed that cinema was only at the beginning of its investigations, and his basic conceptions of cinematic ethics and transformed wholes can certainly be developed and reimagined in later films. The struggle to find ways out of late nihilism must in the Capitalocene also more obviously concern the formation of a new kind of whole on a planetary scale.

The Non-linear Whole of *Vertigo Sea*

Vertigo Sea's vast differential montage, between three screens and between the screens and a layered audio track, extends, updates, and develops some of the struggles and ethical aims of the time-image. It certainly goes beyond the problem of belief in the world, say, in the sense of expressing a kind of un-known that Deleuze finds in some time-image films. It concerns movements towards (and blockages for) more direct new connections between modern subjects and the planetary: not as an organic unity of man and the world (as if only rehabilitating the logic of the movement-image), but in the sense of humans and human societies more openly and productively implicated in planetary multiplicity.

Vertigo Sea oscillates between a semi-harmonious flow and breaking up into clearer differences. There is a profusion of sounds, images and motifs, but also a wave-like rhythm that tends to gradually immerse the spectator rather than, say, confront the spectator with negative dialectical conflict (and key here is the spherical and sometimes dramatic avant-garde music and soundscapes). The immersion, however, is constantly into multiplicity. Co-existing temporalities are expressed in juxtapositions of eras within and across images, in a recurrent motif of different clocks spread out in nature, speed- and slow-motion imagery of plants and animals, and a general opening up of our globalised present to a partly geologic time scale. Graphic connections are made between the screens creating concrete but subtle rhymes and resonances between differences: whale tails and bird wings; submarines and sharks; clusters of baby sharks and clouds; the moon and a whale's eye; the arc of a killer whale jumping over the surface and a similarly shaped rock; butterflies in still/regular/slow motion and a fish corpse rotting into the ground in fast time; flowing aquatic plants and flowing tentacles of sea creatures and eel-like animals crawling in and out of holes in a dead seal.

The tableaus with alternating *Rückenfiguren* join shots of water formations, mountains, deserts, plants and myriads of animals, as well as a historicised Capitalocene – slavery, migrant tragedies, industrial hunting, oilrigs on fire, and so on. These juxtapositions are irreducible to virtuous beautiful nature as opposed to human culture as terror: it all appears as a complex 'whole of Nature' spanning 'the artificial and the natural' (Deleuze and Guattari 1987: 254). A variety of storms, which could be either boosted by climate change or like in the world before man. Slaves thrown off slave ships next to birds diving into the water for fish. Elephant hunters next to alligators attacking gnus and zebras. Striking similarities in colours, patterns and beauty in shots of whale butchering and aerial shots of abstract landscapes. Atom-bomb clouds followed by erupting underwater volcanoes. These juxtapositions seem to aim for an immersive experience of natural and human history that cultivates our ability to be pulled in by the planetary in all its complexity.

Vertigo Sea charts nodes of pain but also nodes of potential for other modes of being. And in the end the latter is slightly more emphasised: the *Rückenfigur* variations, a stand-in for the alienated modern subject, become gradually less frequent and actually disappear from the last parts of the film. There are more

Figure 6.4   *Vertigo Sea*, 2015. © Smoking Dogs Films; Courtesy Smoking Dogs Films and Lisson Gallery.

aerial shots of strangely colourful and abstract-looking patches of land. Some are reminiscent of parts in the Stargate sequence in Kubrick's *2001: A Space Odyssey*, an impression that is aided by a minimal almost industrial soundscape that expands into lightly spherical, swelling, both melancholic and ambiguously optimistic music. This leaves an oblique sense, finally, that within this wondrous sadness something new could come about. Flocks of birds emerge, and close to the very end the man with the heavy eyes reappears, and his gaze is – still subtly, but slightly more extensively – extended by the birds.

Conclusion

We can recognise aspects of what Jameson calls cognitive mapping in *Vertigo Sea*: the emphasis on historisation and focus on capitalism (here extended to the Capitalocene), the use of artistic form to create an experience of a global whole, the need for new artistic form given the complexity of the whole, and the concern in all this with revitalising utopian desire and imagination. But in *Vertigo Sea* those aspects are part of a more subrepresentational mapping venture, which also updates and develops Deleuze's ethics of the time-image, as discussed above.

Vertigo Sea charts the Capitalocene but it also forms potentials – adjusted to a modern lack of belief in the world – for more planetary modes of existence: there is ethical imagination in the map itself. This is different from only charting what already exists and leaving the work of ethical imagination to the through-the-map illuminated spectator, which is largely the case for Jameson. Ideas about 'visualizing' the Capitalocene, however revealing of the deeper causes of the crisis, can remain similarly focused on the past and present of existing states of affairs (e.g. Koutsourakis 2017). *Vertigo Sea* superimposes such visualisations with outlines for the new. It is only a small map in a big world, of course, but it tends to resonate in unexpected and believable ways.

Notes

1. This chapter is one outcome of a larger individual research project called 'Modern Essay Films as Thought-Maps of Globalization' (2015–18), which was generously funded by the Swedish Research Council.
2. 'John Akomfrah, *Vertigo Sea*, 2015, Three channel HD colour video installation, 7.1 sound, 48 minutes 30 seconds.'
3. The 'tend to' is based on reviews, scholarly assessments (e.g. Alter 2018: 3), personal experience and observations during exhibitions, and from screening *Vertigo Sea* for students.
4. E.g. Alter (2016; 2018: 272–87). For a discussion of memory in previous Akomfrah films specifically from the perspective of cinematic ethics see Grønstad (2016: 188–94). See also Demos (2016b) who touches on the topic of nature/environment in *Vertigo Sea* but not its charting of a planetary whole.

5. *Purple* was part of an earlier version of this text and omitted due to a lack of space, but much of what is said about *Vertigo Sea* is applicable to *Purple*. (Akomfrah's *Four Nocturnes* [2019] is related but does not have quite the same planetary scope.)
6. For an examination of interrelated aesthetical-political issues in *Vertigo Sea* centred around its ample use of footage from the BBC Natural History Unit, see Nilsson (2018).
7. *Vertigo Sea* presents a massive web of visual and aural motifs across its forty-eight-minute running time. This text therefore describes and formally analyses only illustrative bits and sequences and otherwise focuses on general aesthetic ideas and logics of connections that recur throughout in different guises. The reader is advised to watch the following two sets of samples from *Vertigo Sea* available online at the time of writing, which, while relatively brief, give clear indications of its sentiments, general aesthetics, and logic of montage: 'Vertigo Sea Highlights', <https://vimeo.com/287537229> (accessed 23 August 2022); 'Akomfrah and Vertigo Sea, video installation © Smoking Dogs Films I Zacheta Gallery Warsaw', <https://www.youtube.com/watch?v=8oHI3OE9FYg> (accessed 23 August 2022).
8. Both terms refer to (what is increasingly recognised as) a new geological era marked by fundamental (negative) transformations of global climate, ecosystems and biodiversity. As often said, however, the term Anthropocene helps conceal what causes these transformations, since it points to the 'human' (*anthropos*) in general rather than specific human conducts. Capitalocene instead foregrounds the main cause, amplifier, and maintainer of this state: global industrial capitalism seen as 'a way of organizing nature [*as a whole*]', 'a world-ecology of capital, power and nature' (Moore 2016: 6, 7, xi). (This includes its colonial and slave-labour build-up starting in the fifteenth to seventeenth centuries, but not preceding causes that go far beyond such as 12,000 years of agriculture.) I also agree with Moore (2015) and Haraway (2015) that Capitalocene is the most apt single term while other terms are useful too, such as, Plantationocene (for its additional/partly alternative explanations of historical causes), Haraway's own Cthulhucene (for its inclusion of additional complexities as well as progressive potentialities), and even sometimes Anthropocene (for being so established). Nevertheless, in this short text I will try to heed more pressing calls – given its ideological obfuscation of causes – to work actively against 'the Anthropocene as a legitimate term [. . .] in both theory and practice' (Demos 2017: 9) simply by keeping as much as possible to Capitalocene.
9. The footage of this man (played by Boris Ranevsky) is taken from Ken Russell's BBC *Monitor* episode on Bartok (1964).
10. Key here is also the spherical, sweeping, and oftentimes fairly dramatic music alternating with a carefully constructed soundscape (made up of nature sounds, e.g. crashing waves or whale song, as well as more artificial sounds).
11. As Deleuze does not talk about this explicitly in terms of ethics, apart from '[w]e need an ethic or a faith' concerning 'a need to believe in this world' (2003b: 173), I am taking a general cue here from D. N. Rodowick labelling this aspect of Deleuze as 'an ethics of cinema' (2007: 63). See also Sinnerbrink and Trahair (2016: 4).
12. More nuanced: (1) Jameson at one point indicates that the 'cognitive' is also to be *in* the map: he references Brecht's poetry as a 'cognitive art' of 'thinking and reflection'

with a 'contemplative distance from historical events' (1988: 348). However, this is talked about in the context of 'the pedagogical function of a work of art' as regarding already existing states of affairs (347). Ethical imagination beyond states of affairs seems confined to the (through-the-map-enlightened) mind of the spectator. (2) And while Jameson, in his ongoing concern with utopia, often writes about fictional narratives and characters expressing utopian ideas or drives, cognitive mapping appears to exclusively concern – apart from the global – what *blocks* utopian ideas or drives. Since cognitive mapping is also a kind of methodology guiding Jameson's own (later) writings, he describes this method as having 'generally [. . .] been a negative one, that is, it's to examine the blockages on the future and on the utopian impulse' (2006: 131).

13. On capturing invisible forces, see Deleuze (2004 [1981]: 57, 58, 61), on something having to emerge from the diagram, see ibid., pp. 103, 138, 156.
14. Deleuze and Guattari conceive of a 'world capitalism' (1994: 98) as a rhizomatic 'worldwide war machine whose organization exceeds the State apparatuses and passes into energy, military-industrial, and multinational complexes' (1987: 387), to which we can add Guattari's labelling of 'post-industrial capitalism' as 'Integrated World Capitalism' (2000: 47ff.).
15. This underexplored aspect of Deleuze's cinema books is analysed in depth in Chapter 3 of Nilsson (2023, forthcoming).

References

Alter, Nora (2016), 'Movements: metaphors and metonymies in the work of John Akomfrah', in *John Akomfrah*, London: Lisson Gallery.

Alter, Nora M. (2018), *The Essay Film After Fact and Fiction*, New York: Columbia University Press.

Deleuze, Gilles (2003a) [1983], *Cinema 1: The Movement-Image*, translated by Hugh Tomlinson and Barbara Habberjam, Minneapolis: University of Minnesota Press.

Deleuze, Gilles (2003b) [1985], *Cinema 2: The Time-Image*, translated by Hugh Tomlinson and Robert Galeta, Minneapolis: University of Minnesota Press.

Deleuze, Gilles (2004 [1981]), *Francis Bacon: The Logic of Sensation*, translated by Daniel W. Smith, New York: Continuum.

Deleuze, Gilles (2006) [1986], *Foucault*, translated by Seán Hand, Minnesota/London: University of Minnesota Press.

Deleuze, Gilles and Felix Guattari (1987) [1980], *A Thousand Plateaus*, translated by Brian Massumi. Minneapolis: University of Minnesota Press.

Deleuze, Gilles and Felix Guattari (1994) [1991], *What Is Philosophy?*, translated by H. Tomlinson and G. Burchill, New York: Columbia University Press.

Demos, T. J. (2013), *The Migrant Image: The Art and Politics of Documentary During Global Crisis*, Durham, NC/London: Duke University Press.

Demos, T. J. (2016a), *Decolonizing Nature: Contemporary Art and the Politics of Ecology*, Berlin: Sternberg Press.

Demos, T. J. (2016b), 'On terror and beauty', in *John Akomfrah*, London: Lisson Gallery.

Demos, T. J. (2017), *Against the Anthropocene: Visual Culture and Environment Today*, Berlin: Sternberg Press.

Grønstad, Asbjørn (2016), *Film and the Ethical Imagination*, London: Palgrave Macmillan.
Guattari, Felix (2000) [1989], *The Three Ecologies*, translated by Ian Pindar and Paul Sutton, New Jersey: Athlone Press.
Haraway, Donna (2015), 'Anthropocene, Capitalocene, Plantationocene, Chthulucene: Making Kin', in *Environmental Humanities*, 6: 159–65.
Jameson, Fredric (1988), 'Cognitive mapping', in Cary Nelson and Lawrence Grossberg (eds), *Marxism and the Interpretation of Culture*, Urbana: University of Illinois Press, pp. 347–60.
Jameson, Fredric (1991), *Postmodernism, Or the Cultural Logic of Late Capitalism*, Durham, NC: Duke University Press.
Jameson, Fredric (2006), 'Live Jameson', interviewed in Ian Buchanan, *Fredric Jameson: Live Theory*, London/New York: Continuum, pp. 120–32.
Koutsourakis, Angelos (2017), 'Visualising the Anthropocene dialectically: Jessica Woodworth and Peter Brosens' eco-crisis trilogy', *Film-Philosophy*, 21: 3, 299–325.
Latour, Bruno (2010), 'An attempt at a "Compositionist Manifesto"', *New Literary History*, 41: 484.
Martin-Jones, David (2016), 'Trolls, tigers and transmodern ecological encounters: Enrique Dussel and a cine-ethics for the Anthropocene', *Film-Philosophy*, 20: 63–103.
Martin-Jones, David (2018), *Cinema Against Doublethink. Ethical Encounters with the Lost Pasts of World History*, London: Routledge.
Mirzoeff, Nicholas (2014), 'Visualizing the Anthropocene', in *Public Culture*, 26: 2, 213–32.
Moore, Jason W. (2015), *Capitalism in the Web of Life: Ecology and the Accumulation of Capital*, New York: Verso.
Moore, Jason W. (ed.) (2016), *Anthropocene or Capitalocene? Nature, History, and the Crisis of Capitalism*, Oakland: PM Press.
Morton, Timothy (2013), *Hyperobjects. Philosophy and Ecology after the End of the World*, Minneapolis: University of Minnesota Press.
Naficy, Hamid (2001), *An Accented Cinema: Exilic and Diasporic Filmmaking*, Princeton, NJ: Princeton University Press.
Nilsson, Jakob (2018), 'Capitalocene, clichés, and critical re-enchantment: what Akomfrah's *Vertigo Sea* does through BBC Nature', *Journal of Aesthetics and Culture*, 10: 1, 1–10.
Nilsson, Jakob (2023 forthcoming), *Cinecepts, Deleuze, and Godard-Miéville. Developing Philosophy through Audiovisual Media*, Edinburgh: Edinburgh University Press.
Pick, Anat (2013), 'Three worlds: dwelling and worldhood on screen', in Anat Pick and Guinevere Narraway (eds), *Screening Nature: Cinema beyond the Human*, New York/Oxford: Berghahn.
Rajchman, John (2000), *The Deleuze Connections*, Cambridge, MA/London: MIT Press.
Rodowick, D. N. (2007), *The Virtual Life of Film*, Cambridge: Harvard University Press.
Sinnerbrink, Robert and Lisa Trahair (2016), 'Introduction: Film and / as ethics', in *SubStance*, 45: 3, 3–15.
Toscano, Alberto and Jeff Kinkle (2015), *Cartographies of the Absolute*, Winchester: Zero Books.

7. MERMAIDS AND SUPERPIGS: LOVING NATURE UNDER GLOBAL CAPITALISM

Chelsea Birks

A number of films of the 2000s and 2010s frame relationships between humans and non-humans in terms of love. *Avatar* (James Cameron, 2009), which follows a human hero as he acquires an environmental conscience through a romantic relationship with the daughter of an alien chief, is the best known and most commercially successful film of this trend. *Avatar* achieved unprecedented worldwide box-office success – a record not surpassed until 2019 with *Avengers: Endgame* (Anthony Russo and Joe Russo, 2019), another apocalyptic blockbuster with environmental themes (Clode 2019; Russo 2019) – as well as significant funds and awareness for environmental causes.[1] Other recent films similarly centre on loving relationships with or between non-human characters and suggest that these relationships are somehow key to human redemption and environmental harmony: in *Bee Movie* (Simon J. Smith and Steve Hickner, 2007), the improbable romance between a bee and a human woman helps the world narrowly avoid ecological catastrophe when bees stop pollinating flowers; in *The Mermaid* (Stephen Chow, 2016), a polluting billionaire falls in love with the mermaid who is sent to kill him in revenge for the destruction of her home, resulting in the billionaire devoting his life and fortune to environmental conservation; in *WALL-E* (Andrew Stanton, 2008), the romance between two robots in an apocalyptic distant future spurs a chain of events that inspires humans to correct their ways and devote themselves to the restoration of Earth's natural systems. That these recent films use the trope of redemptive love to solve environmental problems is not surprising given the preponderance of happy endings in popular and genre cinemas: though *WALL-E*, *The*

Mermaid and *Avatar* all explicitly acknowledge the threat posed by capitalism's exploitation of the environment – all three place the blame on specific corporations or resource extraction processes, from the mining of Unobtanium in *Avatar* to the megacorporation Buy-N-Large in *Wall-E* to the development of an ocean reserve by the billionaire's company in *The Mermaid* – none of these films conclude by leaving the spectator in a state of discomfort about the future. Instead, they assert that ecological catastrophe can be avoided through individual action, a type of resolution that aligns with the neoliberal 'assumption that market individualism is the key to economic and social progress' (Cheshire and Lawrence, 2005: 436).

Though this chapter recognises the problematic neoliberal implications of the Hollywood happy ending in recent environmentally themed genre cinema, its intention is not to mount a criticism of these films. Instead, I want to find something ethically productive and positive about their flawed representations of love. I argue that happy endings in popular eco-films can usefully mobilise a tension crucial to the ethics of the Anthropocene: that between large-scale environmental problems and personal responsibility. I look at two films in particular that evoke this tension between the personal and universal through the trope of redemptive love: *The Mermaid* and *Okja* (Bong Joon-ho, 2017). I focus on these films for two reasons: first, because there is a melancholic undertone to their ostensibly happy endings that betrays the impossibility of reconciling the ethical tension at stake; and second, because they mobilise different forms of love, and therefore offer slightly different ways of imagining human–nonhuman relations. *The Mermaid* draws on the generic conventions of the romantic comedy and therefore articulates its reunification with nature through *eros* (romantic love), while *Okja* imagines human–animal relationships in terms of *philia* (friendship); together, these two films provide a more complex picture of the ethical implications of the happy ending in eco-cinema. To understand the ethical possibilities at play, I read these films in relation to an old philosophical quandary: the problem of divine love that Søren Kierkegaard grapples with in *Works of Love*, and its application to contemporary global politics in Slavoj Žižek's work on the neighbour. *Okja* and *The Mermaid* both articulate this very old problem in the new context of the global ecological crisis, and in so doing mark a shift away from anthropocentrism, even if such a shift is somewhat compromised by the films' neoliberal ideological commitments.

By exploring popular and genre films, I am working against a tendency in film ecocriticism to focus primarily on independent and art cinemas, experimental films, and documentaries,[2] modes of filmmaking that are usually assumed to be better equipped to handle the harsh realities and ambiguities of environmental crisis. There are exceptions: Sean Cubitt (2005), for example, asserts the importance of popular media and ideological critique for film ecocriticism, while Pat Brereton (2004) views American genre films as largely imagining positive – even utopian – visions of humanity's relationship with the environment. However, as Fiona Yuk-wa Law (2020: 166) argues,

> ecocinema studies have been concerned with finding alternatives – alternative representational strategies to illuminate the relationship between human and non-human, alternative ways to perceive beyond our ideological assumptions about the cinematic form in portraying nature, and alternative aesthetics to address the non-human aspects of the Anthropocene.

By focusing primarily on cinema that positions itself against the mainstream, ecocriticism tends implicitly to draw an analogy between alternative ecological perspectives and alternative cinematic ones. However, Law argues the popular films also have a role to play in imagining alternatives for the future, and she reads *The Mermaid* as reflecting a growing awareness of environmental issues in the People's Republic of China. Like Law, I see a positive (albeit imperfect) ethics at work in the film's way of balancing economic and environmental issues; however, while Law reads the film through a local lens, my aim in connecting *The Mermaid* and *Okja* is to explore a more global cinematic ethics of the non-human. I am particularly interested in the ethical compromises the characters in both films make in the name of love for particular non-human subjects; both *Okja* and *The Mermaid* reject universal love and insist on the inevitability of arbitrary choices and preferential love in the context of the environmental crisis.

Universal Love

Both *Okja* and *The Mermaid* stage love in the explicit context of global capitalism. The eponymous character in *Okja* is a 'superpig' bred by the multinational Mirando corporation, which brands the product as an ecologically friendly non-GMO food source. *Okja*'s production and distribution methods reflect its globalised storyline: it was distributed by Netflix and drew funding from both South Korea and Hollywood. Like many transnational Asian co-productions that aim to appeal across international markets (Wei 2011), *Okja* draws from familiar genre tropes and emphasises special effects, and features bilingual dialogue and high-profile stars from both Hollywood and South Korea. *Okja*'s love story is one of friendship rather than romance, and the relationship between Okja and Mija bears similarities to other films focused on relationships between children and misunderstood creatures (*How to Train Your Dragon*, Dean DeBlois and Chris Sanders, 2010; *Free Willy*, Simon Wincer, 1993; *E.T. the Extra-Terrestrial*, Steven Spielberg, 1982). Karen Lury argues that children and non-human animals often have a particular affinity onscreen, and that

Figure 7.1 Eco branding in *Okja* (Bong Joon-ho, 2017).

'some of the most interesting and provocative performances from children in films address or explore how the child is able to "pass" between the (inhuman) animal and the human' (2010: 167). Lury explains this affinity through a shared perceived lack of rationality that marks children and animals as 'other' (2010: 1, 11): because of this other-ness, both are easily inscribed with cultural anxieties and desires.³ *Okja* situates these desires and anxieties in the context of globalisation and its associated environmental problems, using Mija and Okja as symbols of the suffering inflicted by corporate greed. Okja's spectacular CGI animation in particular serves both as a major marketing draw for the film and as a way of concentrating the ethical issues at stake: her expressive eyes and behaviour encourage empathy from Mija and, by extension, the audience, who are implored to reject Okja's categorisation as commodity. *Okja* is therefore fundamentally ambivalent in that it criticises a system upon which it depends, as – like many popular genre films – its globalised marketing strategies are at odds with the critique of global capitalism at the heart of the narrative.

The Mermaid is similarly ambivalent in its relationship to globalisation, though unlike *Okja* it was primarily marketed to a domestic audience. In 2016 *The Mermaid* was the highest-grossing film of all time in China, and it held the record for most earnings over its opening weekend until *The Wandering Earth* (a Chinese science fiction film) was released in 2019. Despite being a less globalised product, however, it, like *Okja*, promotes an environmental message in the context of globalised capitalism. The protagonist of *The Mermaid*, Liu Xuan (Deng Chao), is a playboy tycoon whose use of sonar technology devastates the population of merpeople living in the wildlife reserve he has recently purchased for development. The opening shots immediately establish the film's environmentalist message with grainy stock footage of smoke stacks, felled forests and polluted drainage pipes. This surface-level critique of

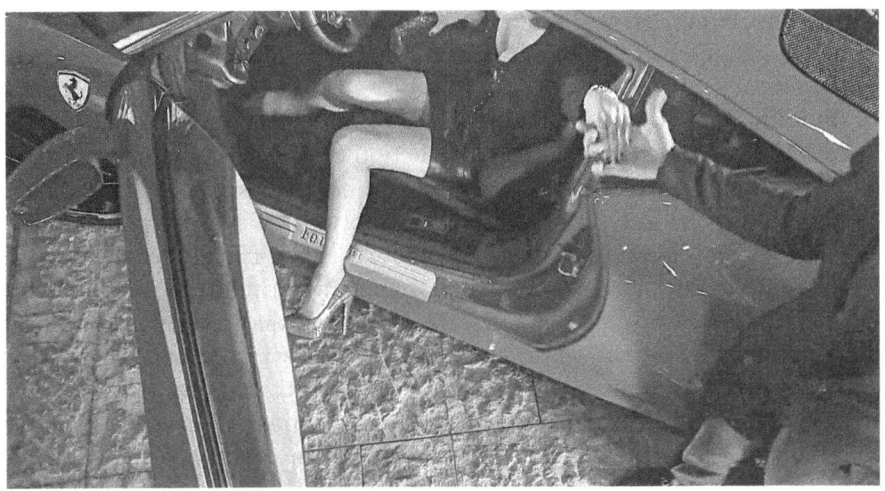

Figure 7.2   Spectacle of global capitalism in *The Mermaid* (Stephen Chow, 2016).

industry is contradicted by *The Mermaid*'s excessive appeal to the pleasures of consumer capitalism: the *mise-en-scène* is crowded with ostentatious designer clothes and shiny branded sports cars, often emphasised by quick zooms, jump cuts or sound effects that echo the frenetic pace of television advertisements. These aspirational articulations of wealth echo the film's context: China is the world's fastest-growing consumer culture, accounting for a third of the market for luxury goods (McKinsey and Company 2019). Audience members indifferent or unsympathetic to the film's environmental critique are nevertheless likely to enjoy the exaggerated spectacle of global brands, from Ferraris to diamond-encrusted watches to Romanée-Conti wine.

Okja similarly exploits the pleasures of consumer capitalism by drawing from the aesthetics of advertising. In the opening sequence, CEO Lucy Mirando (Tilda Swinton) delivers a TED talk-like promotion of the superpig where she explicitly frames the product as a rebranding strategy for the Mirando corporation. Lucy acknowledges the company's history of committing atrocities against workers and the environment and explains that her leadership marks a new beginning driven by environmentalism as a core value; her slide show, 'save the world' messaging and sunny appearance reference the optimism and glossy aesthetics of Silicon Valley companies like Tesla and Apple. The Mirando corporation's branding therefore aligns with consumerist versions of capitalism, which endorse the idea that environmental progress is compatible with – or even only possible through – economic growth, and that change involves individual consumers choosing the right products.[4] Mirando sells the superpig as exactly the right kind of product, one that is non-GMO, produces little waste, requires fewer resources, and – most importantly – 'tastes fucking good'. Consumers are therefore not required to renounce pleasure to affect environmental change.

In both *Okja* and *The Mermaid*, however, the pleasures of capitalism are predicated on suffering, and the disjunction between the branded fantasy of consumption and the reality of exploitation creates the central conflict. Corporate players in both films use environmentalism cynically, as a way to polish their public image: just as Mirando uses eco-friendly rebranding to distance itself from past crimes, Xuan's company justifies the multi-billion-dollar purchase of the wildlife reserve by saying that money is no object for ecologically sustainable development. The glossy consumerist aesthetic in both films is contrasted with a grittier reality that exposes the hypocrisy of corporate branding. In *Okja*, the high-key lighting and pastel colours of Mirando advertisements are in direct contrast to the conditions in the laboratory and slaughterhouse, which are shot with a green filter that emphasises shadows and grime. In *The Mermaid*, the dilapidated ship where the merpeople take refuge after their home is destroyed by pollution and Xuan's sonar is similarly grimy and green-hued, emphasising the scars and mottled skin of the wounded merpeople. Both films also use violence to underscore corporate evil: Okja is subjected to various cruelties in the filthy laboratory, including having flesh extracted for taste-testing and being forcibly bred with another superpig, and the climax of *The Mermaid*, in which Xuan's business rival retaliates against the merpeople, is shockingly graphic in the context of the film's otherwise lighthearted tone.

Figure 7.3   Environmental suffering in *The Mermaid* (Stephen Chow, 2016).

Ethical hypocrisy in both films is therefore articulated as aesthetic discord: the exaggerated glossiness of consumer capitalism is only possible on the condition of a harsh but hidden underlying reality. Because both films remain imbricated in the systems that they critique, however, their ethics are more ambivalent than this binary might suggest. Both films acknowledge the complexity of globalisation and the mutual implication of capitalism and environmental devastation. Further, their ethics are quite complex in that they understand the pleasures of consumerism; by rejecting eco-branding and capitalist-compatible versions of environmentalism, they implicitly reinforce the idea that sustainability involves sacrifice. *Okja* and *The Mermaid* operate on a scale beyond the personal by imagining worlds where actions have widespread implications: while Xuan is sequestered in his mansions and boardrooms, his business dealings cause damage to ecosystems he has never seen or imagined; the decisions made in Mirando offices in New York profoundly affect the lives of a sprawling cast of characters across the world. However, *Okja* and *The Mermaid* have problems reconciling the generalised problems posed by globalisation and the particular love stories at the centre of their narratives.

Arbitrary Choices and Preferential Love

In light of their focus on globalisation, it would seem logical, at least from an ethical standpoint, if *Okja* and *The Mermaid* posed solutions as universal as their problems. Despite the fact that both films indicate a need to either reject or radically revise capitalism, neither film follows through. This is in contrast to films like *Avatar* and *FernGully: The Last Rainforest* (Bill Kroyer, 1992), which do imagine widespread solutions: the entire forest of Pandora in the former revolts against the colonial powers seeking to destroy it, while the fairies in *FernGully* successfully prevent deforestation and pollution by enlightening a human about their cause. In both *Okja* and *The Mermaid*, by contrast, humans choose the love of particular non-human subjects over any kind of general solution. This section will discuss the implications of framing love as a response to environmental crisis, a choice that seems morally suspect but which I argue mobilises a more complex ethics of the non-human than the simplified fantasies that resolve films like *Avatar* and *FernGully*.

Mija's love for Okja is single-minded and absolutely resolute. Her drive to find Okja after the superpig is taken by the Mirando corporation is so strong that it leads her to commit several extreme and dangerous actions, including smashing through a glass wall and jumping off a bridge onto a moving truck. The Mirando corporation decides to exploit Mija's devotion to Okja as a marketing strategy, though Mija resists their seductions, punching through a promotional poster and refusing to smile for photographs. Mija follows Okja all the way to a slaughterhouse, where Mija ignores the other superpigs – who

Figure 7.4   Superpig feedlot in *Okja* (Bong Joon-ho, 2017).

are less anthropomorphised than Okja, with duller eyes and more animal-like behaviours – and finds Okja as she is about to be slaughtered. She barters with Mirando's CEO, first by appealing to her emotions, and then by purchasing Okja with a golden pig previously given to her by her grandfather. Okja's extrication from the supply chain is therefore paradoxically only possible through a re-affirmation of her status as commodity. In this process, Okja is singled out as exceptional: she leaves with Mija as the other superpigs, an undifferentiated mass crowded in the feedlot, cry out mournfully. Only one is saved, a baby pushed through the fence by its parents and hidden by Okja in her mouth.

Michelle Gunawun points to the moral issues implicit in Okja's exceptionalism, which she argues expose our social framework as founded on 'the fiction that *some* animals have a higher moral status than others' (2018: 264). Gunawun points out that Okja traverses the available legal categories for non-human animals, from companion to food and back again, but she never transcends her status as property. Although *Okja* ostensibly promotes a pro-animal rights message – Bong Joon-ho and others involved in the production went (temporarily) vegan, and the film was celebrated by PETA and other animal rights organisations[5] – Okja's exceptional status as companion animal resolves nothing about the power structures conditioning the lives of animals more generally. Despite this lack of resolution, Michelle Gunawan argues that the film's ethics are positive insofar as they point to the absurdity of granting some animals higher moral standing than others: if Okja can be both companion and food, then it follows that the distinction is arbitrary. I want to take a somewhat different approach by arguing that, counterintuitively, ethics requires these kinds of arbitrary choices.

Though *Okja* hints towards a desire for better treatment of non-human animals in general – the butchering of the superpigs is graphic and their suffering is obvious – it cannot move beyond the particular love between one girl and her superpig. This reflects a problem in the ethics of divine love as described by Kierkegaard (1995). Kierkegaard grapples with the biblical injunction to love the neighbour and tries to reconcile this kind of non-preferential divine love (*agape*) with ordinary experiences of love – *eros* between lovers, *philia* between friends – which are always directed towards particular objects; Sharon Krishek (2008) argues that Kierkegaard's failure to reconcile these experiences results in an unresolved contradiction inherent in the structure of universal love. Slavoj Žižek affirms the paradoxical nature of non-preferential love in *The Neighbor*, where he argues that universal love is only possible through an exception:

> The universal proposition 'I love you all' acquires the level of actual existence only if 'there is at least one whom I hate' – a thesis abundantly confirmed by the fact that universal love for humanity always led to the brutal hatred of the (actually existing) exception, of the enemies of humanity. This hatred of the exception is the 'truth' of universal love, in contrast to true love which can only emerge against the background – *not* of universal hatred, but – of universal indifference: I am indifferent toward All, the totality of the universe, and as such, I actually love *you*, the unique individual who stands/sticks out of this indifferent background. Love and hatred are thus not symmetrical: love emerges out of universal indifference, while hatred emerges out of universal love (2005: 182–3)

The world is not totalisable, which means that the concept of the universal itself is necessarily fractured; for Žižek, this means that universal love is only possible through an exception that both conditions and delegitimises it.

Love for both Kierkegaard and Žižek is therefore essentially paradoxical, and an ethics that aims for better treatment for all must account for the exceptions that condition any universal. Gunawan objects to Okja's exceptionalism and favours a more universally empathetic approach. In Žižek's terms, however, *Okja* is ethical precisely because it makes Okja the exception: 'justice begins when I remember the faceless many left in shadow in this privileging of the One' (2005: 182). The contrast between Okja, singled out through her expressive eyes, and the undifferentiated mass of superpigs in the feedlot is the starting point of ethics, since the universal category (suffering superpigs) can only be understood with reference to an exception that proves the arbitrariness of our preference. This is not to suggest that working towards more holistic approaches to ethical problems is undesirable. It is, however, to argue that it is finally unobtainable; there is no universal that is not re-particularised, and therefore dynamic, constantly re-negotiated through new particular objects and contexts. This logic of non-totalisation calls for a more complex ethics of the non-human, which means that resolving the paradox between the universal and the particular is an empty fantasy: the endings of *Avatar* and *FernGully* therefore ring false because they do not acknowledge the complexity of the problems they mobilise. The failure of *Okja* to propose a general solution is therefore ethically productive, despite being flawed and incorrigibly partial.

That the ethics of love is a paradox between the universal and the particular (understanding *agape* is impossible without reference to specific examples that trouble the very idea of the universal) is a structure that we can also read into both *The Mermaid* and *Okja* on the level of form. Jean-Louis Baudry's apparatus theory describes cinema as a seemingly objective perspective predicated on particularity and subjectivity: he writes that the apparent indexicality of the medium is founded on a deeper reification of subjectivity, since the spectator facing the screen is positioned as the 'active centre and origin of meaning' by the ideological forces shaping the apparatus (1986a: 286). For Baudry, cinema only looks real because of this ideological conditioning, and he undermines the illusion of objectivity implied by the camera's apparently inhuman, unfiltered access to the world by tracing a historical lineage back to the camera obscura, the Renaissance and single-point perspective. Thus, Baudry asserts the importance of examining 'the position of the subject facing the image' in understanding the ideological implications of the cinema (1986b: 312), a charge that I take up here by examining *Okja* and *The Mermaid* through the lens of ideological critique. In this I follow Cubitt (2005) in affirming the importance of ideological critique in light of environmental crisis, as well as Cary Wolfe's (2009) assertion that a major aim of posthumanism ought to be the deconstruction of humanism and its associated emphasis on the individual human subject.[6] Because our representational systems are implicated in humanist ideology, Wolfe (2009) argues for the political potential of deconstruction in helping to expose our blind spots and therefore fracture the humanist subject from within. My aim in reading *Okja* and *The Mermaid* through ideological critique and an ethics of love is therefore to undermine totalisation; while neither film provides a solution or positive alternative to widespread environmental crisis, they are subversive insofar as they destabilise any illusion of objectivity.

Okja does this through Mija's seemingly perverse choice of Okja above all else; the film choses a finite intersubjective exchange over a fantasy of complete overhaul or political upheaval. *The Mermaid* also involves the choice of a particular subject, though its ethics involve a different kind of love. If *Okja* revises the child-befriends-animal/monster genre for the Anthropocene, then *The Mermaid* does the same for the romantic comedy: while the former imagines relationships between humans and non-humans in terms of *philia*, the love at stake in *The Mermaid* is *eros*, the kind of romantic love that Leger Grindon (2011) argues often stands in for anxieties about social change. Dedicated analysis of *The Mermaid* is therefore helpful at this point because it illuminates the differences between the two forms of love and how they symbolise the cultural tensions at play in contemporary eco-cinema: while the child/animal pairing acquires its symbolic weight in virtue of their shared other-ness, the couple in the romantic comedy represent a culture's struggle to reconcile progressive ideas with traditional values. *The Mermaid* updates the formula to address conflicts between economic progress and environmental destruction.

For Grindon, each of the romantic comedy narrative patterns he identifies collapses a complex social issue into a specific interpersonal problem, as conflicts between romantic partners or between lovers and their parents embody collisions between tradition and progress. They are therefore expressions of contemporaneous social conflicts about race, class, gender, and politics. *The Mermaid* generally adheres to the master plot outlined by Grindon (2011: 8–16): the lovers meet, obstacles arise, and the couple must eventually choose between their respective social milieus and each other. There is one crucial difference, however: the conflict staged in *The Mermaid* is not social, but ecological, and therefore reflects anxieties not about human interactions with each other, but rather with their environment. This transition from social to ecological anxiety is apparent when we compare *The Mermaid* to the other romantic comedy about a man falling in love with a mermaid: *Splash* (Ron Howard, 1984). *Splash* draws from the misogynist subtext of mermaid mythology to stage its conflict between Allan's (Tom Hanks) desire to get married and his disgust over Madison's (Darryl Hannah) sexual difference, symbolised by her fishy lower half. *The Mermaid*, on the other hand, is less easily read as a parable about negotiating sexual difference; instead, *The Mermaid*'s conflict is between the world of global capital, excessively visible through branded signifiers of wealth, and imperilled nature. This expansion past the anthropocentric bubble of human relations is a significant departure for a genre that is fundamentally about social change and its associated anxieties. The environmentalist themes of *The Mermaid* apply the simplified logic of the romantic comedy to the troubling, paradoxical relationship between humans and nature in the Anthropocene. On the one hand, the impact of human behaviour on the environment suggests that we are overly implicated in nature, that our existence causes excessive harm through impacts such as climate change, ocean acidification and mass extinction. On the other, the very real possibility of our own extinction as a result of these problems implies a world radically indifferent to human thought and action, since it forces us to imagine a universe that carries on in our absence.

Recent philosophies have begun to engage with the existential threats posed by the ecological crisis: Quentin Meillassoux (2011) argues against the implicit anthropocentrism of twentieth-century thought and argues that philosophies like phenomenology and post-structuralism are ill-equipped to deal with a universe that long preceded the human subject's ability to apprehend it. From the other direction, nihilist Ray Brassier (2007) argues that the inevitability of human extinction, if not because of our own actions then eventually due to the death of our sun, implies the radical meaningless of our existence. The rise of non-anthropocentric philosophies in the twenty-first century, which Richard Grusin (2015) describes as the 'nonhuman turn', is in part a response to this paradox between a world that cares both more and less about us than we would like. That *The Mermaid* negotiates these anxieties through the conventions of the romantic comedy, which generally resolves its conflicts through heteronormative union, is ethically troubling because it rests on a reassuring but problematic fantasy of reciprocal love. Shan (Yun Lin), the mermaid, is an anthropomorphised symbol of the trauma inflicted on the oceans by the forces of global capitalism, embodied in Xuan, and as such is a perfect embodiment of 'the innocent', a requisite character in the romantic comedy. We are introduced to Shan at a lavish pool party, where she grins at Xuan with make-up smeared all over her face, seemingly unaware of how out of place she is; Shan is immediately characterised as 'childlike, unsophisticated and naïve, but open to education' (Grindon 2011: 15). By reducing the complex issues surrounding the effects of human behaviour on the environment into the simplified archetype of the innocent, *The Mermaid* plays on associations between women and nature, presenting Shan as the virginal victim of social evils and implying that the solution is merely to love rather than exploit her. Although this resolution demands a sacrifice in the form of Xuan's renunciation of his wealth and lavish lifestyle, the reward for this sacrifice is Shan's reciprocation of Xuan's love – a reassuring fantasy in the context of the environmental crisis, which works against ideas of reciprocal human-nature relations.

Despite these problems, however, there is something subversive in the way that *The Mermaid* stages its conflict. By framing the solution to ecological catastrophe in terms of love rather than masculine bravado or scientific advancement – as is generally the case in genre disaster films like *The Day After Tomorrow* (Roland Emmerich, 2004) – *The Mermaid* suggests new possibilities for an ethics of the non-human. While love inevitably runs the risk of subjective desire and projection, since it raises questions about whether we love the other as they are or as we want them to be (Bell 2014), it also demands a continual process of intersubjective exchange. This process is based in affect rather than reason, as love is often conceived as impossible or outside of our ability to rationalise or explain. Grindon writes that characters in romantic comedies are driven by irrational forces: 'Emotion characterises the lovers, as the instinctual forces of sexuality drive them forward in spite of their vulnerability, inexperience, and foolishness' (2011: 12). While the threat of these instinctual, sexual forces is eventually domesticated through romantic union, the romantic comedy in general deals with anxieties about our inability to restrain irrational feelings through such institutions for long. As the mermaid matriarch in *The Mermaid* explains,

'Love has no law: it is beyond any rules or boundaries'. This means that the conflicts resolved through one romantic pairing inevitably resurface in the next generation, as tensions are renegotiated in relation to changing social attitudes.

The romantic comedy's resolution of these problems through romantic union amounts to a recognition of our inability to solve them at all, because love is a process rather than a final product. Jean-Luc Nancy writes that love is not about infinity – it does not involve tying ourselves to another in some certain way forever – but rather is about finitude: 'Love cuts across finitude, always from the other to the other, which never returns to the same – and all loves, so humbly alike, are superbly singular. Love offers finitude in its truth; it is finitude's dazzling presentation' (1991: 99). This means that love relates us to something in excess of ourselves, thereby recognising the limits that mark our differences and that always prevent certainty in our engagements with each other. Because love is non-totalisable and always predicated on difference, the relationship between the lover and love object is a work in progress that can never be finished or guaranteed: Mathew Abbott writes that 'this "being put to the test" is crucial to it [love], and persists with it at all times; there is no way of proving it once and for all, and so the task it sets is continual' (2011: 140). This is a promising starting point for an environmental ethics of love: though love is inevitably imperfect, it requires a generosity and openness to the other, as well as a willingness to keep trying. By framing encounters between humans and non-humans in terms of love, both *Okja* and *The Mermaid* suggest an ecological ethics based in a continuous and uncertain process of adjustment.

Happily, Ever After?

Though *The Mermaid* hints at the ever-unfinished quality of *eros*, like most romantic comedies it represses the more radical implications of an ecological ethics of love by implying that Shan and Xuan live happily ever after. This means that the film's subversive potential is quite limited; however, there is a hesitancy in the film's conclusion that betrays the impossibility of any kind of complete intersubjective reconciliation. The final act differs in tone from the rest of the film, departing from the romantic comedy's conventional 'self-deprecating stance which signals the audience to relax and have fun, for nothing serious will disturb their pleasure' (Grindon 2011: 2). We witness the bloody massacre of the merpeople, shot in a way that echoes the footage of dolphin slaughter from the beginning of the film – an explicit reference to the documentary *The Cove* (Louie Psihoyos, 2009). This violent intrusion into the film's generic structure emphasises the stakes of the ecological crisis, and throws a shadow over the subsequent staging of the film's happy ending. The final sequence, where we discover that the lovers survived and have been reunited, is in sharp contrast to the rest of the film: Xuan has learned to temper his excessive wealth by living a more moderate lifestyle in muted shades of blue and grey, providing a middle ground between the film's aesthetic binary. This middle ground is extended to other aspects of Xuan and Shan's reconciliation, as we learn that they split their time between his human world and her oceanic one, and the last shot is of them swimming together to the sounds of mournful whale calls.

The shocking violence and abrupt melancholic tone of *The Mermaid*'s conclusion acknowledges what romantic comedies usually disavow: that, as Zygmunt Bauman suggests (quoting novelist Ivan Klima) 'there is little that comes so close to death as fulfilled love' (2003: 2). By domesticating the excesses of romantic love through institutions such as marriage, romantic comedies usually foreclose the difficult process of intersubjective relation. The narrative must end because the 'ever after' is impossible to imagine beyond the confines of the diegesis; the promise of fulfilled and everlasting love is, like *agape*, an empty category. Nancy writes against the idea of love as fulfilment, and argues that love can only exist through the possibility of its negation: 'it is possible that one day I will no longer love you, and this possibility cannot be taken away from love – it belongs to it. It is against this possibility, but also with it, that the promise is made' (1991: 100). Love in the age of the Anthropocene is similarly predicated on negation because our efforts to change our behaviours have no guarantees. The stakes are death and extinction – already of plants and animals in unprecedented numbers, as well as humans killed or displaced by climate change and worsening natural disasters – and we are each called on to make small changes, from protesting to voting to reducing consumption, while also being told that these individual actions are insufficient for addressing the sweeping alterations to our economic systems needed by 2050 to avoid the worst impacts of climate change (IPCC 2019). The ending of *The Mermaid* does not propose a solution, but its concluding tonal shift embraces the ambiguity inherent in the romantic comedy – which both mobilises our societal anxieties about change while also reassuring us in the face of them – and therefore at least partially acknowledges the difficulty of these intersubjective processes of upheaval.

The particular love for a non-human object in *Okja* is similarly potentially subversive, in a limited way, because of its melancholic tone. After Mija brings Okja home to South Korea, the final sequence in the film marks an abrupt shift from the fast-paced international adventure of Mija's quest to find Okja. Mija sleeps by a waterfall while Okja and the superpiglet play; as they go back to the house for dinner, we watch them move around the farm in a wide shot from within the house. There is little dialogue and the music is quiet and sombre, a formal stasis matched by the relative stillness of the camera. The ending literally domesticates the film's sprawling social anxieties by insisting on the personal space of the home as the only refuge against corporate greed. While this conclusion fails to address the suffering witnessed in the previous factory

Figure 7.5 Domestic tranquillity at the end of *Okja* (Bong Joon-ho, 2017).

farming sequence, I inevitably find the stillness of *Okja*'s ending profoundly life-affirming. It is precisely because of its insufficiency that the sequence is moving: its happiness is clouded by the profound suffering that precedes it, and it is the contradiction between these two extremes – the acknowledgement of a problem that it cannot solve – that I find so emotionally resonant.

I see the formal breaks that conclude *The Mermaid* and *Okja* as productive failures to reconcile a tension within which both films are deeply imbricated: global capitalism and personal responsibility. Rosalind Galt argues that failure can be politically subversive in the context of neoliberal capitalism, referring to the defaulted debt of Argentina as a 'powerful statement of refusal' that 'stopped the narratives of capitalism short, refusing to read the situation in terms of the framework offered, forcing a material and representational break' (2013: 63). She also acknowledges the limitations of failure as a response, since 'default is not revolutionary' (63), but she nevertheless argues that refusing the dominant narratives of neoliberal capital is an important aesthetic strategy for contemporary global cinema. Earlier, I linked the films' failure to resolve tensions between subjective and universal perspectives to the formal qualities of the apparatus itself, describing cinema as an illusion of objectivity that is, on closer inspection, deeply humanist and subjective. Yet this is not to suggest that there is no resisting these ideological conditions, or that change is not possible. Instead, my argument here is that resistance occurs through an acknowledgement of our limitations and a commitment to persisting despite uncertainty. *Okja* and *The Mermaid* both reflect a tension that they cannot resolve, either formally or narratively: the aesthetic discord between the pleasures of consumer capitalism and the suffering that conditions those pleasures is not reconciled by the films' ostensibly happy endings. This is because the arbitrary choice of one object over others – this superpig, this mermaid – is grounded in an ethics of preferential love that is inevitably compromised and partial, and therefore cannot offer universal solutions. However, according to the paradox of divine love there are no universal solutions, since *agape* is an empty category that does not acknowledge reality as non-totalisable. In both *Okja* and *The Mermaid*, arbitrary choices are inevitable; but instead of viewing these choices as ethical shortcomings in the face of the global threat of ecological catastrophe, I argue they suggest a starting point for an ethics of the non-human based in preferential love. As with any work of love, this process will be difficult and ongoing.[7]

Notes

1. For an overview of the polemics surrounding *Avatar* as well as a discussion of the positive environmental impacts of *Avatar*, see Ivakhiv 2013: 284–4; for more on *Avatar* and love, see Collins 2014.
2. See Birks 2018; Cahill 2019; Ivakhiv 2013 (though he does consider some popular examples, such as *Avatar*); MacDonald 2001; Martin-Jones 2018; McMahon 2019; Pick 2011.
3. See also Lebeau (2008), who discusses the history of the child on screen in relation to Victorian attitudes about childhood and Freudian notions of childhood sexual development: for Lebeau, the child on screen evokes the 'fascination . . . as well as the anxiety, of looking' (18).
4. Recent social movements such as the call for a Green New Deal in the United States and elsewhere oppose capitalist-friendly versions of environmentalism; see Klein 2019.
5. Bong's vegan period lasted only two months: 'I live in South Korea. Korea is BBQ paradise' (Elwood 2017).
6. I have argued elsewhere for the importance of theories of subjectivity in the context of posthumanism and film ecocriticism: see Birks 2018.
7. The research underlying this project was made possible by funding from the College of Arts at the University of Glasgow.

References

Abbott, Mathew (2011), 'On not loving everyone: comments on Jean-Luc Nancy's "L'amour en éclats" ["Shattered Love"]', *Glossator*, 5: 139–62.
Baudry, Jean-Louis (1986a), 'Ideological effects of the basic cinematographic apparatus', in Philip Rosen (ed.), *Narrative, Apparatus, Ideology: A Film Reader*, New York: Columbia University Press, pp. 286–98.
Baudry, Jean-Louis (1986b), 'The apparatus: metapsychological approaches to the impression of reality in the cinema', in Philip Rosen (ed.), *Narrative, Apparatus, Ideology: A Film Reader*, New York: Columbia University Press, pp. 299–318.
Bauman, Zygmunt (2003), *Liquid Love: On the Frailty of Human Bonds*, Cambridge: Polity.
Bell, Macalester (2014), '*Grizzly Man,* sentimentality, and our relationship with other animals', in Susan Wolf and Christopher Grau (eds), *Understanding Love*, Oxford: Oxford University Press, pp. 15–36.

Birks, Chelsea (2018), 'Objectivity, speculative realism and the cinematic apparatus', *Cinema Journal*, 57: 4, 3–24.

Brassier, Ray (2007), *Nihil Unbound: Enlightenment and Extinction*, London: Palgrave Macmillan.

Brereton, Pat (2004), *Hollywood Utopia: Ecology in Contemporary American Cinema*, Bristol: Intellect.

Cahill, James (2019), *Zoological Surrealism: The Nonhuman Cinema of Jean Painlevé*, Minneapolis: University of Minnesota Press.

Cheshire, Lynda and Geoffrey Lawrence (2005), 'Neoliberalism, individualisation and community: regional restructuring in Australia', *Journal for the Study of Race, Nation and Culture* 11: 5, 435–45.

Clode, Danielle (2019), '"Avengers: Engame" is a climate change movie in disguise', *Quartzy*, 21 May, <https://qz.com/quartzy/1624617/marvels-avengers-endgame-is-a-climate-change-movie-in-disguise/> (accessed 1 October 2019).

Collins, Marsha (2014), 'Echoing romance: James Cameron's *Avatar* as ecoromance', *Mosaic*, 47: 2, 103–19.

Cubitt, Sean (2005), *EcoMedia*, Amsterdam: Rodopi.

Ellwood, Gregory (2017), 'With its real-world messaging, "Okja" and director Bong Joon-ho tap into something special', *Los Angeles Times*, 9 November, <https://www.latimes.com/entertainment/envelope/la-en-mn-bong-joon-ho-okja-20171109-story.html> (accessed 1 October 2019).

Galt, Rosalind (2013), 'Default cinema: queering economic crisis in Argentina and beyond', *Screen*, 54:1, 62–81.

Grindon, Leger (2011), *The Hollywood Romantic Comedy: Conventions, History, Controversies*, London: Wiley-Blackwell.

Grusin, Richard (ed.) (2015), *The Nonhuman Turn*, Minneapolis: University of Minnesota Press.

Gunawan, Michelle (2018), 'Navigating human and non-human animal relations: "Okja", Foucault and animal welfare laws', *Alternative Law Journal*, 43: 4, 263–8.

IPCC Special Report (2019), 'Global warming of 1.5°C', 2018 <https://www.ipcc.ch/sr15/> (accessed 1 October 2019).

Ivakhiv, Adrian (2013), *Ecologies of the Moving Image*, Waterloo: Wilfrid Laurier University Press.

Kierkegaard, Søren (1995), *Works of Love*, translated by Howard Hong and Edna Hong, Princeton: Princeton University Press.

Klein, Naomi (2019), *On Fire: The Burning Case for a Green New Deal*, Toronto: Alfred A. Knopf.

Krishek, Sharon (2008), 'Two forms of love: the problem of preferential love in Kierkegaard's "Works of Love"', *Journal of Religious Ethics*, 36: 4, 595–617.

Law, Fiona Yuk-wa (2020), 'Fabulating animal-human affinity: towards an ethics of care in *Monster Hunt* and *The Mermaid*', in Sheldon Lu and Haomin Gong (ed.), *Ecology and Chinese Language Cinema*, London: Routledge, pp. 166–95.

Lebeau, Vicky (2008), *Childhood and Cinema*, London: Reaktion.

Lury, Karen (2010), *The Child in Film: Tears, Fears and Fairytales*, London: I.B. Tauris.

MacDonald, Scott (2001), *The Garden in the Machine: A Field Guide to Independent Films About Place*, Berkeley: University of California Press.

McKinsey and Company (2019), 'China Luxury Report', April, <https://www.mckinsey.com/~/media/mckinsey/featured%20insights/china/how%20young%20chinese%20consumers%20are%20reshaping%20global%20luxury/mckinsey-china-luxury-report-2019-how-young-chinese-consumers-are-reshaping-global-luxury.ashx> (accessed 1 October 2019).

McMahon, Laura (2019), *Animal Worlds: Film, Philosophy and Time*, Edinburgh: Edinburgh University Press.

Martin-Jones, David (2018), *Cinema Against Doublethink: Ethical Encounters with the Lost Pasts of World History*, London: Routledge.

Meillassoux, Quentin (2011), *After Finitude: An Essay on the Necessity of Contingency*, translated by Ray Brassier, London: Continuum.

Nancy, Jean-Luc (1991), *The Inoperative Community*, edited by Peter Connor, Minneapolis: University of Minnesota Press.

Pick, Anat (2011), *Creaturely Poetics: Animality and Vulnerability in Literature and Film*, New York: Columbia University Press.

Russo, Donovan (2019), '"Avengers: Endgame": the not-so-hidden politics of Marvel's apocalyptic blockbuster', *CNBC*, 21 April <https://www.cnbc.com/2019/04/20/avengers-endgame-the-not-so-hidden-marvel-environmental-politics.html> (accessed 1 October 2019).

Wei, Ti (2011), 'In the name of "Asia": practices and consequences of recent international co-productions in East Asia', in Vivian P. Y. Lee (ed.), *East Asian Cinemas: Regional Flows and Global Transformations*, London: Palgrave, pp. 189–210.

Wolfe, Cary (2009), *What Is Posthumanism?*, Minneapolis: University of Minnesota Press.

Žižek, Slavoj (2005), 'Neighbors and other monsters', in Slavoj Žižek, Eric L. Santner and Kenneth Reinhard, *The Neighbor: Three Inquiries in Political Theology*, Chicago: University of Chicago Press, pp. 134–90.

8. DREAMING OF JOYCE VINCENT'S LIFE: CAROL MORLEY'S INTERSECTIONAL ETHICS OF CARE

Lucy Bolton

In this chapter I will revisit Carol Morley's 2011 film *Dreams of a Life* and approach it from the perspective of contemporary feminist ethics, drawing on intersectional feminism and the ethics of care. Morley's film focuses on Joyce Vincent, a woman whose decomposed body was found on the sofa in her flat in Wood Green, north-east London, above the 'Shopping City' centre, in 2006, nearly three years after she had died. The electricity supply was still connected, with the television still on, mounds of post lay by the door, and a collection of wrapped but unlabelled Christmas presents surrounded the woman's body. The story of Joyce's death was met with shock in Britain at the time and was perceived as evidence of the disconnected London lives being led in the noughties. Critical reception of the film focused on the film's perceived message as being that we should check on our friends and family, and not lose touch with people. Many critics described how, despite failing to solve the mystery of what happened to Joyce Vincent, the film actually told a 'universal' story about loneliness and modern society.

In this chapter, I will shift the emphasis of the film back onto Joyce Vincent, and argue that the film enacts an intersectional feminist ethics of care, taking into account Joyce's specific social identity in terms of race, gender and class. Further, I will argue that Morley's pursuit of the project can be looked at in light of an ethics of recognition of Joyce's story, rather than an attempt to 'solve' it, and that Zawe Ashton's performance as 'Joyce' in the film's powerful and affecting reconstruction scenes can be viewed as an embodied performance of care. I thereby seek to reposition the film in relation to contemporary feminist ethics, rather than consigning it to the status of an urban cautionary tale or inadequate investigative documentary. In assessing the ethics of the film as a gesture of care, it is important to consider Morley's motivations for making the film, and the process which she undertook to compile the film's contents. This will enable us to assess whether the project was undertaken as a gesture of care towards Joyce, in line with the recognition that Joyce was a person who existed in 'mutually interconnected, interdependent, and often unequal relations with each other' (Hankivsky 2014: 252).

Antecedence

Morley's first film was *The Alcohol Years* (2000), a self-reflexive documentary about her hedonistic 'Madchester' days in the 1980s at the famous Hacienda club in Manchester (Bainbridge 2012). The film is a compilation of reminiscences and anecdotes told by friends from those days who she reconnected with by advertising in a newspaper. Morley brings together a quite excoriating collection of testimonies, which range from critical and angry to resentful and pathologising. Morley presents talking head testimonies, edited together in a poetic and evocative style, intercut with recreated images of her dressing table and bedroom, handheld footage of various locations, and fake footage of a young Morley played by an actress, interspersed with photographs of the real Morley at the time. It is a compellingly masochistic exercise, as Morley's camera records people saying that they hated her, or thought she was ridiculous, or recounting debasing and depressing stories, including how she had sex for money, and was considered to be, in one man's opinion, 'sexually ill'. Several contributors challenge her for making a film about herself, seeing it as typically self-centred. One says 'aren't you interested in anybody else? Is nobody else worth making a film about?'

Joyce Vincent, it seems, was worth Morley making a film about. Morley writes about how she came across the account of Joyce Vincent's death in a small report in *The Sun* newspaper, which she picked up on the London Underground, and how she became fascinated with the woman's story (Morley 2011). The newspaper revealed that the only reason Joyce's body had been discovered was because housing officials eventually came to repossess her bedsit, her rent having fallen substantially into arrears. Morley discovered similarities between her life and Joyce's: they were the same age, both lost a parent at the age of eleven, and at different times had even lived on the same street. Joyce's middle name was Carol. Morley said she "couldn't let go. I didn't want her to be forgotten. I decided I must make a film about her" (Morley 2011).

Investigating Joyce

So, Morley began a similar process of research as she had undertaken for her film about herself. She placed an advertisement in the local paper asking if anyone remembered Joyce Vincent. She researched Joyce's life, and recorded people's opinions about Joyce as a woman, their experiences with her, and what might have happened to her. A woman emerged who was not the type that many of us might think would die and decay in such circumstances: she was physically beautiful, desired by many men, and with an active social life. She had friends and lovers, a good job, and four sisters. She mixed in various social circles, including with high profile people in the music industry, and wanted to be a singer. Morley researched all this material but still found Joyce elusive, until she caught sight of her in backstage footage from the Nelson Mandela International Tribute concert in 1991, where Joyce met Mandela. In this clip, Joyce turns round, looks past the camera, and turns back: and for Morley, this was a mesmerising moment, with which she chooses to finish *Dreams of a Life* (see Figure 8.1). Morley writes, 'It was Joyce – moving and alive. I had found her. The power of the moving image hit me, the power to resurrect' (2011).

Dreams of a Life weaves traces and testimonies about Joyce Vincent into an evocation of her life, relationships, desires and potential. The similarities between the methodologies and structures of *Alcohol Years* and *Dreams of a Life* are striking, as is the form of the finished films. This not only suggests Morley's satisfaction with the methodology of compiling the testimonies of others as a way of conveying a certain impression of a person's life, but also points to just one of the ethical issues this film raises: is Joyce Vincent's life one about which Morley is entitled to dream in this way?

Records of Joyce

Morley's commitment to discovering more about Joyce led to a five-year film-making project of research, discovery, frustration and creation, but ultimately she was unable to explain why Joyce had died and been left undiscovered for so long. Morley explains that, in the days before smart phones, there were very few photographs of Joyce available, and hardly any video footage (Nick Bradshaw 2012). Morley cast Zawe Ashton to play the adult 'Joyce', and Alix Luka-Cain to play the child 'Joyce' (see Figure 8.1), in imagined sequences that sometimes re-enact the stories told to Morley by people who had known Joyce but on other occasions simply depict Morley's imagination.

It was this element of *Dreams of a Life* that offended people when the film came out: the depiction of imagined events, such as the little girl 'Joyce' gazing longingly out of her window at her departing father, or the lonely, unwell adult

Figure 8.1 Alix Luka-Cain plays young Joyce gazing longingly after her father.

'Joyce' sitting on her sofa, or crying, in the hours leading up to her death. Critic Tim Robey is typical of many when he writes,

> Her recreations of Joyce's last days [. . .] jar quite ruinously: they're feebly speculative and in poor taste, getting us nowhere closer to understanding her . . . neither dream nor séance, it makes the film mutate into something dangerously self-serving – closer to an art project. (Robey 2011)

While some of the recreations are accompanied by corresponding descriptions of events by interviewees, such as Joyce in high spirits at an office party, or dressed in a French maid's outfit, others seem to spring entirely from Morley's imagination. Most notably, the imaginings of Joyce's final hours, as she appears unwell, tired and sad, embodying lethargy and isolation. This risks conveying the suggestion that these images are grounded in authenticity, and there is no accompanying evidence to support this belief. Considering the film's mixture of verbal and visual texts, its impressions and creations, it is important to assess the status of the film's contents in order to consider how we are to respond to what we are witnessing. This is where philosophical approaches to teasing out the specific ontologies of documentary films can help to further our understanding.

Assessing 'Joyce'

Analytic philosophers have grappled with the status of non-fiction films, and some of their observations are pertinent to Morley's project. For Gregory

Currie, a direct testimony is a record of what someone thought of something, such as the people who say that Joyce was really attractive: but a trace, such as a photograph or video recording, is independent of belief in a way that paintings and other testimonies are not. Currie claims that documentary films are made up primarily of traces (Currie 1999). Trevor Ponech (1997) argues that documentaries are cinematic assertions that consist at their core of the action of indication. And Noël Carroll (1997) employs the term 'intention-response' as a model for documentary film, that is, the film is intended to produce a particular response. Taking these observations in turn, Morley's film consists mainly of testimonies and includes far fewer traces of Joyce Vincent or her life; Morley's stated intention was to not let Joyce be forgotten (2011), and we are invited to respond to the film by considering those that we haven't heard from in a while, and perhaps reflect upon the ties we have kept up and the relationships we have allowed to lapse. It is not a documentary film which resembles investigative journalism, in that it does not assert an explanation of what happened to Joyce, or the reason for her death. Journalist Ryan Gilbey states that the film has invented a new genre: the speculative documentary (2011: 85). Gilbey claims that the film 'is more about what isn't there and what can't be known than what is and what can' (85). Thomas Austin proposes that the film is 'intended as a memorial to someone who can never be interviewed', and 'can also be understood as a self-reflexive study of the means by which documentary might lay claim to the absent other, and the ultimate restrictions on such a project' (Austin 2016: 416). Viewed in light of these documenting, problem-solving criteria, the film can only ever be partially successful, and, as Fionnuala Halligan considers, pose more questions than it answers (2011).

Figure 8.2 Some of the very few photographs of Joyce that Morley found and which act as traces of Joyce in the film.

As analytic approaches to traces and testimonies only partly help to explain how the film works, a deeper ethical analysis is called for in light of the difficult problems the film poses and does not solve. As briefly noted above, *Dreams of a Life* was widely interpreted as a devastating comment on contemporary London life: 'How can a person disappear for two years without some inquiry?' (Kauffmann 2012); 'it is a chilling idea that someone could fade away to skeletal remains mere feet away from dozens of living, chatting, laughing humans' (Walker 2015); 'it gives feature-length attention to an unknown soldier of 21st century urban life: a woman who was ignored until she disappeared' (Hasted 2011). This conception of Joyce as emblematic of disconnected modern city life leads most critics to agree with Peter Walker's conclusion that 'the sting comes with the universality' (2015). This approach says that Joyce's story confronts us all with the lingering fear, 'how many more Joyce Vincents are out there, alone, unloved and unremembered? (Peter Bradshaw 2011); and, perhaps, there but for the grace of God go we (Nick Bradshaw 2012: 1).

Despite the shots where the camera glides across the pages of the *London A–Z* street atlas, and the surveillance camera footage of Shopping City, and indeed the indefinite article in the film's title, this film is not simply a story of urban living – it is specifically focused on Joyce Vincent. Some critics found that Joyce was not the heart of the film, or even its subject, preferring instead to focus on ex-boyfriend Martin's evident guilt and grief; but I propose this is to misread the film's foundations. Joyce is present in every moment of the film, albeit mediated by the recall of others, the technology of video or sound recording, the camera, or the re-enactments. Sometimes shots or items in the film act like Currie's traces, such as the photographs Morley was able to find, or the footage of Joyce at the Mandela tribute concert in 1990; but the affective power of that piece of footage has a devastating emotional impact at the end of the film in a conceptual and ethical way, not simply an evidential one. It had that impact on Morley:

> Joyce, who died alone in her bedsit, anonymous and seemingly forgotten, had once had her image transmitted live to millions of living rooms in the 61 countries where the show was broadcast . . . She had her whole life ahead of her but in 13 years she would die, and nobody would know and nobody would notice. (Morley, 2011)

Morley carried on watching the tape as she was 'eager to experience what Joyce once had'. This highlights where *Dreams* exceeds the analytic definitional elements. Although the audience response cannot actually be predicted or assumed, the express intention of Morley's film is not to prove any narrative or resolve any mystery. It is to 'dream up Joyce's life and ambitions through the information I gathered and the people who knew her' (Morley 2011). This 'dreaming up' is what creates the specific ethical conundrum presented by this unique film. Although *Dreams* is less caustic than *Alcohol*, and markedly more poignant, this does not obfuscate the fact that *Alcohol* is Morley's investigation of her own past, whereas *Dreams* is her evocation of somebody else's: somebody dead, who could not give their consent. We must move beyond the analytic definitional framework to consider the ethical ramifications of *Dreams of a Life* in the context of this specific woman's life, in its phenomenological and ethical realities. It is more akin to the idea of a 'documentary fable' as described by Ilona Hongisto, in the way that it 'opens up the possibility of framing and rewinding fragments of the past' (2015: 59). Hongisto's analysis of the way that, in such a film, 'ethics intertwines with creating' is pertinent to the ways in which *Dreams of a Life* creates possible pasts for Joyce (2015: 135). I suggest that it is in the speculative, performative elements of the film that the ethical challenges and possibilities emerge, and it is here where the rich potential of the film can begin to be unearthed.

The Ethics of 'Joyce'

The ethical framework for Morley's filmmaking project was complex when she made the film in 2011, but it is even more complicated to analyse today. The ethical challenges that the film presents include the fact that Morley did not include the family of her deceased documentary subject, and the methods used by Morley, including recreations and dramatisations of events that may never have happened, imbue the film with a strong element of fiction. Joyce Vincent is a woman of Indian and African heritage, and her bi-racial identity plays a strong part in the film's depiction of her somewhat bifurcated life, seemingly split between two friendship circles of white colleagues and black musicians. Integral to the film's depiction of Joyce's life and death is the presence of a variety of screens: the lens of Morley's camera and the screen of the television or computer monitor, or cinema, on which we see her story told, but also the few captured photographic images of Joyce which feature in the film, both still and moving, and the appearance of Joyce, or the character 'Joyce' as played by Zawe Ashton within the film. Also, the recreations of Joyce's childhood and adult life involve visual narrativisation which turns possible events into filmic images, which we receive as if watching a more straightforward narrative film or reconstruction. All these elements, along with the role of editing and montage in the construction of the film, create a uniquely intricate web of ethical encounters through a provocative system of screening and suggestion.

The film begins with an extreme close-up of a newspaper headline about 'a woman'; the camera scans the *London A–Z*, and we see surveillance footage of the Wood Green shopping centre. Then we see a tall, slim woman, walking slowly, with shopping in carrier bags. The film develops by showing us the inside of a dirty, dusty flat, with post piled up, and bailiffs banging on the door. As we hear journalists describe the story of what happened to Joyce as 'the one everyone wanted but no one could get', we see the bailiffs come in and respond with shock and revulsion to whatever it is that they find in the lounge. We then hear an answer machine recording of Carol Morley's voice explaining that she is enquiring after Joyce, and see the advertisement that she put in the newspapers. The film then begins to relay the testimonies made by the various contributors who either responded to Morley's advertisements or were tracked down by her across the period of three or four years. The array of contributors includes the journalists who worked on the story of Joyce's death, her local MP, ex-colleagues from her job in the City, a friend from junior school, ex-lovers and their friends, and a couple of old friends. The range of interests in Joyce, from professional to personal, and platonic to sexual, convey a variety of impressions of her, some of which are contradictory in their accounts of Joyce but all of which reveal how the speakers saw Joyce, what they thought of her, and how they were orientated towards her in terms of competition, affection, kinship and care.

The journalist explains that it is in his 'clutch of stories that I will remember for a lifetime', and for the local MP, Lynne Featherstone, it was a case that baffled her despite contacting the utilities companies and local authority, who 'washed their hands of her'. Joyce's schoolfriend cries, upset that 'she was that alone'. Ex-boyfriend Martin comments that it is 'horrible, annoying', and other friends and ex-colleagues, when shown the newspaper reports about the inquest, comment on how impossible it is to believe that this person was the Joyce they knew. Some suggest foul play, one believes she must have been murdered, and another, despite the fact that the inquest ruled out any suspicious circumstances, concludes somewhat implausibly that 'you'll probably never find out the true story – it'll be another JFK, all the way'.

The contributors then begin to describe Joyce. Martin's group of friends saw her as lively and beautiful, and an odd match for him. John says that Martin turned up with Joyce at a hunt ball, and she was wearing what he describes as 'a spray-on dress', which made him think about Martin as a 'jammy bastard'. Martin says he knows that his friends fancied her and that he was 'really chuffed to go out with her'. One of his friends describes her as – 'petite, and yet a good figure, small feet, I should imagine, great hair, lovely eyes, well-manicured hands – yeah – pleasing'; and another 'maybe my heart was a little a flutter as well because I secretly fancied her . . . she was just lovely'.

Morley cuts to shots of 'Joyce' played by Zawe Ashton, unpacking her shopping from carrier bags and placing things in the fridge. The accompanying soundtrack music is bleak and ominous in tone, reminiscent of a crime drama. As someone describes how 'she was always the centre of attention . . . people gravitated to her like a magnet', we see 'Joyce' alone in her flat, putting on the light, with a melancholy acoustic guitar soundtrack. She moves slowly, almost lethargically. The contrast is driven home: the Joyce people thought they knew was not the sort of person whose life would end in the circumstances that it did. Mysterious inconsistencies emerge, such as Joyce having few qualifications, including an 'ungraded' maths O level, and yet holding down a responsible job in finance; her having told friends that her father had died and yet it emerges that he unknowingly outlived Joyce.

Recreations, or reimaginings, as Morley describes them (Bradshaw 2011), of 'Joyce' as a little girl show her cooking with her mother, skipping and singing in the playground at school, singing for her mother and sisters, and looking wistfully out of the window at her departing father as he heads down to the pub to flirt with other women. Joyce's mother was Indian and father was from Grenada, and her mother died when Joyce was eleven. Her four older sisters then brought her up. One of Joyce's friends from the music scene, her ex-landlord Kirk, describes how he 'always thought she was well brought up in the Caribbean style of well brought up – what we call "well broughtupsy"'. A shot of a 'Post-it' note on Morley's detective-style research board says 'met Joyce's sister, family want to remain anonymous'. The role of the family matters here because there is a glaring absence of her sisters in her later life, and it is noted that when she was admitted to hospital in 2003 she gave her bank manager as her next of kin. Several contributors muse over why her family was not more involved in her life. The film shows little 'Joyce' putting a record on a turntable, and older 'Joyce' putting on the same record. The connection is drawn between the two eras of Joyce, and linked to the descriptions being given about her, especially as people mention that she had a lovely singing voice and wanted to be a singer. The film drives home the contrast between the young Joyce surrounded by love and support, and the adult Joyce living in isolation.

In one particular sequence, Morley presents a confrontation between trace and testimony. We see a recreation of Joyce singing in Kirk's recording studio (see Figure 8.3), called 'Nice', and then we hear a clip of Joyce's voice saying, 'Hi it's Joyce, and that's nice'. Joyce is introducing herself and using her name, and also performing for Kirk as he wanted the jingle to sound. Morley plays and replays the clip to her assorted contributors, and their responses reveal the multi-faceted ways in which a person is perceived and assessed by others. The journalist is shocked by how vibrant and playful the person sounds, as opposed to 'a stain on the carpet'; Martin laughs at how she's 'trying to sound more street' but he says it isn't working; her ex-flatmate says it doesn't sound like her, whereas two men who fancied her say 'yeah that's her flirtatious', and 'sexy weren't she, she was sexy'.

There are layers of ownership over Joyce Vincent at work here. Kirk has recorded her voice, so the machine bears the trace of that; Morley has taken the recording to use in the multi-interview process, but also to capture it on film, and to replicate the cassette in a fresh, new state saying 'Joyce Vincent Demo',

Figure 8.3   Zawe Ashton plays Joyce recording a demo tape.

as well as to replicate the state it was in when it was found, being picked up by a hand covered in a forensic glove. The recording also hijacks the testimonies about Joyce being given in the film by confronting the speakers with a trace of Joyce. The contributors then form opinions in relation to their recollections, having their instant reactions to this highly mediated snippet of Joyce captured on film. Opinions about Joyce are being formed at the time of filming, and then of course edited into the impression Morley wants to convey. And we are also arrested by the sound of Joyce's voice: does it sound like the Joyce we have formed in our heads? This is one of the most complex encounters in the film. Morley is directly confounding the dreams of Joyce's life we may have been forging and forcing us to acknowledge her embodied existence.

How people talk about Joyce displays a range of kindness and degrees of care towards her. Her school friend says Joyce had a very lovely voice, saying 'you'd put her in with your Shirley Basseys, Donna Summers'; singer Alton Edwards says Joyce had star quality like Aretha Franklin, but record producer ex-boyfriend Alistair says 'Joyce was no singer – I told her she could mime in the background'. Alistair's contributions are uniquely harsh amongst all the voices. When he states that Joyce died alone because she wanted to be alone, that she was 'emotionally retarded' and that she has to take responsibility for the way her life ended, it sounds the only critical note in the film. Her flatmate Catherine says that Joyce 'had the whole Sade thing – tight trousers, high waistband, hair tied back, v exotic, beautiful, everybody fancied her . . . Sade was huge at the time . . . she got that quite a lot, "oh you look like Sade"'; and Catherine pulls a face of irritation which perhaps suggests jealousy.

My descriptions of these moments and observations convey how the film combines the testimonies from those who knew Joyce or worked on her story with shots of ephemera (newspaper cuttings, Post-its, *A-Z* pages) which convey her 'case' and Morley's apparent investigation of it, along with more durable objects arising from the diegesis (cassette tape, vinyl record, hairbrush, Christmas presents) which are not genuine articles that belonged to Joyce but which are props used in the sequences where Joyce is played by actresses as part of the film's production design. There are also several types of film footage, such as surveillance camera shots of the shopping centre and the exterior of Joyce's flat, the conventional 'talking heads' of the interviewees, the dreamlike recreations, and the moments where the interviewees are shown to be on the television screen in 'Joyce's' flat (see Figure 8.2). In these particularly disorientating scenes, the effect of witnessing Martin and others on 'Joyce's' television screen ties into the fact that her television was still on when her body was discovered, and conveys the disconnection between Joyce and everything and everyone in her life. In these scenes, 'Joyce' is seen alone, soon to be dead, contemplating her mediated, inauthentic relationships with people who are no more aware of her than anything else contained by the four walls of the television set.

Joyce's Intersectionality

What emerges from the film's treatment of Joyce Vincent's life is a complex and incomplete picture of a very particular woman. Morley undoubtedly had more material than made it to the final cut, but her selection and editing of the film enables us to build a picture of Joyce informed by the major elements of her identity: her gender, her race and her class. It is in this way that the film calls for an intersectional approach to its subtle political and societal subversions. The dominant interpretation of the film was its finger-wagging about urban citizenship, but the power relations in Joyce's life call for more nuanced understanding. Vivian M. May explains how, as a critical heuristic

> in the interests of deciphering power, [intersectionality] directs our attention to gaps, inconsistencies, opacities, and discontinuities and insists that such omissions or silences be treated as (potentially) meaningful and significant, not just as obstacles to work around or anomalies to set aside. (May 2015: 227)

Engaging in this matrix thinking that intersectionality demands enables a reading of the film that is more germane, and less overarching. As May further explains,

> A focus on the interstices, on context, and on interacting forces renders meaning and crafts renderings at the boundaries where (supposed)

opposites meet: it also requires that the background (which the eye/I is often trained not to note or attend to) be brought to the foreground. (May 2015: 228)

Using 'intersectionality's matrix lens' (May 2015: 228) to look at Joyce Vincent in *Dreams of a Life* focuses attention on all the elements of her identity and lived experience. Her identity as both Indian and African is emphasised through the scenes that show actors playing her parents, and the ways in which friends describe her looks as 'exotic' and her upbringing as typically Caribbean. Her friends fall into two distinct groups: the white 'office types', as Kirk calls them, and the Black 'musos' as Martin calls them. The Black musicians say that Joyce was 'not into the black thing', and that meeting Nelson Mandela was to her like meeting Princess Diana: he was a famous person, but not important to her because of his status as a Black icon. Kirk and Catherine say that they both used to joke with her that 'what she needed was a good black man', and another friend says 'she didn't go out with black guys'. They also say that when friends came to Kirk's house they would say 'she didn't want to be black, that she was pretending to be something that she wasn't'. When she was going out with Martin, some of them said 'what are you doing going out with a white honky?' When she did go out with Alistair, she was surrounded by high profile black musicians, like Isaac Hayes, Betty Wright and Jimmy Cliff, so she was part of a scene where Black culture and Black music were strong in her life.

With Martin and his friends, she appears to have been the only person of colour amongst them. Joyce is described as clearly adoring Martin, who reveals that she did ask him to marry her, and he turned her down. John relates how, when he asked Martin why he had never married Joyce, Martin had replied that 'it wouldn't be fair because they'd have tinted children'. John explains, 'he didn't mean it in a racist way, he just – at the time, there was a lot of racism around and half-caste kids get it worst don't they'. John's account of Martin's words, and his attempt to justify them, as well as Martin's account of how his own father queried whether he had seen Martin with a black woman, convey racist attitudes in Martin's friendship and family group. The discussions of both friendship groups suggest that racist microaggressions, now understood as a significant cause of racial trauma, were part of Joyce's life from the circles that she mixed in but which did not mix with each other (Nadal et al. 2019). Her close family relationships were clearly ruptured, and the closest relationships she had were with social groups where she perhaps did not feel she fully belonged; it certainly appears that she was perceived as an outsider on the grounds of her racial identity by both friendship groups.

Joyce's attractiveness is a topic that everybody waxes lyrical over (see Figure 8.4). Men and women describe her beauty and loveliness, with her ex-colleague saying she would like to be like her, and men saying they wanted

Figure 8.4 A photograph of Joyce Vincent.

to go out with her. For many she seemed to play the role of a fantasy woman: whether it was deliberately, as when she dressed up as a French maid to bring tea to Captain Sensible, or unwittingly, as when Martin's friend imagines that she had small feet, or John perceives mounting sexual tension between them. Morley discovered that Joyce had sought help from services for women who had experienced domestic violence and was housed by a refuge for abused women. Colleagues recall an incident where a boyfriend had locked her in her flat for a whole day, and that on another occasion they had to 'rescue her from the clutches' of a lecherous colleague. Catherine describes how 'guys were so focused and possessive with her', that she wasn't surprised to hear that Joyce had been in an abusive relationship. It appears Martin asked her if she wanted to get back together, and she said not, but that she had asked Alasdair if they could get back together, and he had said no. These two men represent very different types of masculinity and therefore convey how Joyce was caught between various men who offered and wanted different things from her and who treated her in a variety of ways.

Class also features notably in Joyce's story. Friends describe how she had elocution lessons, and 'spoke not common but not posh'. Images of young 'Joyce' walking with a book on her head to practice deportment are accompanied by voiceover saying that she was taught to walk and speak nicely. Martin's friend says that she 'was the same class as the rest of us, middle class'. People assumed she was well educated and qualified and are amazed when they find out that she had a secret cleaning job towards the end of her life. Martin is really hurt that she didn't tell him about it, and ex-colleagues are unable to envisage the well-dressed Joyce they remember pushing a hoover around. We see 'Joyce' cleaning toilets, so that we do not have to try to envisage it. Rose Deller writes that this job role 'suggests the return of those relentless social forces that erode the pursuit of "respectability", and dreams of the good life' (2014: 292); in other words, Joyce slipped from someone seemingly trying to live above their class into a secret 'subterranean labour force of urban London' (292).

This reading of the elements of race, gender and class in the film enables a matrix-like approach to thinking about Joyce's life, rather than a linear chronology. The gaps in her story, the secrets, the unknowns, have many possible explanations, and the film does not attempt to pin down explanations. Constructing these elements in this criss-crossing, intersectional way enables Morley to carry out a project which is understandable as an expression of care, rather than an unsuccessful and incomplete investigation.

Caring for Joyce

The ethics of care, as Olena Hankivsky explains, 'now occupies a central position within moral and feminist theory' and can be 'enhanced through critical engagement with intersectionality' (Hankivsky 2014: 252). A full account of the development of care ethics is beyond the scope of this chapter, but it has come to be concerned with how we recognise that 'humans are concrete beings, who exist in mutually interconnected, interdependent, and often unequal relations with each other' (Hankivsky 2014: 253; Okano 2016). Care ethics is concerned with the prevention of harm and suffering, and the demonstration that caring for others is fundamental to living as humans in society. Originating as an ethics of women's work, care ethics has tended to prioritise gender as the determining factor in its scope of concern. Rather than seeing oppression in hierarchical terms, Patricia Hill Collins describes the intersecting systems of oppression as a 'matrix of domination' (2000: 21). Bringing care ethics and intersectionality together results in a focus on 'dependency and vulnerability' (Hankivsky: 262), which is an insightful approach to Joyce Vincent. This enables recognition of the vulnerabilities that existed in Joyce's life as a result of the intersecting systems of oppression and exclusion to which she was subject.

Maurice Hamington writes about embodied care, or 'the framing of feminist care ethics in terms of its physical elements' (2015: 79). Hamington draws on the idea of embodiment as a 'common denominator among humans despite the strength of intersectional differences' (ibid.). He suggests that the body is a means of connectivity and therefore a possible basis for a shared understanding. Hamington's main point is that 'a performative understanding of care ethics can be an important tool for engaging intersectional differences of identity . . . with the aim of ameliorating identity-based injustice' (81). This helps explain the role of the reimaginings of 'Joyce' in the film. Hamington says, 'powerful distinctions that divide humanity may be socially constructed and inscribed on the body, but there is always a body' (84–5). Except, in the case of Joyce Vincent, there is no body – just a stain on the carpet (Deller 2014).

As Hamington writes, 'caring performances can come in many forms' (2015: 87), and I suggest that Zawe Ashton's performance as Joyce can be understood in this light. Ashton describes how Morley did not allow her to see any of the interviews, but rather gave her the facts of Joyce's life, the photographs, dates, events and places. Ashton says that the first thing to strike her was how many addresses Joyce had,

> so that sparked something in my head about someone who keeps moving, who maybe doesn't want to be found. Then I just started to apply my imagination. A lot of it had to come from being really honest about my own experience of isolation, love, friendship, family. (Saner 2011)

In this way, Ashton says she focused on the idea of 'coping' as a way of understanding how Joyce went from the kind of girl people would remember to the kind of girl they all forgot. Coping, Ashton believes, is a difficult thing for women: 'we're supposed to be all right with all the different roles we're born with and are piled on us later on . . . I suppose I let myself imagine what it would be like not to cope' (Saner 2011). Ashton undertakes what Hamington calls the 'embodied and imaginative endeavour' of acting (2015: 90). Hamington sees potential for moral progress in reflective character acting, as it demands new ways of developing skills to care for others with differently complex webs of relational identities. Ashton's embodied performance of Joyce stands in for Joyce's own body, as does Alix Luka-Cain's, and these enactments support our attention to Joyce's life and hopefully our care for her.

Morley's dedication to Joyce's story can also be understood along these lines, in terms of care and attention: she says 'I couldn't let her go. I didn't want her to be forgotten' (2011). The title of her project, after all, is not 'What Happened to Joyce Vincent', but rather reflects Morley's wish to 'dream up Joyce's life and ambitions through the information I gathered and the people who knew her' (2011). Morley felt strongly that Joyce did not belong to her family, and there was nothing to prevent her from exploring Joyce's life in this way (Nick Bradshaw 2012). There is a question about whether a white person is entitled tell a black person's story, and this is an issue here. As Naomi Vogt writes when analysing Celine Sciamma's *Bande de Filles*, 'beyond the question of whose space a filmmaker represents, that of whose story they tell is crucial' (2017: 41). Morley feels connections with Joyce, but she has a different racial identity and is engaging with communities and populations that she is not a part of. However, when Morley began the project, she did not know anything about Joyce's identity, so should she have stepped away from the project when she discovered that Joyce was a woman of colour? I suggest that Morley's approach can be seen as an attempt to highlight Joyce's life without imposing her own narrative on it. Morley is drawing attention to Joyce Vincent and the complexity of her identity, without closing anything down or offering any explanations. Morley's work here is more akin to the feminist praxis described by Talila Milroy et al. than a white saviour or 'do gooder' enterprise. This work entails 'listening without expecting to comprehend or fully "grasp" the Other' (2018: 405). Milroy et al. describe this recognition-based praxis as being 'stopped in our tracks' by what cannot be articulated through coherent, narrative linearity or documentary evidence' (2018: 405). Viewed in this way, Morley's approach is not a misguided 'imaginative act of psycho-archaeology', as it was called by *Guardian* critic Peter Bradshaw (2011), and does not 'both solicit[s] viewer engagement in a search for truth and confront[s] audiences with the inevitable inadequacy of the "evidence" and the failure of any such quest' (Austin 2016: 426). Far from a failure to find all the answers to a mystery, it is rather an attempt to enact an ethics of care towards Joyce Vincent, inviting us to pay attention to her life, by drawing on performative embodiment, recognition and intersectional thinking. In this way, in the words of Hongisto, the film's ethics are 'integrally woven into analysing the composition of actuality captured in documentary frames and proposing alternative lines of life in the face of deadlocked or unliveable circumstances' (2015: 136). Joyce's life may have ended, but the reasons for its unlivability are not fixed, and the film shows that we should never close them down.

References

Austin, Thomas (2016), 'Interiority, identity and the limits of knowledge in documentary film', *Screen*, 57: 4, 414–30.

Bainbridge, Lucas (2012), 'Madchester remembered: 'There was amazing creative energy at the time', *The Guardian*, 21 April, <https://www.theguardian.com/music/2012/apr/21/madchester-manchester-interviews-hook-ryder> (accessed 19 November 2021).

Bradshaw, Peter (2011), '*Dreams of a Life* review', *The Guardian*, 15 December, <https://www.theguardian.com/film/2011/dec/15/dreams-of-a-life-film-review> (accessed 6 August 2020).

Bradshaw, Nick (2012), '*Forget Me Not*', *Sight and Sound*, 22: 1, 44–5.

Carroll, Noël (1997), 'Fiction, non-fiction, and the film of presumptive assertion: a conceptual analysis', in Richard Allen and Murray Smith (eds), *Film Theory and Philosophy*, Oxford: Oxford University Press, pp. 173–202.

Currie, Gregory (1999), 'Visible traces: documentary and the contents of photographs', *Journal of Aesthetics and Art Criticism*, 57: 3, 285–97.

Deller, Rose (2014), 'The body that "melted into the carpet": mortal stains and domestic dissolution in Carol Morley's *Dreams of a Life*', *InterAlia: Pismo poświęcone studiom queer*, 9: 280–303.

Gilbey, Ryan (2011), 'Known unknown', *New Statesman*, 19 December to 1 January, p. 85.

Halligan, Fionnuala (2011), '*Dreams of a Life*', 17 October, *Screen Daily*, <https://www.screendaily.com/dreams-of-a-life/5033360.article> (accessed 10 August 2020).

Hamington, Maurice (2015), 'Care Ethics and Engaging Intersectional Difference through the Body', *Critical Philosophy of Race*, Vol. 3, No. 1 (2015), pp. 79–100.

Hankivsky, Olena (2014), Rethinking Care Ethics: On the Promise and Potential of an Intersectional Analysis, *The American Political Science Review*, May 2014, Vol. 108, No. 2, pp. 252–264.

Hasted, Nick (2011), '*Dreams of a Life*', *The Arts Desk*, 14 December, <https://theartsdesk.com/film/dreams-life-0> (accessed 6 August 2020).

Hill Collins, Patricia (1999), *Black Feminist Thought: Knowledge, Consciousness, and the Politics of Empowerment*, New York and London: Routledge.

Hongisto, Ilona (2015), *Soul of the Documentary: Framing, Expression, Ethics*, Amsterdam: Amsterdam University Press.

Kauffmann, Stanley (2012), 'Worlds and their women', *The New Republic*, 13 September, pp. 17–18.

May, Vivian M. (2015), *Pursuing Intersectionality, Unsettling Dominant Imaginaries*, New York and Oxford: Routledge.

Milroy, Talila, Leanne Cutcher, Melissa Tyler (2019), 'Stopped in our Tracks: From "giving an account" to an ethics of recognition in feminist praxis', *Gender, Work & Organization*, Vol. 26, Issue 4, May 2019, pp. 393–410.

Morley, Carol (2011), 'Joyce Carol Vincent: how could this young woman lie dead and undiscovered for almost three years?', *The Guardian*, 9 October, <https://www.theguardian.com/film/2011/oct/09/joyce-vincent-death-mystery-documentary> (accessed 6 August 2020).

Nadal, Kevin, Tanya Erazo and Rukiya King (2019), 'Challenging definitions of psychological trauma: connecting racial microaggressions and traumatic stress', *Journal for Social Action in Counselling and Psychology*, 11: 2, 2019.

Okano, Yayo (2016), 'Why has the ethics of care become an issue of global concern?', *International Journal of Japanese Sociology*, 25: 85–99.

Ponech, Trevor (1997), 'What is non-fiction cinema?', in Richard Allen and Murray Smith (eds), *Film Theory and Philosophy*, Oxford: Oxford University Press, pp. 203–20.

Robey, Tim (2011), '*Dreams of a Life*, review', *The Telegraph*, 15 December, <https://www.theguardian.com/film/2011/oct/09/joyce-vincent-death-mystery-documentary> (accessed 6 August 2020).

Saner, Emine (2011), 'Life and soul', *The Guardian*, 6 December.

Vogt, Naomi (2017), 'Divine Girlhoods: Filming Young Women in France's Banlieues', *Cineaste*, Vol. XLII, Issue 3 (2017), 38–42.

Walker, Peter (2015), 'The film that makes me cry: *Dreams of a Life*', *The Guardian*, 27 March, <https://www.theguardian.com/film/filmblog/2015/mar/27/the-film-that-makes-me-cry-dreams-of-a-life> (accessed 21 November 2021).

PART FOUR

LOOKING ANEW

9. EMPATHY MACHINES, INDIFFERENCE ENGINES AND DIGITAL EXTENSIONS OF PERCEPTION

Nick Jones

What is the relationship between digital media and the material world, and how might our use of the former change our understanding of and place within the latter? A central concern of digital media theory from the late-1990s onwards, the ethical aspects of this technological and (potentially) ontological change in relation to film is summed up by Markos Hadjioannou in *From Light to Byte: Towards an Ethics of Digital Cinema* (2012). As he describes, analogue cinema's indexicality 'enables a realization on the part of the spectator of her or his existential position within the world and so qualifies an ethical implication in the image as the potential for responding to, and acting in, the world' (2012: 177). Digital media, by contrast, offer not indexical trace but interactive, present-tense simulation, and so, for Hadjioannou, 'cannot conjure up an image of the world as an existential guarantee' (2012: 177). While assertions around the radical differences between analogue and digital capture have been challenged (see, for instance, Cubitt 2011), it is certainly the case that digital images and the networks that produce them offer a new kind of visual modality. In a digital age, vision becomes a method of filtering, rather than encountering, and the image becomes interactive and navigable (Manovich 2001; Verhoeff 2012). Images are no longer only observed, they are swiped, clicked, tagged, filtered, and shared. If they provide evidentiary proof, it is less as an authentication of a past moment than a trace of a flexible present, a conditional marker of temporary conditions.

All of this alters our ethical relationship to images. The new digital visuality is not principally voyeuristic or scopophilic but rather cartographic, defined by an informatic mode of automated recording and registering that seeks legibility and apparent usefulness. This is not to say that this is entirely novel: the digital's 'cartographic gaze' of remote presence certainly inherits impulses to catalogue and quantify familiar from colonial visual modalities – image-making and image-circulation remain methods for distant control and ideological persuasion (Specht and Feigenbaum 2019). Through interactive digital images, the perception of the user is extended beyond their temporal-spatial confines. This is achieved through the digital generation of an algorithmic world, one which is less concerned with aesthetic appreciation than it is with bodily immersion and virtual presence. These images do not offer ambiguity or the invitation for interpretation, and Jordan Crandall terms them 'operational media' to emphasise the utility which is so central to them (Crandall 2005). Added together, all the operational media which shape our experience result in what media philosopher Vilém Flusser refers to as a 'universe of technical images': reality itself is restructured into a 'global image scenario' in which simulation is always preferred to its alternative (Flusser 2000: 10; see also Flusser 2011).

If digital theory often questions the ethical potential of this 'image scenario', then elsewhere in cultural and industrial discourse alternative claims are made, including that digital simulations can amplify impressions of ethical obligation, or that they can entirely sidestep them. In what follows I consider such claims, attempting to explore the ethical dimensions of digital mediation in ways that do not position it in opposition to indexical media or more 'authentic' experiences, but which deconstruct the statements about ethics, empathy, and access that are made about digital mediation in some specific contexts beyond cinema. Rather than analyse particular media texts and their presentation of ethical challenges, I instead explore three technological frameworks that are used to deliver images today. I begin by looking at virtual reality and its promises of immersion. Labelled an 'empathy machine', strong ethical arguments are made for VR by content makers, financiers and consumers, and I unpack these claims and question the presumed automaticity of the ethical viewing position of 'immersive journalism', arguing that (at present) VR offers only the illusion of an ethical situation, one in which technological marvelling often overrides moral engagement. I then move on to consider less hyped – but equally fundamental – visual systems of the digital age, namely the maps offered by Google Earth and Google Street View. I survey the work of key artists who use Earth and Street View in their practice and alight on the ethical issues posed by these world-simulations, and who by doing so reveal that the indifference these technologies assert is itself also a fiction. Finally, by way of conclusion, I connect both these examples to contemporary drone warfare, a site in which affirmations of either empathy or indifference otherwise associated with the digital are rendered much more complex. In this way the chapter ends by looking (briefly) to the larger ethical and political concerns raised by the extended perceptions of digital mediation.

SIMULATING EMPATHY

Virtual Reality (VR) has recently become one of the more culturally visible sites of machinic visual perception, conspicuous not necessarily because of its actual pervasiveness, but rather thanks to its imagined possibilities. For a long time a speculative rather than practical technology, in the 2010s VR became more firmly established as an entertainment form and as a tool for a variety of instrumental ends. It is telling that as early as 1991, Howard Rheingold began his survey of VR with a description of virtual 'molecular docking', a programme simulating the interactions of proteins, designed to assist in medical research. Here the simulated three-dimensional space of VR was being used like a microscope, giving access to a miniscule, abstract realm in order to engender its better scientific understanding and manipulation. Today, VR continues to be employed operationally, being used to aid surgical procedures and for medical training (Barad 2019), as well as to treat military post-traumatic stress disorders (Friedrich 2016). Nonetheless, most VR users will have experienced it in entertainment contexts. Commercial VR content is available for download or free to stream online, VR games have been released for major consoles (Crecente 2018), and film festivals and art galleries regularly feature a VR component among more 'traditional' visual material.

For all that earlier media such as panoramas, stereoscopes and cinema (especially large-format screens) sought to replace the visual field of the viewer with the constructed visual experience of the media object, VR appears a quantum leap in this regard, and so is hyped as a great leap forward for moving image entertainment media. Observers can see nothing but the virtual space and can navigate this space by moving their head, as well as, in some cases, their body (albeit within a restricted area). This involvement is total and enveloping. In the words of Pasi Väliaho, 'there is no distinction in virtual reality between screens and how subjects intuit themselves in space as dynamic, kinetic, affective beings; no distinction, to put it in neuroscientific terms, between the image and the brain's simulation of its surroundings' (Väliaho 2014: 74–5). The screens of other media, no matter how immersive, are nonetheless perceptible as screens, surfaces which deliver content within a wider visual field. By bringing its screen surface extremely proximate to the user, VR effaces this separation (see Jones 2019).

Partly as a result of this proximity, VR is considered by many to provide a kind of unmediated mediation. This misapprehension is common when media technologies first enter the mainstream. For instance, photography and cinema were both considered by some at the time of their early use to remove the guiding or interfering hand of the artist. But with VR this rhetoric is particularly strong. As Marie-Laure Ryan sums up such claims:

> In its ideal implementation, VR is not merely another step toward transparency that will be 'remediated' by future media, but a synthesis of all media that will represent the end of media history. [. . .] The 'virtual reality effect' is the denial of the role of hardware and software (bits, pixels and binary codes) in the production of what the user experiences as unmediated presence. [. . .] [C]omputers [. . .] serve as pure media – as largely hollow channels for the circulation of information. (2015: 42–3)

VR's envelopment, then, might not just be a quantitative shift, but a more foundational re-alignment of media and viewer. This apparent immediacy has led to VR's use for documentary and documentary-like projects aimed at raising awareness or exposing injustice, often termed 'immersive journalism' (de la Peña et al. 2010). These experiences seek to provide 'first-hand' knowledge of contemporary events, which often involve disenfranchised individuals whose experiences are presumed to be very far from that of the viewer. Examples of this kind of VR, some of which I will mention shortly, are founded upon the supposed ethical engagement wrought by VR's immersion and immediacy. If many theorists of digital media have argued that it robs us of some core connection to the world, then VR seems to overcome, or eradicate, that issue. In immersive journalism, digital meditation apparently becomes not the *barrier to* but the *condition of* ethical witnessing and understanding.

Emblematic of this problematic manoeuvre is the labelling of VR as 'empathy machine', a phrase intended to indicate its ability to rouse viewer engagement, excitement, and, indeed, compassion (McStay 2018: 95–111; Milk 2015; Robertson 2017). In her summary of VR's potential to deliver 'witnessing texts' – those which call attention to the viewer's presence, and that seem to thus call for a moral response to the presented material – Kate Nash stresses VR's 'ability to promote an imaginative transportation': that is, its generation of a believable imaginary space (Nash 2018: 120). Through this transportation VR can claim to 'foster a moral response to distant others' (Nash 2018: 120). The space it generates, while imaginary, is verisimilitudinous to the extent of being a document of time and space, and this prompts an encounter which – it is thought – can be distinctly ethical in nature.

VR's success as a tool to prompt empathy, then, is reliant upon its technological capacity to render environments and their occupants. If it is an empathy *machine*, then the machine's primary function is its ability to transport. VR acts as a temporary extension of perception into a virtual realm of ethical presence, from which one is, in an immersive journalism context, encouraged to return to the real with some new lessons learned and an expanded sense of one's obligations to the other. This empathetic education can occur by taking on the embodied perspective of somebody else. For instance, VR has provided users with the experience of having different and marginal sensorial perceptions (such as colour blindness), of being different ages, or of coming from different racial backgrounds (Louie et al. 2018). Here, though, I want to focus not on bodily transference but on the more widely disseminated VR content which places the viewer alongside or within an unfolding scene and which seeks to create empathetic investment primarily through a spatial transportation – you are still you, and you are placed among surroundings that are new and somehow ethically weighted.

In 2015 the United Nations initiated a series of ongoing VR projects with the stated intention of 'bring[ing] the world's most pressing challenges home to decision makers and global citizens around the world, pushing the bounds of empathy' (Anon. n.d.). These sites of challenge included an Ebola epidemic in West Africa, and the Gaza strip, among others. The collapse of time and space is here presumed to engender empathy, as global citizens – the mobile, connected and affluent – are confronted with the spatially distant, disconnected and disenfranchised of the world. Part of this VR slate, *The Last Goodbye* (2017) provides users with a tour of the Majdanek concentration camp in Poland delivered by Holocaust survivor Pinchas Gutter. Directed by Gabo Arora and Ari Palitz, *The Last Goodbye* places emphasis on the forensic accuracy of its location, this then being allied with some explicitly ethical filmmaking choices – viewers of the experience are shown a gas chamber, but are not taken inside (see Figure 9.1).

Figure 9.1   *The Last Goodbye* (2017) screengrab.

For Joshua A. Fisher and Sarah Schoemann, this allows viewers 'to determine their own engagement' with the subject matter (2018: 583). (This is only true to a small extent, though – Gutter's recounting and the spaces through which the viewer is guided are stable, meaning that spatial repositioning is possible but minimal).

Meanwhile, *Carne y arena* (2017), a VR experience directed by Alejandro G. Iñárritu, situates the viewer alongside an illegal border crossing from Mexico to the US. Reviews foreground the technological experience of the apparatus: 'You're *there*', states Owen Gleiberman, before calling it a 'genuine fiction' which prompts a 'primal empathetic connection' (Gleiberman 2017). Similarly praising its effectiveness, Peter Bradshaw calls *Carne y arena* 'a dynamic, kinetic experience in which the audience can roam freely about, looking up and down, and around in a 360-degree circle' – a freedom which results in a greater understanding of the plight of undocumented migrants (Bradshaw 2017). Technology begets immersion, which is inevitably yoked to ethical contemplation and cross-cultural understanding (or the possibility thereof). While Gleiberman proposes that the installation 'isn't "political"', he nonetheless argues that it makes a political statement, namely that whatever the viewer's political position on illegal immigration, 'the people risking their lives to cross the border are human beings, so know their experience' (Gleiberman 2017).

In these examples, it seems as though 'we are there', and we get to 'know the experience' of another. The experiences rely on an 'auratic rhetoric' – the sense that the aura of an individual and place has been retained, delivered to the user in some authentic fashion (Fisher and Schoemann 2018: 586). Nash (2018: 126–7) notes how much of the UN content consists of guided tours of spaces occupied by those deemed deserving of humanitarian attention, such as the widely-reported on *Clouds Over Sidra* (2015), in which a young Syrian refugee tells her story from within a Jordanian refugee camp. The viewer's empathy is apparently activated as a result of their new surroundings and the way they are directly addressed by a local occupant of this novel space (see Figure 9.2). Yet such telepresence is always coloured by the technological: Nash (2018: 128) flags up the tension between focusing on the subject of the experience on the one hand and looking around to revel at the completeness of the spatial illusion on the other. This speaks to a broader issue with the tenor of the ethical claims made regarding this kind of VR content, and it is to this subject that I now turn.

For VR filmmaker Chris Milk, VR is an empathy machine because 'through this machine we become more compassionate, we become more empathetic, we become more connected, and ultimately we become more human' (Milk 2015). Through the apparatus we are ethically improved – although it is not clear in Milk's words whether this is because we witness what we otherwise would not, or if the very act of seeing content in VR makes us inherently more compassionate subjects, the machine's mode of address reshaping our capacity

Figure 9.2 *Clouds Over Sidra* (2015) screengrab.

to understand the other. Either assertion is questionable, and they are often conflated, the content of experiences being intrinsically yoked to the mode of their experiencing. Granting temporary access in a disembodied fashion, VR material like *Carne y arena* and *Clouds Over Sidra* places excessive emphasis on the fact that this access is possible – and from and through that access ethical understanding is thought to flow.

In some senses, VR repeats and extends the 'distant suffering' of television news coverage. In this mode of representation, as various scholars have shown, images of others in pain are instrumentalised in order to defuse the political charge of the situation that has led to that pain, including the situation of viewing itself (Downing and Saxton 2010: 67). Luc Boltanski (1999: 114) has suggested that the insurmountable gap between television viewer and viewed sufferer results in a kind of enforced viewer inactivity, and it is this inability to intervene that results in the production of pity. However, the rhetoric of VR asserts that the viewer – now an *experiencer* in VR terminology – can in some senses intervene. VR users are encouraged by the fact of 360-degree immersion to look and sometimes move around, and in immersive journalism we are often directly addressed by a calm and unthreatening individual from within the mediated world. The spatial access and presence granted by the medium, then, operates under the sign of intervention, seeming to emplace us in an active way. Industrial and journalistic discourses presume that this apparent immersion then *automatically* engenders a more ethically engaged viewer. The machine, it seems, performs or encodes the presence of empathy through a facsimile of intervention, relieving us of this burden. Moreover, those ethical claims that are being made regarding access and immersion ignore the disembodiment inherent in mediation. Apart from choosing our spatial viewpoint we are not active within the mediated scene, our presence implied but in no way authenticated. Indeed, the technological excitement of VR is precisely that *we are not there*, even though we feel like we are. We may be able to move and look around, but we do so touristically.

This is not to claim that the technological dimension of the screening situation straightforwardly compromises the ethical intentions of these experiences. If it did, then any mediated content would suffer the same fate. What is different is the nature of agency, and the way this is discussed. In her book about ethics and cinema, Michele Aaron describes how 'spectatorial agency' is 'a marker of socio-political responsibility', as the film viewer is prompted to consider moral frameworks and their own lived ethical experiences as a result of certain content (Aaron 2007: 88). In VR, this agency remains present, and, as we have seen, claims can be made that the increase in agency engendered by spatial emplacement leads in turn to an increase in ethical engagement. If ethical media (of any kind) prompt us to consider 'our personal powers of reasoning and choice' and our relationship to moral conditions (Aaron 2007: 109), then VR is certainly capable of such encouragements.

However, VR discourse conflates this power of reasoning with the power of spatial agency and immersion. Our 'choice' to look and move where we like in a virtual environment rings much louder than more internalised choices about response and engagement. If the content of a VR experience operates in a register of empathetic presence, this still functions to highlight the actual absence that the VR technology is overcoming, and so revels in this technological competence and implicitly creates further distance. Even though the viewer is granted some semblance of experiential access, this is always pegged to the distance between the coordinates of the experience and the viewer's own circumstances – whether socio-political or, in the case of body-swapping experiences like *Notes on Blindness* (2016), sensorial. Digital media are able to ask the same ethical questions as analogue media, but in the case of VR, the rhetoric of technological presence put forward by both the apparatus itself and the discourses which circulate around it make these questions harder to discern. As a result, content that most visibly and explicitly functions in this ethical manner – immersive journalism – might be considered more *machinic* than *empathic*.

For game designer Robert Yang, VR is less an empathy machine than an appropriation machine, experiences like *Clouds over Sidra* being 'refugee tourism simulators' that furnish little real compassion let alone political understanding (Yang 2017). An ethical situation is operationalised and technologised – a fact which may not be unique to VR, but which is relentlessly effaced in the conjoining of empathy and technological hype. Ultimately, VR has been mobilised in the entertainment sphere as both a method of collapsing spatial and temporal distance (making us feel 'as if we are there') and of cinematic amplification (taking us 'within the image'). In empathetic terms, the viewer is offered an illusion of an ethical situation – like the computer-enabled space they find themselves in, this is a virtual, perhaps convincing, but ephemeral simulation. Though the content of VR documentaries like *Carne y arena* and *The Last Goodbye* may be shocking or upsetting, their technological transportation might only add to the distance between the user and the ethical challenges presented by their content.

Report a Problem

If VR takes us to another place in a fashion that can claim amplified ethical gravitas, then what of other virtual spatial navigations which place far less emphasis upon the viewer's ethical subject positioning? Applications like Google Street View and Google Earth provide VR-like transportation – indeed, they are available on VR platforms alongside desktop, tablet, and mobile screens – but rather than solicit emotion they seek to function as neutral aids. The spaces they present are empty of other people, or those other people have been de-emphasised through facial blurring. Virtual presence, in these cases, apparently involves no encounter with the other. The authenticity of the world they provide is measured not through empathic stakes, but neutral objectivity. However, a range of artists working with these programmes have uncovered the limits and unexpected potency of this supposed neutrality, as I will show after briefly discussing the technologies themselves and their histories.

Google's navigation technologies allow users not just to *see* a visual representation of a potential journey or far off landscape, but encourage them to feel as though they are undertaking this journey or visiting this landscape in a virtual fashion. To do this, space must be digitally recreated. In the case of Street View, vehicles mounted with 360-degree cameras collect countless pictorial reference points for many of the world's roads, amalgamating these to present something of a navigable virtual world, accessible to the user on the screen of their chosen device. Google Earth, meanwhile, uses satellite and aircraft imaging in a similar manner, stitching this together to generate a holistic globe that can be navigated via a mouse or touchscreen. Like a scanned, digital version of a text document or other piece of media, these technologies allow instant access for the sake of convenience. They present 'the world as fact, mapped and documented, and reconstituted online' (Gilge 2016: 469). As a response to privacy concerns, the faces of those caught on camera are blurred out, resulting in a world depopulated of recognisable people. If VR has been termed an empathy machine, then by contrast we might call these 'indifference engines': they assert their own neutrality (and by extension the user's) in relation to the world they depict.

The scale of the cultural shift to digital mapping has been described by Laura Kurgan, who uses several examples of images of planet Earth – from those taken in the 1970s with a mechanical camera, to more recent images digitally composited from satellite data – to stress the ambiguity that comes with this supposed totality and objectivity. The recent digital images of Earth are 'composites of massive quantities of remotely sensed data collected by satellite-borne sensors', and so do not represent anything that a human could see with their own visual apparatus, whether aided or unaided (Kurgan 2013: 11–12). Such images, whether produced by NASA (in her examples) or Google, indicate how the 'truth' of an image is now bound up with assessments of resolution and the accuracy of data. What was once, in the Apollo 8 image *Earthrise*, one kind of signifier of totality (the common cause of a species living on a single, precarious globe) becomes, in the digital age, quite another. Now, what we look at is 'a patchwork of satellite data, artificially assembled – albeit with great skill and an enormous amount of labor' (Kurgan 2013: 11–12). As in VR, the technology of capture supersedes the content that is captured, asserting a new visual modality of interactivity and the composite rather than a pre-existing reality. Here is cinema's indexical debate, restaged on cartographic terrain.

Consumer products and conveniences, these mapping technologies arose through military research and development. The Global Positioning System upon which they rely was created by the US military in the 1960s, while the specific technology now known as Google Earth was bought by a CIA-funded venture capital firm in 2003, at which point it was used to plan elements of the invasion and subsequent occupation of Iraq (Anon. 2012). As Caren Kaplan (2006) stresses, attending to this lineage reveals how these technologies remain undergirded by a militaristic form of visuality. This can be traced to their efforts to increase distance while amplifying access. Extending the user's perception in profound ways, Street View et al. engender a 'shift from experiencing place to the image of place as experience' (Gilge 2016: 471). Our primary perceptual experience of space occurs through Street View's navigable virtual space; only secondarily do we experience the physical location (if at all). This filters our vision, shaping what we perceive, what we expect to discover, and what we can observe at all.

A growing body of work by artists seeks to reveal the mediation at work in these programmes and the ethical challenges they raise. Perhaps the most famous is Clement Valla. His *Postcards from Google Earth* (2010–ongoing) exposes moments when Google Earth's algorithmic image-processing does not produce what we would recognise as a realistic simulation of terrain or human infrastructure. This occurs through the apparent incompatibility between the texture mapping employed to wrap photographic material around 3D models of buildings and landscapes, and the content of these satellite photographs. This results in images such as *Postcard from Google Earth (40°26'29.66"N,*

79°59'32.91"W), in which a series of overlapping highways in Pittsburgh, PA, seem to melt and sag into one another, cars appear flattened into the roads they sit upon, and spikes in pixilation erupt from unexpected portions of the image. These and other depictions of warped space in Valla's work – including numerous bridges melting into the valleys they span, but also buildings frothing into unusual, psychedelic shapes – reveal that the amalgamation of visual material and geological contours is not always as successful as Google's rhetoric suggests.

If, in Valla's images, 'the illusion of a seamless and accurate representation of the Earth's surface seems to break down', then what they show are nonetheless *not* glitches or errors exactly. They are rather, as he states,

> the absolute logical result of the system. [. . .] They are seams which reveal a new model of seeing and of representing our world – as dynamic, ever-changing data from a myriad of different sources – endlessly combined, constantly updated, creating a seamless illusion. (Valla 2012)

These seams arise from the persistence of a non-human agency at work in the intersection of 2D and 3D data. The human eye knows from experience what a bridge looks like from multiple angles; Google Earth's texture mapping software, at the time it produced the images Valla has excerpted, does not. It is confused or misled by the nature of the shadows and undulating terrain of a given location. But *Postcards* represents a miniscule fraction of the visual material available on Google Earth. The rest of this content can as a consequence be overwhelmingly be taken as factual, a 'true' accounting of the surface of the planet, featuring spaces which align with our expectations of images and the world. Valla's revelations then act as strange reassurances of the general accuracy and usefulness of Google's virtual reality – apart from the occasional slip-up, here is a navigable, believable world, accessible from one's desktop or mobile.

Marion Balac similarly identifies what might be considered a glitch in Google's approach to space, one which again stresses the occasional imperfection of the automated systems being employed. In *Anonymous Gods* (2014), she collects images of large-scale statues from Google Street View – many of which are religious icons – in which faces have been automatically blurred out by the software (Balac n.d.). The distinction between the human and the divine, the human-sized and the towering emblem, is effaced: the algorithm employed is sophisticated enough to recognise a face peering out from within a complex image, but not so advanced that it can discriminate between living flesh and inert stone. *Anonymous Gods* thus highlights the impersonality of this app. Like Valla, Balac reveals the non-human perception beneath the user-friendly layer of information-interpretation that is the databased image. But rather than show this at the level of infrastructure, she zeroes in on Street View's intriguing and telling relationship to the human face, a relationship which gets closer to the ethical complications offered by these systems and their images.

In *The Nine Eyes of Google Street View* (2010–ongoing), Jon Rafman pushes further in this direction. Again a collection of unexpected images from the spatial navigation app, Rafman describes how *Nine Eyes* – named for the amount of cameras embedded within the periscope that erupts from atop Google capture cars, but perhaps also a serendipitous reference to the Nine Eyes intelligence alliance – was initially focused on the apparent neutrality of the images. Here, the artist states, was 'true docu-photography', fragments of reality shorn of artistic interpretation or intent (Rafman 2009). But this preliminary thinking gave way to a related but more pessimistic impression of Google as a kind of 'indifferent being', one witnessing a world 'absent of moral dimension' (Rafman 2009).

If this is, as Rafman describes in a later interview, like 'looking at a memory that nobody really had' (quoted in Recinos 2018), then these memories can be quietly troubling. Snapshots of glimpsed violence or (potential) abuse or abject poverty sit alongside those of absurdity, hostility (individuals with blurred faces sticking one finger up at the Street View camera), and occasional technical poetry (glitched images of distorted colour and space). All contain traces of the apparatus: the digital haze of the zoomed-in frame and the annotations automatically provided by the app, including directional cursors in the top left corner. Rafman himself draws attention to the still-present invitation for the Street View user to 'report a problem' that he leaves in many images. In the live app, this button allows users to request something to be blurred (their face, a licence plate, their home), or to report misplaced navigation arrows or poor image quality. As of checking in 2022, it offers no option to 'report' something more systemic – all we can do is blur those portions of the image that offend us (or, rather, ask Google to undertake this blurring). Rafman's images are *images*, not nodes of an active database, so this hyperlink is inactive, burned in and inert, and this encourages the reading that all these images present a 'problem' of some kind, one which is epistemological and ethical, and which we are alerted to as viewers but have no way of expressing within the machinic logic of Google's platform.

The images in *Nine Eyes* recapitulate, in their own strange way, Google's claims of accuracy and objective mapping. But they do so in a manner that calls direct attention to the claims such objectivity makes upon the viewer – many images appear to prompt ethical action, or at least concern. And yet, these are not scenes captured by a photographer with an artistic or moral intention, but interactive fragments collected by an automated process which hides them in plain sight (that is, among billions of other images). The absence of an authoring agency may lead in general terms to operational mediation and functional navigation, but also results in unexpectedly challenging content. For Rafman, these images express a tension 'between our uncaring, indifferent universe and our search for connectedness and significance' (Rafman 2009). We see the repressed of technology: we just want to know how to get from A to B, but if we look through Rafman's lens we can also see how this machinic perception has transferred the strange and the troubling into the virtual realm. Valla may identify unfeasible architectural malformations, manufactured oddities unique to this interface, but many of Rafman's images show us actual events. *Nine Eyes* highlights the passivity with which these moments have been recorded, the tell-tale blur operating as a kind of moral claim on behalf of Google – the app is for viewing streets, not their occupants, and so the smudge of the faces in these scenes functions as a kind of metonymy of total erasure, the removal of strangers from the world in order to enable our complete and frictionless navigation of it. But the strangers remain, and the moments of their lives that have been selected by Rafman call for some kind of response, whether mild curiosity or a sense of shock and outrage. It is the very neutrality of the platform which seems to call on us to make up for its blankness.

As Ila Nicole Sheren argues, work like that by Rafman, Balac and Valla 'confronts the techno-utopian illusion of standardized space' (Sheren 2018: 397–8). Valla describes Google Earth as 'essentially a database disguised as a photographic representation', and the projects described above ironically amplify our awareness of the former by reframing these mapping tools as more explicitly the latter (Valla 2012). That is, where Google Earth and Street View assert the comprehensive navigability of the 3D environment, these artists alight upon the still image, plucking it from this spatial milieu. Valla, Balac, Rafman and others reinstate a frame into a system that seeks to be frameless – these images are single pictures, fixed landscapes which must speak as and for themselves (Becking 2018: 312).[1] To an extent this is crucial to the art practice context of these pieces – excerpted images can be displayed on websites and hung in galleries as discrete works, the artists' interventions into the technology indicated by their choice of image and their wrenching of these from their normally navigable context. But more than this, framing the virtual image in such a way forces its contemplation as a distinct artefact. This is not an invitation to click or continue navigating around, but a demand to linger and consider. Like VR, Google's mapping programmes endow the user with agency. We are presented with a navigable, interactive setting; in VR, this is used to imply presence and connection, while in these mapping programmes it is used to stress functionality. These artists stall this interactivity, and, ironically, in so doing they cultivate precisely that ethical dimension of spatial access that VR commentators take for granted in relation to that technology. By using these mapping programmes against the grain of their intent, the indifference engine is rendered closer to the empathy machine many claim VR to be. In the images selected by these artists we face an object or a trace, rather than a use or a function. And if this associates the stilled with the revelatory, then the virtual environment we navigate on our desktops (as opposed to the images we peruse in a gallery) is itself shown to be a system of concealment, obscuring the databased and integrated nature of these environments under the veil of spatial unity, and burying the machinic logic and its ethical consequences beneath the sign of operational neutrality.

Conclusion

Both VR and Google's mapping programmes claim to extend our perception beyond previous limitations, but in so doing they displace our perception into a simulated mode of visuality which is dominated by operational imperatives. In VR this occurs under the sign of empathy, in Street View that of indifference. In either case, these claims must be tempered through attention to the realities of the technology and the nature in which its presence shapes that which is presented. To further demonstrate this, I would like to conclude by briefly applying the preceding work to a more explicitly political site, namely the use of unmanned aerial vehicles, or drones, by today's military forces.

Drones extend the military capacity of their users into foreign territories – indeed, the scale and use of contemporary drone warfare has led scholars like Grégoire Chamayou (2015) to propose that nowhere is now exempt from a militaristic gaze, rendering the whole world a perpetual battlefield. In this, drone warfare is the weaponisation of Google's consumer mapping applications – although, as noted, the military history of GPS and tools that use its data mean that Google Earth and Street View are possibly better considered the commercialisation of an inherently martial system of targeting. Meanwhile, drone pilots may observe the live feeds that make their job possible on screens rather than headsets, but like VR they are plunged into a virtual space through which they can navigate at will, and which assures them at some level of their co-presence with the screened content thanks to their ability to disrupt it at the squeeze of a trigger.[2] If the unexpected or the combative is encountered when telepresently traversing terrain (as it was in Rafman's *Nine Eyes*), then the injunction to 'report a problem' in effect remains: the remote operators are invited to apply their own blur to the screen, an action which has grave real-world consequences but which, on the screen, is just an erupting smudge. But VR's empathy model does make an appearance here too, as the emotional stress felt by drone pilots serves to 'apply a layer of humanity to an instrument of mechanized homicide' within circulating discourse (even if the shift work and endless tedium of this remote piloting is what might actually be producing stress, as opposed to the moral consequences of tactical actions) (Chamayou 2015: 108). Drones expand the perception of the pilot and by extension the military in which she serves, providing virtual access to distant space in a manner that does not conceal the power asymmetries and empathetic gaps in play between here and there, but which actively relies on and exploits them.

As moving image media, drones, VR and consumer mapping apps point to the scale and diversity of digital images, but also reveal consistent traits of virtual access and technologised presence. The ethical weight and potential of these images and image-systems is tied to these operational contexts. Crucially, colonial models of visual power seem to be restated here, and even made more emphatic, as the impulses to conquer space and categorise its contents now occur through virtual remediations (Specht and Feigenbaum 2019). Spatial access is marketed as increasing presence and empathy (in VR) or as helping us get around our local area and even explore the world as a virtual agent (Google Earth and Street View), but in either case the technological reshaping of perception needs to remain in our field of view. We need, in short, to maintain a healthy scepticism towards claims that these media encode either compassion or indifference as an automatic function. The same is true beyond these examples, and I hope that by attending to the wider ecosystem of digital images, I have helped reveal an array of pressing ethical issues that may not be uncovered when focusing on digital cinema alone.

Notes

1. Similar claims might be made of the work of other artists who employ Street View and other mapping tools, such as Douglas Rickard, Kyle Matthews, Halley Docherty and Michael Wolf.
2. In another expected confluence, VR is consistently being tested as a method of improving drone piloting (Smolyanskiy and Gonzalez-Franco 2017).

References

Aaron, Michele (2007), *Spectatorship: The Power of Looking On*, London: Wallflower.

Anon. (2012), 'CIA's impact on technology', *CIA*, <https://www.cia.gov/about-cia/cia-museum/experience-the-collection/text-version/stories/cias-impact-on-technology.html> (accessed 22 August 2019).

Anon. (n.d.), 'About UNVR', *United Nations Virtual Reality*, <http://unvr.sdgactioncampaign.org/home/about/> (accessed 22 August 2019).

Balac, Marion (n.d.), 'Anonymous Gods', *Marion Balac*, <http://www.marionbalac.com/works/anonymous-gods/> (accessed 22 August 2019).

Barad, Justin (2019), 'Virtual and augmented reality can save lives by improving surgeons' training', *Stat News*, 16 August, <https://www.statnews.com/2019/08/16/virtual-reality-improve-surgeon-training/> (accessed 22 August 2019).

Becking, Jessica (2018), 'Records of representation: Clement Valla's *Postcards from Google Earth*', *Media Theory*, 2: 1, 307–15.

Boltanski, Luc (1999), *Distant Suffering: Morality, Media and Politics*, Cambridge: Cambridge University Press.

Bradshaw, Peter (2017), 'Carne y arena review', *The Guardian*, 22 May, <https://www.theguardian.com/film/2017/may/22/carne-y-arena-review-inarritu-virtual-reality-refugee-cannes-2017> (accessed 22 August 2019).

Chamayou, Grégoire (2015), *Drone Theory*, London: Penguin.
Crandall, Jordan (2005), 'Operational media', *CTheory*, <http://www.ctheory.net/articles.aspx?id=441>.
Crecente, Brian (2018), 'Sony: 3 million Playstation VR sold, 21 million PSVR games', *Variety*, 16 August, <https://variety.com/2018/digital/hardware/psvr-sales-2018-1202907159/> (accessed 22 August 2019).
Cubitt, Sean (2011), 'The latent image', *International Journal of the Image*, 1: 2, 27–38.
de la Peña, Nonny, Peggy Weil, Joan Llobera, Elias Giannopolous, Ausiàs Pomés, Bernhard Spanlang, Doron Friedman, Maria V. Sanchez-Vives and Mel Slater (2010), 'Immersive journalism: immersive virtual reality for the first-person experience of news', *Presence*, 16: 4, 291–301.
Downing, Lisa and Libby Saxton (2010), *Film and Ethics: Foreclosed Encounters*, Abingdon: Routledge.
Fisher, Joshua A. and Sarah Schoemann (2018), 'Toward an ethics of interactive storytelling at dark tourism sites in virtual reality', in *Conference Proceedings of the 11th International Conference on Interactive Digital Storytelling*, New York: Springer, 577–90.
Flusser, Vilém (2000), *Towards a Philosophy of Photography*, London: Reaktion.
Flusser, Vilém (2011), *Into the Universe of Technical Images*, Minneapolis: University of Minnesota.
Friedrich, Kathrin (2016), 'Therapeutic media: treating PTSD with virtual reality exposure therapy', *MediaTropes*, 6: 1, 86–113.
Gilge, Cheryl (2016), 'Google Street View and the image as experience', *GeoHumanities*, 2: 2, 469–84, doi.org/10.1080/2373566X.2016.1217741.
Gleiberman, Owen (2017), 'Cannes virtual reality review: Alejandro G. Iñárritu's "Carne y Arena"', *Variety*, 20 May, <https://variety.com/2017/film/reviews/carne-y-arena-review-alejandro-g-inarritu-1202438293/> (accessed 22 August 2019).
Hadjioannou, Markos (2012), *From Light to Byte: Towards an Ethics of Digital Cinema*, Minneapolis: University of Minnesota Press.
Jones, Nick (2019), 'The expansive and proximate scales of immersive media', *International Journal on Stereo and Immersive Media*, 2: 2, 36–49.
Kaplan, Caren (2006), 'Precision targets: GPS and the militarization of U.S. consumer identity', *American Quarterly*, 58: 3, 693–713.
Kurgan, Laura (2013), *Close Up at a Distance: Mapping, Technology, and Politics*, New York: Zone.
Louie, Alan K., John H. Coverdale, Richard Balon, Eugene V. Beresin, Adam M. Brenner, Anthony P. S. Guerrero and Laura Weiss Roberts (2018), 'Enhancing empathy: a role for virtual reality?', *Academic Psychiatry*, 42: 6, 747–52.
McStay, Andrew (2018), *Emotional AI: The Rise of Empathic Media*, Thousand Oaks, CA: Sage.
Manovich, Lev (2001), *The Language of New Media*, Cambridge, MA: MIT Press.
Milk, Chris (2015), 'How virtual reality can create the ultimate empathy machine', *TED*, March, <https://www.ted.com/talks/chris_milk_how_virtual_reality_can_create_the_ultimate_empathy_machine?language=en> (accessed 22 August 2019).
Nash, Kate (2018), 'Virtual reality witness: exploring the ethics of mediated presence', *Studies in Documentary Film*, 12: 2, 119–31.

Rafman, Jon (2009), 'IMG MGMT: the nine eyes of Google Street View', *ArtFCity*, 12 August, <http://artfcity.com/2009/08/12/img-mgmt-the-nine-eyes-of-google-street-view/> (accessed 11 July 2019).

Recinos, Alec (2018), 'Towards a postinternet sublime: Jon Rafman's Street View romanticism', *Rhizome*, 4 January, <http://rhizome.org/editorial/2018/jan/04/towards-a-postinternet-sublime/> (accessed 10 July 2019).

Rheingold, Howard (1991), *Virtual Reality*, New York: Touchstone.

Robertson, Adi (2017), 'VR was sold as an "empathy machine" – but some artists are getting sick of it', *The Verge*, 3 May, <https://www.theverge.com/2017/5/3/15524404/tribeca-film-festival-2017-vr-empathy-machine-backlash> (accessed 22 August 2019).

Ryan, Marie-Laure (2015), *Narrative as Virtual Reality 2: Revisiting Immersion and Interactivity in Literature and Electronic Media*, Baltimore: Johns Hopkins University Press.

Sheren, Ila Nicole (2018), 'Standardization, censorship, systems, surveillance: artist perambulations through Google Earth', *GeoHumanities*, 4: 2, 397–416.

Smolyanskiy, Nikolai and Mar Gonzalez-Franco (2017), 'Stereoscopic first person view system for drone navigation', *Frontiers in Robotics and AI*, 4: 11, doi.org/10.3389/frobt.2017.00011.

Specht, Doug and Anna Feigenbaum (2019), 'From the cartographic gaze to contested cartographies', in Pol Bargués-Pedreny, David Chandler and Elena Simon (eds), *Mapping and Politics in the Digital Age*, London and New York: Routledge, pp. 39–55.

Väliaho, Pasi (2014), *Biopolitical Screens: Image, Power, and the Neoliberal Brain*, Cambridge, MA: MIT Press.

Valla, Clement (2012), 'The universal texture,' *Rhizome*, 31 July, <http://rhizome.org/editorial/2012/jul/31/universal-texture/> (accessed 12 July 2019).

Verhoeff, Nanna (2012), *Mobile Screens: The Visual Regime of Navigation*, Amsterdam: Amsterdam University Press.

Yang, Robert (2017), '"If you walk in someone else's shoes, then you've taken their shoes": empathy machines as appropriation machines', *Radiator*, 5 April, <https://www.blog.radiator.debacle.us/2017/04/if-you-walk-in-someone-elses-shoes-then.html> (accessed 22 August 2019).

10. DO YOU SEE WHAT I SEE? THE ETHICS OF SEEING RACE IN *GET OUT*

Berenike Jung

The complex relationship between race and visuality extends from matters of representation – the erasure or distorted depiction of racially marked characters – to the way in which we *learn to see* in racialised ways. As Donna Haraway puts it: 'eyes are a technology, too' (1988: 583). In this chapter, I argue that Jordan Peele's *Get Out* (2017) addresses both the problem of racist representation – the hyper- and invisibility of the black body in US culture – and the ways in which cultural norms, themselves shaped by race relations, condition what emerges, and how, in our field of vision. 'The very concept of seeing and being seen – or of not being seen – ', remarks Richard Brody, 'emerge in 'Get Out' as essentially racialised experiences' (2017). The film also foregrounds the mediation of racial representation, working through cinema's complicity in the stereotyping of black bodies and the establishment of racist viewing conventions, but ultimately challenging such 'established ways of seeing' (Sinnerbrink 2011: 141). This visual approach corresponds to what Keith Harris has called a 'dialogic' representation of visualisation, a methodology that engages with 'the iconography and image discourse of pre-existing representations' (Harris 2012: 41–2). As *Get Out* invites its audience on a journey of intentional engagement with such media frames and with our own patterns of looking, the film factors in different habits, experiences and viewing positions. Specifically, I argue that rather than a homogeneously imagined 'modern subject' (Choi/Frey 2014: 3), *Get Out* carefully addresses both white and black audiences[1] in different ways, using film-specific cues to disrupt dominant looking conventions. The analysis will focus on how markers of the horror genre, emotional and sonic alignment, visual address, and narrative economy help to translate different non-dominant experiences of embodied seeing into drama and aesthetic form and to motivate a broad engagement with questions of perception and mediation.

Strategies of Seduction

Get Out tells the story of black photographer Chris Washington, who takes a weekend trip to meet Dean and Missy Armitage (Bradley Whitford and Catherine Keener), the parents of his white girlfriend Rose (Allison Williams), a wealthy, politically liberal couple. When they arrive, the parents reveal that an annual gathering is to take place that very evening. Chris endures not only a barrage of minor and major racist incidents at the hands of Rose's family and their largely white friends but also encounters strange behaviour by the black household staff and a lone black visitor. Chris is forcibly hypnotised by Rose's mother, supposedly to help him quit smoking. Increasingly feeling paranoid, Chris eventually discovers that he has fallen into the hands of a cult who entrap and kidnap black people to serve as hosts for their ailing white members. The victims are sold in an auction and undergo the so-called 'Coagula procedure' after which their bodies are made to do their new white owners' bidding. At the last minute, Chris is able to break the hypnotic spell that kept him bound. In his attempt to escape, and to stop the cult, he kills most of the Armitages, and is ultimately rescued, at the last-minute, by his black friend Rod (Lil Rel Howery).

In the film's prologue, we see a lone black man trying to navigate a deserted suburban community. He is lost in a space that is clearly unfamiliar and threatening to him: when a white car slowly approaches, he mutters 'Not today', and turns around to walk in the opposite direction. The car stops; we hear the 1930s song *Run Rabbit Run* playing.[2] Suddenly, a masked person jumps the man from behind and from offscreen, drags him to the car and throws him into the trunk. As the car door closes with a *thud*, the music – which had increased in volume – switches from diegetic to a high-pitched violin string, as if to anchor us with the fearful victim. With the next cut, the credits run over a long shot which pans along trees as if looking out a fast-moving car or train, accompanied by the song *Sikiliza Kwa Wahenga* – a drawn out 'Bro-o-o-ther', followed by Swahili lyrics – that begins, intersects and ends the film. Named after a Swahili phrase that translates to 'listen to (your) ancestors', the song speaks of a looming danger. The point of view (and of audition) of this shot is not yet diegetically anchored – later, we can ascribe it to Chris's gaze out of the car window on the drive up to the Armitage residence. Retrospectively, the lyrics might be read as a sonic warning from the voices of Africans kidnapped and enslaved in the New World, telling Chris to run, just as he is entering the 'white space' of suburbia (Anderson 2015: 1). This song will recur, as nondiegetic sound, to signal the link to historical black trauma. Its Swahili lyrics, presumably inaccessible for a broad audience, offer a cached warning, yet the sound, often whispered, transmits a sensation of unease and tension.

In the next shot, the camera scans black and white photographs on the wall of Chris's stylish urban apartment – a pregnant woman, a child holding a mask in front of its face, a man holding an aggressive white dog on a leash; photographs of community, place, and imminent change – before panning to the right, where we see Chris shaving. Thus, the audience is first introduced to Chris's way of seeing the world – and arguably, historical consciousness – and to Chris's body second. The sonic anchor remains with Chris, with *Redbone*, in which singer Childish Gambino speaks of distrust towards their lover and warns to 'Stay Woke'. The next shots show Rose buying pastries and coffee, followed by the couple discussing their weekend plans.

Driving up to the Armitage residence, Rose accidentally hits a deer. The visceral shock of unexpected collision serves as jump scare and ominous alert to dangers to come. We, and Chris, hear a wailing sound and he enters the wood to search for the deer. Rather than a monster, he finds a dying animal with large Bambi eyes. The next shot shows Rose explaining the accident to a white policeman, who then proceeds to ask for Chris's licence. While Chris is ready to comply with weary familiarity, Rose zealously calls out the cop. This detail pretends to follow the movie convention of establishing a character as the 'good white', in distinction to the 'bad white' cop, and her behaviour cements trust between the couple. Only in retrospect do we realise that she also prevented the tracing of her future victim.

When Chris and Rose arrive at the Armitage residence, Rose drops her bag, squeals '*Daddy!*' and runs into her father's arms, while Chris hangs back a little, his modest duffle bag over his shoulder. We observe these family greetings in a wide-angle long shot. With a front porch and columns, looking out over an impressive estate, the house appears Southern and colonial, while the Armitages, in their words, are tolerant, cultured and liberal, connecting the trope of the racist white South with the more subtle racism of the genteel, upper middle-class, North-eastern Whites. The camera does not move closer during this theatrically staged scene. In its stillness, towering over the characters as they exchange hugs and greetings in a performance of social roles and rituals, the house evokes the social and material structures that precede and encompass the characters as individuals. While Chris appears financially comfortable, the Armitages' wealth and property suggest 'old money' – status and money gained over generations, at the expense of suppressed communities of colour, thus benefitting from what George Lipsitz termed the 'possessive investment in whiteness'. Slowly, the camera retracts to reveal that this shot is the perspective of black groundkeeper Walter (Marcus Henderson), who seems to be staring with hostility or resentment at the arrivals. But later Walter's body is revealed to have been colonised by a white man, and his hostility towards Chris has in fact been a *white* perspective. The shot tricks us, just as Chris is being tricked, aligning our experiential journeys.

Already these first scenes complicate multiple typical horror framings: instead of the trope of a scantily clad female teenager (Clover 1992), here a young black male is the first victim, and rather than repeating the notorious horror trope of the lone black person being the first to die,[3] he will neither die nor remain the only black character. The scenes also reverse the cultural discourse that contrasts a violent, racialised inner city with safe, white suburbia, a 'spatial metaphor for whiteness itself' (Wiese quoted in Patton 2019: 351) and reframes the horror dichotomy of urban/rural divide (Clover 1992). Here, it is the suburbs that emerge as site of danger.

The evocation of horror tropes not only serves to provide a familiar pleasure to the discerning fan, but registers also among the strategies of seduction offered by the film to a racially diverse audience. In interviews, director Peele emphasised that his intention was to offer recognition to black horror fans. He also explained that the film purposefully sets up a fairly 'universal' experience to create empathy with its protagonist: the apprehension of meeting your partner's parents for the first time; the unpleasant experience of being singled out at a party. The star images of the film's main characters might further entice an audience of liberal white viewers: Dean is played by Bradley Whitford, best known for his well-intended if self-absorbed liberal character in the television show *The West Wing* (1999–2006); Missy is depicted by 'indie goddess' Catherine Keener (Holmlund 2016: 263), known to portray women who are 'flawed but . . . not unlikeable' (259); Rose is portrayed by Allison Williams, whose star persona from the TV show *Girls* (2012–7), belatedly criticised for whiteness, is that of a privileged ingénue, tone-deaf but harmless; and Chris is embodied by British actor Daniel Kaluuya, who was at the time not yet widely known in the US.

Most seductive, perhaps, is how this biting critique of white privilege begins as *satire* of 'colour-blind' practices of the Armitages and their friends.[4] A former member of the successful comedy duo *Mad TV* and *Key & Peele*, Peele aims at what Eduardo Bonilla-Silva calls 'racism without racists' (Bonilla-Silva 2003: 2–4), which function to maintain white domination, while denying the lived embodied experience of black people. As the satire shifts towards horror – not coincidentally, Chris's friend Rod, the character whose outlandish ideas initially provide comedic relief, turns out to have been right in the end – we move towards questions of perception. While Chris's camera gives him hints throughout, registering odd behaviour in the black people around him, this eye alone cannot reveal the truth to him, just as 'skin-deep' surface viewing will not reveal it to the film's audiences.

As the horror genre allows, even invites, crossing established patterns of identification often revolves around seeing too much or too little (e.g. Clover

1992), it seems a particularly apt genre to punctuate normative manners of perception. Choosing the frame of horror genre allows Peele to give cinematic recognition by representing what reality feels like for marginalised communities, particularly a constantly heightened awareness of and tension around potential danger. For white-identified audiences, this reveals blind spots, offering what George Yancy has called the '*gift* of a black countergaze, a gaze that recognizes the ways of whiteness' (Yancy 2013: 135, emphasis in the original). *Get Out* carefully plots to seduce white audiences 'to see the world through the eyes of a black person for an hour and a half' (Zinoman 2017). While the film remains uncompromising and consistent in its affective visual and sonic alignment with its black protagonist, its formal strategies simultaneously serve to enable non-blacks to perceive structural whiteness as terrorising.

Whiteness as Horror

There is a reparative element to this emotional and visual alignment with Chris, as it undermines and reframes what has historically been the white control of the black gaze. As bell hooks explains:

> [Slaves] could be brutally punished for looking . . . To be fully an object then was to lack the capacity to see or recognize reality . . . black people learned to appear before whites as though they were zombies . . . To look directly was an assertion of subjectivity, equality. (2014: 168)

hooks explores these looking dynamics, from white people's inability to see themselves through the eyes of the other, the terror of whiteness in the black imagination, to white desire for the other, which she even describes in terms of consumption: 'It is by eating the Other . . . that one asserts power and privilege' (hooks 2014: 36; cf. Dyer 1988). White desire to possess, to appropriate and discard non-white culture, is literalised in *Get Out* as a kind of cannibalism As Zadie Smith describes it, 'the white people in *Get Out* want to get inside the black experience: They want to wear it like a skin and walk around in it' (Smith 2017). To foreshadow this cannibalistic appetite, we first see Rose eyeing pastries which she will bring to her boyfriend, intercut with scenes of Chris grooming himself. Later her brother tells stories about Rose's semi-cannibalistic voraciousness: as a child, she had a toenail collection, and she allegedly bit a date's tongue. Chris will eventually discover her trophy photos of previous victims, symbols of black fungibility. When he seeks to flee, the family circles and moves in on him like prey. Rose's penchant for trophies is shared by her father, who proudly gives Chris a tour of the house, oblivious to the uncomfortable parallel between his assortment of objects collected from foreign countries and the decorative heads of killed deer, which he proclaims to be a pest.

At night, unable to sleep, Chris steps out, and when he returns, Rose's mother Missy calls on him to sit with her in their opulent living room, plush with leather and velvet furniture, rugs and low-lit lamps oozing golden wealth and subtle hints of orientalism. They face each other in opposing armchairs, a domestic duel. As Missy stirs a spoon in her teacup, the clinking against fine bone china initiates an auditive focus. Although he repeatedly declines her offer, Missy tricks him into being hypnotised, allegedly to help with his nicotine addiction. She inquires details about the night his mother died in a hit-and-run, and tells Chris to search for his memory of being a little boy, waiting for his mother to come home, in front of the TV, listening to the rain. Like Chris, the audience hears not only the insistent clinking of Missy's spoon but also the rain. As Chris recedes into his mind, we see him as a little boy sitting in front of a television, foreshadowing the varied use of this medium later on. Intercut with these images of his memory are shots of Chris's hands scratching the armchair, then of his hands scratching a different chair as the boundaries of reality are collapsing. As Missy's distorted voice commands, 'Sink into the floor', Chris's body and face freeze, and he falls backwards into a black void. We are positioned behind Chris, as if we are *already inside*. The diegetic world is shrunk to a small-screen TV, on which Missy tells him 'Now you're in the Sunken Place'. The cinema audience, gripping their seats in a dark room and a state of suspended disbelief, are experientially aligned to Chris's immobilised body and his wide-eyed stare, the character acting as 'instructive mirror' (Clover 1992: 167). *Sikiliza* plays again in the background, accelerating in volume until with a start, Chris wakes up in bed.

The next day, at the Armitages' gathering, Chris endures a barrage of racist micro-aggressions, remaining silent and quickly reassuring Rose afterwards rather than letting her think that her family is hurting him and that she put him into this position. Along with Chris, our curiosity is roused as to the odd behaviour, frozen or belated reactions and general out-of-sync quality of the few black people around, which none of the white people seem to notice. Housekeeper Georgina fills Chris's glass until it spills over, staring off into the distance; Walter sprints towards Chris as if to attack him; both smile in a forced or menacing way. When Chris addresses Logan, the sole other black guest at the Armitages' gathering, as 'brother', he looks at him blankly, shakes his hand rather than responding to a fist bump, and immediately blabs to his elderly white partner that Chris felt uncomfortable being the only person of colour. Later, Logan twirls for a white audience of admirers and, upon request, comments that 'the African-American experience' has been 'overall, good'. These black zombies hyperbolically and comically enact what Kristen J. Warner describes as 'plastic representation': the writing of contrived black characters performing 'normatively white characters who happen to be of color' (Warner 2017: 37). These zombies represent those flavourless, epidermically black characters in mainstream media who lack any interest in or awareness of black culture: as audiences, we supposedly see black characters, but it is really only the skin colour that changes. Once again, this aligns the gaslighting experienced by Chris with that of the viewing audiences who tend to be offered only such 'plastic representation' in mainstream media. And again, the invitation to the audience is to question visual representation as self-evident.[5]

What gives Walter, Georgina and Logan away, more than their stiff behaviour, is the way they speak. The zombies do not recognise Black English Vernacular nor do they code-switch. 'It's not what he [Walter] says, it's how he says it', Chris tells Rose. Dressed and speaking as Logan, Chris does not recognise his acquaintance André. But awakened by Chris's phone camera's flash, André briefly takes over and shouts at Chris to 'Get Out!'. Only then does Chris *see* him and admits, disturbed: 'I felt like I knew him'. Chris texts the cell phone picture to Rod, who recognises André (LaKeith Stanfield) and, unbeknown to Chris, sets off a search. After the incident, as the Armitages announce a game of bingo, Chris and Rose decide to go on a walk. The audience remains sonically aligned with the couple's conversation, set in an idyllic romantic landscape, but these scenes are crosscut with the Armitages' silent game. Slowly tracking out from a medium shot of Dean, the camera reveals a huge photograph of Chris propped up behind him: he is sold, as if at a slave auction. A blind art dealer, Jim Hudson, wins the auction. We now know more than Chris about the danger he is in, and we fear for him.

Breaking the Frame

The current renaissance of Black Cinema continues to recuperate historical excisions and distorted representations of black people on film and television. Above and beyond, there is a reimagination, a reinvention of blackness in cinema, a process which began with black independent filmmakers in the 1960s (e.g. Snead 1994). The distrust of the camera as being a purveyor of violence is rooted in a long racist history of distorting images in audio-visual entertainment forms, from minstrelsy, vaudeville and peep shows to postcards of lynching and racist tropes in television and cinema. The limited and distorted representation of African-Americans ranges from the blatant stereotypes of minstrelsy (e.g. Bogle 2016) to the white actor in blackface depicting a rapist in *Birth of a Nation*, the passive victim of the abolitionist tearjerker *Uncle Tom's Cabin*, to the liberal projections of post-war 'race message' films and the buddy cop films. All of these examples have been widely discussed in terms of their origin in or appeal to a white gaze and their function of creating whiteness and a *white* self-identification. Blaxploitation films of the 1970s (Guerrero 1993b) and the 'hood' films of the 1990s reinforced the racialised myth of black males as menacing. The black male body in particular has largely been confined between a pathological monster and a beautiful, erotic spectacle, between containment and excess (Harris 2012: 42).

> It is the young black male body that is seen as epitomizing this promise of wildness, of unlimited physical prowess and unbridled eroticism. . . . it is this body that is most represented in contemporary popular culture as the body to be watched, imitated, desired, possessed. (hooks 2014: 34)

Peele's film liberally taps into cinematic history, referencing *Stepford Wives* (Bryan Forbes, 1975), *Night of the Living Dead* (George Romero, 1968), *The Invasion of the Body Snatchers* (Philip Kaufman, 1978), and especially *Guess Who's Coming to Dinner* (Stanley Kramer, 1967) with its attempt at puncturing the taboo of miscegenation (Yaquinto 2008; Guerrero 1993a). *Get Out*'s narrative initially evokes a similar tension around an interracial relationship, but the film also intervenes in the persistent containment of black male sexuality. Contrary to both the desexualised Sidney Poitier in *Guess Who's Coming* or the hypersexualised blaxploitation films, Chris and Rose are seen in romantic activity, sexual foreplay as well as domestic intimacy.

At the outset of her discussion of respectability politics and the 'racialized politics of aesthetics', Racquel Gates reflects on the often-remarked visual connection between stereotypical minstrelsy images and the tightly framed close-ups of Kaluuya's wide-eyed, frozen face as he is falling into the Sunken Place (Gates 2017: 38), asking, 'Can an African American character's fear ever inspire empathy, rather than ridicule, from an audience?' (38). I would like to suggest a different interpretation of precisely those scenes that evoke the stereotypical frames Gates responds to, one that implicates the viewer in questions of perception.

Chris's paralysis functions as symbolic expression of being imprisoned in the Armitages' possessive and object-based white gaze. It is relevant that these various medial frames – from photography to television to cinema – appear around the Sunken Place. Chris seems strategically badly lit in specific moments, such as when Rose's brother Jeremy taunts him to fight, or when Missy catches him smoking. His skin barely illuminated, we see just his teeth and the whites of his eyes gleaming in the dark hallway (see Figure 10.1). Following Harris's 'dialogic' manner of representation, these shots use the history of a visual discourse 'as a process of making visible the discursive means of the visual' (Harris 2012: 41–2). They gesture to both cultural and technological frames: Chris's awareness of the way in which he is being seen in a white gaze – what W. E. B. Du Bois, in *The Souls of Black Folk*, termed 'double-consciousness' – and the ideology inscribed in a cinematic technology that initially fixated only on illuminating Caucasian skin well, resulting in dark-skinned actors' faces portrayed as near-black blobs (Dyer 1988).

Figure 10.1 Protagonist Chris Washington, seen through a white gaze.

These aesthetics are reversed in the scene where Chris finds out the truth. Awakening from being knocked out, he finds himself strapped to a chair in the Armitages' basement, an old television set in front of him. The TV snaps on to a corny home movie of the Armitage family. The narrating Armitage grandfather appears a parody of white 'voice-of-god' documentary, explaining the history of the family and the Coagula procedure over images of metamorphosis. Next the TV functions as a sort of videocall, in which Hudson explains the current situation. The audience sees and shares Chris's flashbacks to his interactions with the black zombies, as we and he put everything together. Hudson is a former 'wilderness' photographer, a profession which symbolically alludes not only to the taxidermy in the house but also evokes settler colonialism's myth that the territory of today's US was uninhabited, or land in which 'savage' nature, animal and indigenous were to be subdued or consumed. In line with this tradition, Hudson wants to take Chris's eyes, his artistic sensibility, without the existential experiences that shaped the way Chris inhabits the world.

The appearance of these various media frames – from photography to television and cinema – is significant here. The scene juxtaposes beautifully shot images of Daniel Kaluuya's distressed face with the poor quality of the television screen (see Figure 10.2). Transmitted via this clearly antiquated television set, Hudson's white face appears washed out, flat, distorted by static and noise, in stark contrast to the carefully illuminated shades of brown, golden, ochre of Chris's face, lit to register minute details of his facial expression, the desperation in his eyes, beads of sweat and the texture of his skin (see Figure 10.3).

Both the television as a physical object, the home movie and the family's privileged heritage evoke the 1950s ideal of a of white suburban family: as

Figure 10.2 Former photographer Jim Hudson, viewed on a grainy television image.

Figure 10.3 Chris, captured and in close-up.

Lynn Spigel points out, when television ascended to dominant mass medium between 1948 and 1955, discourses on suburbia, television and whiteness became deeply intertwined (Spigel 1992). Through this 'old' medium of television and the home movie quality, the film links the loss of white privilege and patriarchal virility to the loss of visual hegemony.

Chris's camera had previously acted as a barrier between his body and the invasive behaviour of those around him but also as artistic expression of Chris's own perception, picking up on fissures and disjunctures in the facades of his surroundings. Now without the camera, Chris is 'force-fed an audiovisual diet … that is the very essence and tool of his captivity and his subjection' (Brody 2017).

By showing such different media's effects and framings, *Get Out* reflects on the ways in which these have shaped and limited screen blackness.

When he is hypnotised again, there is a cut to Chris falling downward into a dark space as well as a point-of-view shot from Chris looking up towards a small, receding television screen. We hear the thumping of Chris's heartbeat and the Armitages talking; then these sounds recede, as if we 'lose connection' (Figure 10.4). A shot of Chris screaming silently is followed by one showing us both the TV and Chris falling backwards. These shots invite a listening subject as much as a viewing one, and while we move our visual position, we remain sonically aligned with Chris. The metaphor of the Sunken Place invites and has generated various interpretations. It reconfigures W. E. B. Du Bois's image of the colour line as a transparent or glass walled chamber, with whites outside and black people inside. Speaking of the psychological meaning and consequences of segregation, Du Bois writes:

> It is as though one, *looking out from a dark cave* in a side of an impending mountain, sees the world passing and speaks to it; speaks courteously and persuasively . . . the people passing do not hear; . . . They still either do not hear at all, or hear but dimly, and even what they hear, they do not understand. Then the people within may become hysterical. They may scream and hurl themselves against the barriers, hardly realizing in their bewilderment that they are screaming in a *vacuum* unheard and that their antics may actually seem funny to those outside looking in. (2007: 66, emphasis added)

Figure 10.4 Falling into the Sunken Place, from Chris's point of view.

The overdetermination of the black body includes an inscription as inherently performative and entertaining, endowed with emotional expressiveness. In a discussion between bell hooks and Arthur Jafa on how black filmmakers may break free of and reframe 'the colonised black body under surveillance', Jafa described this capacity as 'glamorising'. Rather than an innate ability, it is a performance that is tied to survival, mesmerising those in power in a situation of powerlessness (hooks and Jafa 2014). In *Get Out*, Chris's powerlessness in white space is indicated by his immobilisation, paralysed by hypnosis and thrown into a liminal state.[6]

The shifting emphasis to the aural field subverts this visual overdetermination and reveals the sonic dimension as a major 'expressive possibility for blacks to articulate subjectivity' given how they had been 'confronted with vision as a hostile realm of significance' (Fleetwood 2011: 18). In addition to this hostility, material obstacles to access and archiving meant that 'the *images* of black American culture remain unclaimed and in flux' (Jafa in da Costa 2016, emphasis added). Rather than performing the exaggerated 'black sound' that Nina Eidsheim called 'sonic blackness', the film offers examples of a rich sound heritage, positioned at strategic moments in relation to Chris's emotions (for more on the songs, see Ryan-Bryant 2020). In addition, through the zombies' 'white voices', the film makes sonic *whiteness* hear-able. Racialised voice-performance as a form of sonic 'passing' is a dominant motif in recent black film, for instance, in *Sorry to Bother You* (Boots Riley, 2018) or *BlacKkKlansmen* (Spike Lee, 2018). This *performance* of racial voices draws out a non-essentialising politics on the difference between epidermal racial alignment and culturally rooted 'deep' alignment, between inhabiting a body and putting one on for show, and therefore calls it out as a cultural construction. Voices might be *of* the body, but they are shaped by culture. Although the voice in general is too changeable to be a stable determinant of identity, in US culture, 'sonic phenomena and aural stereotypes . . . can function without their correlating visual signifiers and often stand in for them' (Stoever 2016: 11).

Endings

Rather than Clover's archetype of the Final Girl, we have here a 'Final Boy': Chris not only survives but slays the monsters – and the audience participates in, even longs for this cathartic release. This ending inverts the stereotypical negative image of black male bodies as inherently dangerous or bestial or its attendant taboo of showing a black man justifiably aggressive in self-defence (Yaquinto 2008: 6). Chris manages to escape the house by closing his ears with cotton stuffing peeled out of his leather seat's arms, which he had scratched open in his anguish. Through this symbolic reversal of past bondage and slave labour (cotton-picking), he not only reclaims his body but also 'historical consciousness . . . [the] political, psychological, experiential . . . reality of the black experience' (Brody 2017); here, before his counterattack, he finally knows more than the audience.

Chris kills most of the family and then faces a final battle with his former girlfriend. Close-ups alternate between Rose's malevolent smile, and Chris's pained face, as he attempts to strangle her, ultimately unable to go through with it. We hear sirens, red and blue lighting is reflected on Chris's face, and his facial expression immediately changes, both we and him assume a police car off-screen. A shot from behind Chris tilts up to show the lights on the car. A long shot shows the scene from the point of view of the driver, in what would correspond to the racist visual imaginary: a dark-skinned black male kneeling over a white female, both covered in blood, shiny on the woman's white clothes, corpses scattered around them. In a medium close up, Rose stretches out her arm, immediately back in character, feebly squeaking 'Help . . .'. A medium close-up shows Chris as he gets up and raises his hands, the resigned look on Chris's face illuminated by the rotating beacon lights mounted on the police car: he knows, we know, how the scene looks. What we expect is that Chris will be arrested, perhaps killed on the spot, perhaps imprisoned for life. This moment brings the film into the non-diegetic reality of police violence and vulnerability of black life.

In the original ending, a paratext widely available online, Chris *does* kill Rose and it *is* the police who arrive. We find Chris in orange prison jumpsuits, talking to Rod over prison intercom. 'It doesn't matter,' he says, 'what matters is that I stopped them.'[7] Yet in the released ending, too, the weight of unseen reality – the deaths of many African-American men at the hands of police, the institutionalised system of mass incarceration and its devastating effects on black communities – bears down on the screen. The shot lasts long enough for the audience to be horrified at this shattering of disbelief. And then the film releases us into a happier ending. We see a close-up of the word 'Airport' on the car door, which opens to reveal TSA agent Rod coming to save Chris. Black friendship and community, rather than the police or romantic love, provide the remedy and sanctuary for self-assured black identity 'that is informed by race but not crushed under the weight of racism' (Fuentes Morgan 2020: 123). And yet, even in the released, arguably happier ending, the moment remained of reality piercing through serves as final puncture to any complacent disengagement of its movie audiences, the wish to be relieved of any moral demand or ethical need for intervention, or what Stanley Cavell referred to as the 'burden of acting' (in Choi/Frey 2014: 4). This is what makes *Get Out* an example of 'social horror' or a 'documentary,' as Peele provocatively tweeted after the 2017 Golden Globes nominations.

In her reading of the film as *horror vérité*, Alison Landsberg suggests that *Get Out* provides a truthful horror which 'operates on the logic of revelation, enabled by technologies of the visual' (Landsberg 2017: 630). Yet rather than a straightforward reveal, the film in fact *questions* to what extent different media technologies reveal the world to us fully. Photography brings out the truth when Chris's cell phone flash activates the African-American hosts; and photographic evidence of Rose's exploits guides Chris – and the audience – towards uncovering the Armitage family's secrets. Both recall the use of camera phones and video recordings for African Americans as evidence for police violence. But the photographs offer only a flash, a glimpse of the real. Another mediation, television, is used to paralyse Chris.

Showing how different media technologies are historically and culturally shaped and embedded adds further layers of complexity to the spectrum of racial (in)visibilities on the movie screen. In questioning such medial frames as well as our habits of looking, *Get Out* contributes to the conversation on the ethics of seeing and insists on the whole body as medium of historical experience and cultural expression. By pointing to the limitations of what we can know *just* by seeing, the film highlights the limitations of a 'skin-deep' perception of racial identity, which implicates medial frames but also an epidermal-based identity politics and an iconography trapped in binary stereotypes. The film's carefully constructed alignment with the embodied experience of its main character and his journey makes an emancipatory and educational demand towards the viewers. Chris's last name, *Washington*, though never said in the film, conjures the history of America's founding fathers as slave-owners, the unrealised goal of freedom and self-determination for all its citizens. Chris needs to free himself of misperceptions, and the film suggests that the audiences, too, need to cleanse their perception, question their habits of looking and shed any facile belief in the transparent truth of the visual image, and in the narratives such visual discourses are telling: we, too, need to escape the Sunken Place.

NOTES

1. Black and white audiences are used as a heuristic, not to suggest these are homogenic and separate communities.
2. Written for a comedy revue show in 1939, *Run Rabbit Run* became famous during the Second World War, when a British comedy duo changed the lyrics to ridicule Hitler.
3. The film's title is derived from an Eddie Murphy sketch in which he parodies this convention by shouting *Get Out!* to any black character in a horror movie.
4. Filming began during the Obama era when the notion of a 'post-racial' society was widely shared.
5. Additionally, we can also consider these figures in relation to a contemporary media landscape which allows for various forms of racial ventriloquism, or digital blackface, in emojis, GIFs and video game avatars (Gray and Leonard 2018).
6. Rebecca Barnett reads the zombies as an expression of how vulnerable and compliant Chris's life already is (2019: 208). A different creative intervention on this

glamorising is offered by the constantly moving and role-slipping protagonist in Childish Gambino's viral music video *This is America*.
7. <https://www.youtube.com/watch?v=A3JS7_OcPWQ> (posted 24 January 2018; accessed 3 September 2021).

References

'bell hooks and Arthur Jafa discuss transgression in public spaces at the New School' (2014), <https://www.youtube.com/watch?v=fe-7ILSKSog>, 16 October (accessed 15 December 2019).

Anderson, Elijah (2015), 'The white space. sociology of race and ethnicity', *Sociology of Race and Ethnicity*, 1: 1, 10–21.

Barnett, Rebecca (2019), 'On *Get Out* and the problem of racialized aliveness', *Studies in Gender and Sexuality*, 20: 3, 204–8.

Bogle, Donald (2016), *Toms, Coons, Mulattoes, Mammies, and Bucks: An Interpretive History of Blacks in American Films*, New York: Bloomsbury Academic.

Bonilla-Silva, Eduardo (2003), *Racism without Racists. Color-Blind Racism and the Persistence of Racial Inequality in the United States*, Lanham, MA: Rowman and Littlefield.

Brody, Richard (2017), '"Get Out": Jordan Peele's radical cinematic vision of the world through a black man's eyes', 2 March, <https://www.newyorker.com/culture/richard-brody/get-out-jordan-peeles-radical-cinematic-vision-of-the-world-through-black-eyes> (accessed 2 March 2020).

Choi, Jinhee and Mattias Frey (2014), 'Introduction', in Jinhee Choi and Mattias Frey (eds), *Cine-Ethics: Ethical Dimensions of Film Theory, Practice and Spectatorship*, New York/Oxford: Routledge, pp. 1–14.

Clover, Carol J. (1992), *Men, Women, and Chain Saws, Gender in the Modern Horror Film*, Princeton/Oxford: Princeton University Press.

da Costa, Cassie (2016), 'The Profound Power of the New Solange Videos', 24 October, <https://www.newyorker.com/culture/culture-desk/the-profound-power-of-the-new-solange-videos > (last accessed 11 January 2023).

Du Bois, W. E. B. [1940] (2007), *Dusk of Dawn*, edited by Henry Louis, Jr. Gates, Oxford: Oxford University Press.

Dyer, Richard (1988), 'White', *Screen*, 29: 4, 44–64.

Fleetwood, Nicole R. (2011), *Troubling Vision: Performance, Visuality, and Blackness*, Chicago: University of Chicago Press.

Gates, Racquel (2017), 'The last shall be first. Aesthetics and politics in black film and media', *Film Quarterly*, 71: 2, 38–45.

Gillespie, Michael Boyce (2016), *Film Blackness: American Cinema and the Idea of Black Film*, Durham, NC: Duke University Press.

Gray, Kishonna L. and David J. Leonard (eds) (2018), *Woke Gaming. Digital Challenges to Oppression and Social Injustice*, Seattle: University of Washington Press, pp. 231–51.

Guerrero, Ed (1993a), 'The black image in protective custody. Hollywood's biracial buddy films of the eighties', in Manthia Diawara (ed.), *Black American Cinema*, New York: Routledge.

Guerrero, Ed (1993b), 'The rise and fall of blaxploitation', in *Framing Blackness. The African American Image in Film*, Philadelphia: Temple University Press, pp. 69–111.

Haraway, Donna (Autumn 1988), 'Situated knowledges: the science question in feminism and the privilege of partial perspective', *Feminist Studies*, 14: 3, 575–99.

Harris, Keith (2012), 'The burden of the beautiful beast,' in Mia Mask (ed.), *Contemporary Black American Cinema. Race, Gender and Sexuality at the Movies*, London: Routledge, pp. 40–55.

Holmlund, Chris (2016), 'Mutual muses in American independent film: Catherine Keener and Nicole Holofcener, Michelle Williams and Kelly Reichardt', in Linda Badley, Claire Perkins and Michele Schreiber (eds), *Indie Reframed: Women's Filmmaking and Contemporary American Independent Cinema*, Edinburgh: Edinburgh University Press, pp. 257–75.

hooks, bell (2014), *Black Looks: Race and Representation*, New York; Oxfordshire: Taylor and Francis Group.

Landsberg, Alison (2017), 'Horror vérité: politics and history in Jordan Peele's *Get Out*', *Continuum*, 32: 5, 629–42.

Morgan, Danielle Fuentes (2020), 'How long has this been goin' on, this thang?': centering race in the twenty-first century,' in *Laughing to Keep from Dying : African American Satire in the Twenty-First Century*, Champaign, IL: University of Illinois Press, pp. 123–50.

Patton, Elizabeth A. (2019), '*Get Out* and the legacy of sundown suburbs in post-racial America', *New Review of Film and Television Studies*, 17: 3, 349–63.

Ryan-Bryant, Jennifer (2020), 'The cinematic rhetorics of lynching in Jordan Peele's Get Out', *Journal of Popular Culture*, 53: 1, 92–110.

Sinnerbrink, Robert (2011), *New Philosophies of Film: Thinking Images*, London and New York: Continuum.

Smith, Zadie (2017), 'Who owns black pain', *Harpers Magazine*, 24 June, <https://harpers.org/archive/2017/07/getting-in-and-out> (accessed 26 October 2019).

Snead, James (1994), *White Screens/Black Images: Hollywood from the Dark Side*, London and New York: Routledge.

Spigel, Lynn (1992), *Make Room for TV: Television and the Family Ideal in Postwar America*, Chicago: University of Chicago Press.

Stoever, J. (2016), *The Sonic Color Line: Race and the Cultural Politics of Listening*, New York: NYU Press.

Warner, Kristen J. (2017), 'In the time of plastic representation', *Film Quarterly*, 71: 2, 32–7.

Williams, Linda (1991), 'Film bodies: gender, genre, and excess', *Film Quarterly*, 44: 4, 2–13.

Yancy, George (2013), '"Now, imagine she's white": the gift of the black gaze and the reinscription of whiteness as normative in *A Time to Kill*', in Mary K. Bloodsworth-Lugo and Dan Flory (eds), *Race, Philosophy, and Film*, New York: Routledge, pp. 134–48.

Yaquinto, Marilyn (2008), 'Denzel Washington: a study in black and blue', *Black Camera*, 22: 1/23: 2, 3–23.

Zinoman, Jason (2017), 'Jordan Peele on a truly terrifying monster: racism', *New York Times*, 16 February, <https://www.nytimes.com/2017/02/16/movies/jordan-peele-interview-get-out.html> (accessed 2 March 2020).

11. DON'T LOOK AWAY: PRODUCTION-ASSEMBLAGES OF RAPE CULTURE IN MIDI Z'S *NINA WU*

Jiaying Sim

This chapter examines cinema's potential to ethically regard sexual and gendered violence and film aesthetics' capacity to screen rape culture without subjecting women to essentialised visual modes of subjugation, or similar sexual violence, in the context of Asia's media and film industries. It explores *Nina Wu* (2019), a psychological thriller about an aspiring Taiwanese young actress, Nina Wu, who moves to Taipei from her rural hometown. After juggling insignificant media odd jobs for eight years, Nina finally gets an opportunity to audition for a lead role in a 1960s spy romance thriller, *Spy Romance*. To her dismay, Nina learns that this role requires her to get naked in a risqué sex scene. Whilst she lands the part, the audience eventually learns that the film's executive producer, Fat Cat, drugged and raped Nina during her audition. A film about making a film, *Nina Wu* interrogates the circumstantial contexts, psychological aftermaths and other consequences that enable sexual and gendered violence against women within Taiwan's media and film industry. Initially the chapter considers *Nina Wu* in relation to the #MeToo movement and the specificities of its Taiwanese context, establishing in the process how the film's engagement with rape culture relates to ongoing debates concerning cinema, ethics, the gaze and affect. For the remainder of the chapter the film is analysed in terms of its aesthetic features (especially its shot composition, *mise-en-scène* and cinematography, self-reflexive storytelling, and the tracking shot), drawing out thereby both *Nina Wu*'s illumination of how rape culture is enabled in the Taiwanese film and media industry and as a consequence, the insights this particular film offers concerning the correlation between screen ethics and cinematic affect.

'This is not a #MeToo film'

At the 2019 Singapore International Film Festival, Midi Z introduced *Nina Wu* to the audience, reminding them not to think of the film as part of the #MeToo movement that enabled female survivors of sexual violence within Hollywood film industry to speak out against their male perpetrators and have their stories heard. When survivors of sexual violence and domestic abuse began using social media to testify and voice their allegations of sex crimes, it represented a shift for feminism in the digital age where women's voices were finally heard and taken seriously through the potentials offered by online platforms.[1] The #MeToo movement is thus characterised by its challenge against mainstream media that often celebrate stories of men, their morality and dominance in culture, instead of exposing patriarchal violence and injustices (Boyle 2019: 21).

While the success of #MeToo has emphasised victim-survivors' bravery in calling out sexual crimes, there may be a tendency to neglect the fact that besides physical injuries, victim-survivors of the sex crimes also carry scars from sexual assault that are invisible (Bowdler 2021: 10). Furthermore, the emancipatory power depends on a culture of open, direct communication which is attributed to one's ability to 'narrate' and 'speak out' against traumatic sexual abuse. The act of speaking out may prioritise a notable event of sexual trauma that can be represented or identified. As such, trauma theorists like Gabriele Schwab also question one's 'ability to write or express what resists representation', especially when sexual abuse may be inscribed in misogyny, sexism, and patriarchy that have become normalised by societies (2006: 102). If *Nina Wu* is, as Midi Z asserts, not a #MeToo film, it could be due to the lack of a triumphant moment of empowerment where women speak up against their abusers: the film ends with no sign of Nina reporting or speaking of the rape against her. However, Midi Z's disclaimer does not relieve the film from ethically engaging with the complex topic of rape culture in the Taiwanese film and media industry. Midi Z clarifies in another interview with *Variety* that '[*Nina Wu*] is not about real people who are going to feel uncomfortable. But it is timely. The position of female filmmakers in Asia, Japan and Korea is still so troublesome' (Frater 2019). The reference to time here coincides with #TimesUp, where there is urgency today to hold persons publicly accountable for past sexual misconduct, even if those actions might have been commonly excused or ignored before as the way things are (Dempsey 2021). I address the context-specificity of rethinking rape culture in Asia further below. More than ever, regardless of region, it has become imperative to question what is no longer acceptable within the discourse of sexual consent, coercion and exploitation. Similarly, Wu Ke-xi (screenwriter and lead actress) shares that she had simply drawn from her own personal experiences as a young and vulnerable actress working her way through the cinema industry rather than to allude to actual events or persons through fiction.

Beyond Hollywood and outside Anglo-American contexts, *Nina Wu* problematises rape culture as a symptom of deep-seated misogynist and patriarchal structures of power that protect perpetrators within the Taiwanese film industry. In *Media Ethics: Cases and Moral Reasoning*, Clifford Christians and co-authors argue that the #MeToo movement expresses itself differently in socially conservative cultures within Asia, especially because social barriers and gender inequality make it difficult for women to speak up about sexual violation and assault (2020: 80). As such, #MeToo or #TimesUp in Asia may manifest differently, where empowering individual women to speak out about specific incidents of sexual harassment and assault is insufficient (i.e. to think beyond the dichotomy of perpetrator/victim as the construct of rape culture). Rather, it is timely that dynamic structures of violence and collusion, which perpetuate rape culture in the specific contexts of Taiwanese media industry, are made visible and challenged as status quo.

As Alexandra Fanghanel ascertains in *Disrupting Rape Culture*, there is an 'interplay between culture – rape culture – as a vernacular category (as something that just *is*), and rape culture as an analytical category (how we come to understand the world)' (2019: 9). Normalised acts of sexual exploitation from catcalling to victim blaming for sexual abuse constitute the wide spectrum of social experiences and violence that define rape culture, which requires unpacking and reconsideration (Fanghanel 2019: 8). It follows that definitions of rape culture should be reassessed, rather than taken for granted, so as to uncover, examine, and problematise the systemic structures that produce sexual violence and exploitation. This is where a specific ethical consideration arises. The fair treatment of women and sexualised violence on screen has been a concern for film ethics since Lisa Downing and Libby Saxton observed more than a decade ago that there was a considerable lack of scholarship surrounding an 'ethical gaze theory' that could account for audience relationship to images on screen (2009: 2). More recently, the increased interest in film ethics has largely coincided with the affective turn in theories of film spectatorship, where ethical potentials of film encounters unfold through audiences' sensorial perceptions (e.g. Choi and Frey 2014; Sinnerbrink 2015; Sinnerbrink and Trahair 2016). Particularly, Sinnerbrink contends that the cinematic medium parallels an ethical experience when we consider 'film-spectator-context' holistically, 'linking style and content, creation and reception, context and interpretation in ways that enable us to explore cinema's ethical potential to enhance and extend what we understand by ethical inquiry' (2006: 13–14). In other words, rather than to focus primarily on the representation of morally coded images on screen, film as ethics also considers how the cinematic medium expresses and evokes ethical experiences through cinema's formal aesthetics, as well as the process of meaning-making that reflects ethical thinking. Insofar as *Nina Wu* portrays morally coded images and regards themes of sexual violence on screen, the film also offers insights to the correlation between screen ethics and cinematic affects that are evoked through specificities surrounding pre-production, production, reception and other material conditions related to filmmaking and how film produces meaning.

Particularly, I attend to *Nina Wu*'s metacinematic reflexivity and film aesthetics that produce cinematically mediated affects of rape culture; a feminist mode of thinking anew about the production of rape culture through film (as) ethics. This type of attention requires a close reading of the formal aspects of cinema, which compels one to 'look both hard and askance at the norm' (Freeman 2010: xvi). As such, this chapter begins by restating that the question is less about what rape culture looks like in the Taiwanese film and media industry, as this inquiry presupposes a predetermined and normalised definition of rape culture. Instead, it begins by asking how, why and when rape culture is produced. Specifically, given the different degrees of sexual coercion, exploitation and abuse that Nina experienced, what kinds of assemblage and affects would have to be in place to produce rape culture within the context of Taiwanese media industry? In order to consider the material specificities of assemblages, I attend to *Nina Wu*'s self-reflexive, non-linear and aesthetic mode of cinematic storytelling that regards the complexity of rape culture as an amalgamation of sexual coercion, exploitation and violence by reassembling different stages of behind-the-scenes filmmaking processes on screen.

The Limits of Positive Affects: Female Empowerment Through Social Media

Even though *Nina Wu* is set within the context of Taiwan's movie industry, the film also grapples with the notion that the relationship between social media and digital culture's role in enabling sexual objectification and exploitation is a complex one. Prior to Nina's big break as a movie actress, her everyday life includes her participation on social media platforms where she streams content to engage and entertain her followers. While Nina may appear to commodify and co-opt her femininity into the visual digital economy that objectifies her, the use of film editing reframes the female body as an active producer of empowered subjectivities within the specificity of the Taiwanese entertainment media industry. Specifically, shot composition and film editing destabilise the primary significance of visuality in digital media engagement by foregrounding Nina's gestures and internet persona, which produce female subjectivities that are multiple, decentered and empowered. For example, a few minutes into the opening of the film, the audience observes Nina as she prepares a table of dumplings made from scratch in her cramped and dark old Taipei apartment. Listlessly, she sits alone in her living room eating the dumplings before walking to her neon red-lit room to switch off her phone alarm. Like clockwork, Nina puts on a corseted outfit, applies babydoll makeup style (see Figure 11.1), and begins live streaming from her phone. Simpering down at the front-facing camera of her phone, Nina greets her online fans with cutesy peace and heart signs before daintily taking a bite of her handmade dumplings (see Figure 11.2). In this juxtaposition it is clear that, whilst digital mediation evokes positive affects of female subjectivities, material and social constraints still systematically constitute parts of Nina's embodied lived experiences. Emphasising this, *Nina Wu* illuminates a degree of complexity behind Nina's online persona and female agency by framing her offline lived conditions in contrast with her virtual presence to cinematically visualise the different layers of mediation.

The complexities at stake in this aesthetic play with image and reality through shot composition and editing, in the Taiwanese context, can benefit from further

Figure 11.1   Nina putting on make-up before livestreaming.

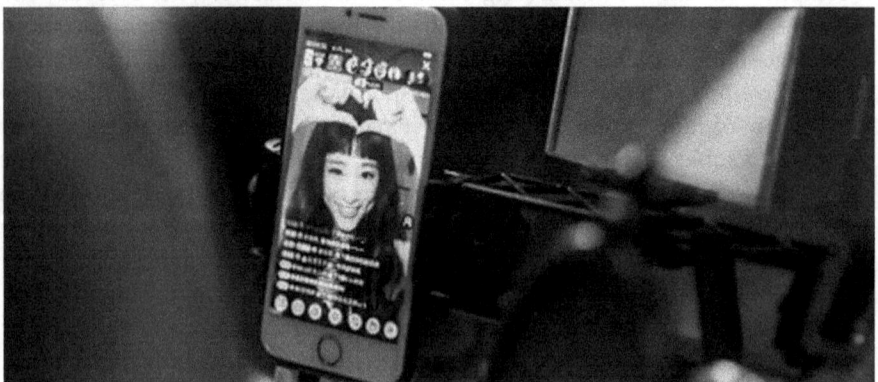

Figure 11.2   Nina in the midst of her livestream session.

unpacking. Nina is an internet personality (*wanghong*) who has gained a substantial number of followers over the years. Later in the film, she is also recognised by one of her spa treatment specialists, who happened to watch her live streams too. In Taiwan, internet celebrities are known as *wanghongs* who achieve fame online for different reasons (Guan 2020). Some perform make-up tutorials for their fans, others share other everyday routines in their live streams. Internet personalities may earn substantial income from advertisements, endorsements, number of views and other internet modes of payment unique to the digital platforms. Specifically, Nina is famous for consuming steamed dumplings on screen as her fans watch. Her internet persona also performs cuteness by expressing a sense of innocence, emphasising baby-like expressions when interacting with her online audience.

Hsin-I Sydney Yueh notes in *Identity Politics of Popular Culture in Taiwan: A Sajiao Generation* (2016) that ideal femininity in Taiwanese popular culture encourages 'young female public figures [to] play cute and imitate children's behaviour' (Yueh 2016, 17). Furthermore, a crucial criterion related to performing the ideal female image is the ability to *sajiao*, which is the expression of cuteness through speech, gestures, physical appearances and disposition (Yueh 2016: 43). *Sajiao* is also understood as a mode of feminine persuasion that serves multiple functions from 'accomplish[ing] communication goals, whether they aim to greet someone, to negotiate or to apologise' or even to function as 'a woman's weapon to manipulate a man in a heterosexual relationship' (Yueh 2016: 81). Through the use of her childish yet querulous tone of voice and persuasive gestures, the effective use of *sajiao* can be seen when Nina manages with little trouble to persuade her fan, '007', to purchase and send her 100 love rockets icon as an expression of his affection for her; Yueh rightly asserts that 'cuteness is a business', but it is a decentralised one that is enabled through social media (Yueh 2016: 102). Insofar as Nina becomes a participatory agent in producing cuteness through the evocation of feminine desire, the model of a centralised and corporate way of commodifying the female body is also subsequently challenged and destabilised.

In this scene, the female image on screen barely functions as a passive object 'to-be-looked-at' as seminally theorised by Laura Mulvey (1975) but takes the form of an active body that produces affective power through *sajiao* performativity. As she playfully forms heart signals with her hands, her online fans are enthusiastically responding to her by clicking on their phones to send out virtual signs of affection to her (made possible only by their tactile response to her). Nina's gestures and physical presence are felt on-screen by her fans through 'haptic visuality' (Marks 2000: xi). Laura Marks explains this manner of regarding a film as skin in *Touch: Sensuous Theory and Multisensory Media* (2002). For Marks, the audience 'perceiv[es the image on screen] with all the senses . . . thinking with [one's] skin, or giving much significance to the physical presence of an other as to the mental operations of symbolization'

(Marks 2002: 18). The animated icons of hearts and love rockets with their accompanied sound effects also emphasise a permeable and sensuous connection between the offline and online spaces that may otherwise separate Nina from her fans, thus bridging their inherent distance. The mobile screen's materiality thus evokes a multisensory mode of address that goes beyond decoding audiovisual cues. Following Marks, Jennifer Barker explores the tactility of cinematic experiences in *The Tactile Eye* (2008), which opens up the audience-screen dichotomy into an assemblage of multiple embodied encounters. Thus, the ability to *sajiao* and engage in cute-production works effectively as 'the tactic of the weak' by destabilising dominant heteronormative gendered roles that celebrate feminine submissiveness in relation to masculine obligation to provide and give (Yueh 2016: 168). Digital images are thus not passively consumed but they rely on Jonathan Beller's theorisation of the attention economy that 'latches onto a nascent aspect of the commodity in circulation – the productive potential of its fetish character – and circulates it through the sensorium with a new intensity: the objects speak' (2006: 21). Here, Nina's image on screen is fetishised through the affective persona on screen that is articulate and active in capturing and perpetuating the desires of her fans. Nina's embodied online presence hence subverts top-down modes of female commodification within consumerist-driven media industries when she reclaims women's position as producer-consumer of her own femininity.

Nina's livestream session is briefly interrupted by a call from her manager, Marco, who tells her that he has received a call for an audition that could be the big break her acting career needs. Assuming her cute persona as she returns momentarily to her livestream, she waves goodbye to her fans, thus ending the session abruptly as she wishes. Even while Nina engages with online social media activities, her body is not limited to the digital space but may engage with other bodies in the material world. As Elizabeth Grosz asserts in *Volatile Bodies: Toward A Corporeal Feminism* (1994), '[t]he limits or borders of the body image are not fixed by nature or confined to the anatomical "container", the skin' (Grosz 1994: 70). Extending Grosz's argument, we see that Nina's body is not constrained by a certain fixed corporeality (i.e. the physical mobile screen itself, or her physical body before the screen) but includes immaterial aspects (i.e. the sensuous affectivity of media engagement and experiences as mediated through the screen) that constitute affective experiences insofar as they produce the bodies involved in the complex processes of meaning-making. The quick shifts in Nina's subjectivities reposition her in relation to location and place – from being at home, to livestreaming, and back in her room by herself – evoke dynamic and fluid trans-sensorial cinematic encounters where the audience reorientate themselves alongside Nina's embodied becomings on screen. This cinematic mode of address keeps the audience abreast with the (dis)placements that Nina faces, and the multiple spatialities of which Nina has to navigate and make sense.

Notably, the film does not idealise social media as a site for female empowerment, where women escape capitalist subjugation as passive, sexualised objects of desire. The film uncovers Nina's choice to leave her livestream as ultimately illusory, and so should not be confused with neoliberal ideals of individual agency. Despite having the autonomy to exercise control over her own femininity, Nina's role as an online personality is an interim position she takes up while waiting for her big cinematic break. Nina is also subjected to the market demands of the cinematic industry as she shuffles between both virtual and cinematic industries of commodification. As Rosalind Gill explains through the concept of 'feminist sensibility', 'today's media culture has a distinctive postfeminist sensibility organised around notions of choice, empowerment, self-surveillance, and sexual difference, and articulated in an ironic and knowing register in which feminism is simultaneously taken for granted and repudiated' (Gill 2007: 271). Gill emphasises the importance of paying attention to and acknowledging other ways in which individuals are 'subject to pressures, constraints or influence from outside themselves' (Gill and Scharff 2011: 7). These constraints, pressures, or influences may be understood as most evident in the way Nina's enlivened online persona juxtaposes her dazed and disconnected disposition as she attends to her everyday activities. Subtle changes in her expressions reveal Nina's own alienation from her affective and sensual labour. In other words, the virtual space, while deterritorialised, is not a sustainable assemblage of positive affects as Nina's capacity to enter into relations of empowerment is not translated into her everyday life beyond a limited time online. As seen, the film presents a nuanced mode of rethinking social media's role in mediating emancipation and entrapment of female subjectivities within a Taiwanese culture of female commodification and sexual objectification.

Mise-en-scène and Cinematography: 'Your feeling is most important'

Analysis of the *mise-en-scène* and cinematography further illustrates how *Nina Wu* performatively disorientates the audience's encounter, drawing attention to problematic and coercive power dynamics between Nina and her managing agent, Marco. In an encounter early in the film, Nina meets with Marco in a restaurant after hours to discuss her initial impressions of *Spy Romance*'s script, which involves a nude scene where the lead actress is sexually violated by two men on screen. Importantly, the directions of the scene describe the lead actress as first resisting the sexual violence only to give in to the pleasure of the encounter. As Nina expresses her apprehension and discomfort towards filming such a problematic scene, in the otherwise empty restaurant the camera tracks in slowly from a long focal shot. Instead of adopting a clear static framing of the scene, the slow movement of the camera creates an unsettling and eerie establishing shot of the restaurant after hours. Marco asks Nina if she has had any other significant roles besides being in small commercials and taking on side gigs. Nina shakes her head and says no. With the camera closing in on Nina's earnest and sincere look, we hear Marco offscreen in assured and measured tones: 'If you don't feel like acting, we will reject the role. If you have even the slightest discomfort in your heart, we will not even audition for the role. How you feel is most important.'

Appearing significantly worried but resolute, Nina seeks to find solutions to alleviate her discomfort from having to perform those nude scenes. Nina asks, 'Can I ask how the director will film this? Even though the script states front nudity.' Off screen, Marco replies, 'Of course you can.'

This response gives Nina a small glimmer of hope as she breaks into a tiny smile and sits up eagerly.

Marco continues: 'Let us be clear here. There are now many people competing for this role, which is why at this point if you have any hesitation or unwillingness, you might as well not go for the audition at all.'

The camera cuts to a medium closeup of Marco and Nina's side profiles while they face each other in conversation. A lampshade and two cups of untouched coffee sit between the two of them. The scene is pregnant with a palpable sense of unease and tension. To which, Marco chimes:

> Of course you can, but let us be clear here, is the act of taking off clothes for the sake of it, or is it for the needs of the scene? All the actresses in Hollywood who you often mention take on these types of roles for two reasons – one, for the sake of a good role; another, for good money. This time is indeed a good role.

Marco, who is positioned off-centre in a medium closeup, looks away from Nina and smokes a cigarette leisurely before lamenting: 'What's more, I don't believe any Hollywood professional actors would reject a good role because of a *little* exposure of their flesh. Still, I respect your decision. The decision lies in your hands.' (See Figure 11.3.)

The skewed framing of Marco, coupled with his words that should be comforting and supportive but do little to instil any sense of confidence, create a sense of dissonance. This incongruity forces the audience to doubt Marco's sincerity because the jarring visual cues disrupt any sense of clarity, drawing one's attention to the double meanings implied in his communication instead. Whether it is the ornate but dated wallpaper and carpeting, or the elaborate but gaudy lampshades on each dining table that characterise the antiquated choice of decor in the restaurant, the *mise-en-scène* of the film alerts the audience to the anachronism that is embodied by the restaurant, and by extension, Marco.

Film aesthetics function as a transferred epithet that comments on the underlying coercion that defines the subtle but prevailing modes of (sexual) pressure

Figure 11.3   Marco convinces Nina to take the role.

Figure 11.4   Silhouette of a lizard writhing under the heat of a lamp.

and lack of consent in the media industry. First, Marco's blasé attitude towards Nina's discomfort with frontal nudity on screen is underscored through the similarly jarring old-fashioned *mise-en-scène*. The audience is made to contemplate through visual storytelling that it is time for such irresponsible coercion and apathy to end.

Second, lip service and words are not enough in times of providing support to female actresses who might feel vulnerable when it comes to making decisions about a potential role they have to take. The film also suggests that it is the agent's responsibility to properly represent and protect the talents they manage. Instead, Marco's apathy toward Nina's reticence in taking on the role leaves her alienated. Even though Marco claims to support Nina's decision, he invalidates her concerns by implying that choosing not to take on the role would mean that Nina is unprofessional.

As the camera pans to Nina's face from a tilted low angle where she looks at Marco with forlorn eyes. The lampshade is off-focus and occupies the foreground of the shot. The camera zooms in on Nina as the audience hears a soft sizzle while Marco continues smoking. The camera cuts to a close-up of the lampshade with a silhouette of a lizard on its underside and zooms in as the lizard writhes and appears to struggle and turn a luminous red under the immense heat of the lamp. With the threat of losing a significant role in play, Nina's precarious position in this moment is embodied by the lizard being burnt alive under intense danger. Her experience is thus rendered affectively through the sound of the sizzle and the heat apparent in the redness of the lizard, which acts as a transferred epithet for Nina's difficult ethical position. The ethical dimension of Nina and Marco's conversation is startling, as the audience experiences the affects of coercion that are felt beneath the surface. The unspoken coercion she faces may be attributed to Marco's concern with Nina's profitability as a client rather than her personal well-being and protection. While Marco has technically uttered all the morally and politically acceptable lines that imply Nina has the agency to make her own career choice, the film aesthetics foreground Marco's hypocrisy to show how Nina is effectively coerced into taking on the role, regardless of her desires and reservations.

Self-reflexive Cinematic Storytelling: Real-Time Unfolding of Narrative Events

Besides Marco, Nina's interactions with the casting director for the *Spy Romance* proved futile even as she strove to speak up for herself and express her reservations and lack of consent in shooting the nude scene in the film. The importance of intimacy coordinators in filming cannot be overstated; they seek to create spaces that empower actors, create equitable work environments where 'intimate moments are created through discussion and collaboration' (Szlawieniec-Haw 2019: 15). Surprisingly, the crucial point of support here is not about giving actors the space to voice their opinions, rather it is best if 'actors are not required to speak about their experiences – in the workplace or outside it – but where they are able to if they want or need to, knowing that this material will be kept in confidence (Szlawieniec-Haw 2019: 19). Intimacy coordinators act as confidantes to actors who are required to perform sexual or romantic scenes, so that actors on set feel safe and comfortable. One of their key job scopes is to ensure that 'actors are continually consenting to all scenes of intimacy and that all scenes of intimacy are performed according to a previously agreed-to choreography. Such agreements are put into writing' (Gage 2021: 2). While screen industries outside Taipei, such as HBO, have made the employment of an intimacy coordinator compulsory, such safety practices are unheard of in the context of *Nina Wu* and the Taiwanese industry in which it is set (Sørensen 2021; Horeck 2021). Film editing creates a sense of continuity between three separate events that occurred at different times to evoke non-linear sense making, enabling the audience to question the lack of support and absence of intimacy coordinators when attending to difficult shoot scenes for actors on set.

The extended montage sequence begins with Nina standing in the middle of a spacious conference room. Seated in front of her is a female casting director smoking a cigarette while looking up at Nina with a look of annoyance. In response to the question of whether the nude scenes are necessary, the casting director answers in a measured and contemplative tone while smoking a cigarette:

> I really quite like your acting, and I have seen your short films. Cinematic performance is all about being natural. When you're showering, do you think about whether you will have to take off clothes? When you're going to make love, do you think about whether you'll be naked? Being natural is most important. My camera has started rolling. Do you want to say your lines?

Just like that, the casting director shuts down any budding discussion and Nina is not given any say in how a scene might be shot. At this moment, Nina snaps into character and recites her lines with feeling as tears well up in her eyes:

> I really can't take it anymore. Not only do they want to destroy my body, they want to destroy my heart too. Take me away. Anywhere will do. Only when I am with you will I have freedom.

Rather than a sense of collaborative filmmaking between casting director and actor, Nina is simply required to mechanically regurgitate lines on cue. This dialogue will also be reprised throughout the film as a refrain, each time taking on a different meaning when Nina expresses the words in different scenarios. The shot cuts away to Nina in her bathroom at home, with a towel wrapped around her, where she rehearses her lines. Determined and disciplined, Nina stares directly into the mirror and emotes her lines with a sense of suffering. The female casting director justifies the need for nude scenes as a way of ensuring scenes are as natural as they can be. However, by juxtaposing that scene with Wu Ke-Xi in the shower without being nude, Midi Z emphasises how it is possible not to avoid the visual pleasure which may be afforded through the spectacle of the female body on screen. The question of need is also quickly problematised by cross-cutting scenes of Nina in the shower and her discussion in the conference room. Through which, the film's meta-reflexivity clarifies cinema's potential to produce natural scenes without compromising the comfort or safety of actors.

In another beat, Nina is back in the conference room, now wearing a red dress. This time, she is auditioning in front of the male actor, executive producer, director, casting director and the director of photography. With more emotions than before, she delivers the same lines to perfection. The camera pans across the casting committee, stopping at the executive director who looks at Nina with awe, before pausing at the director. While he looked impressed, a definitive cross was quickly drawn over Nina's application in red marker. Nina does not make the cut. In the next scene when it is dark outside, Nina walks along an empty walkway in the same red dress, dishevelled, demoralised, crying and hopeless. She crosses the zebra crossing haphazardly and abruptly lies down in the middle of the road. Suddenly, an offscreen voice shouts, 'Cut!'. The director thanks the production crew for their hard work and calls it a day, leaving Nina where she is. While the audience previously assumes that Nina is devastated after failing to make the audition, the continuity editing ultimately reveals that filming for *Spy Romance* has already begun, and Nina has been cast as the female lead. Thus the film's self-reflexivity astutely reveals the power structures in place that may have resulted in the way Nina had been treated, where decision-making is unequally distributed within the hierarchy of filmmakers. In the case of *Spy Romance*, executive producers have more say than directors in casting an actor because of the money they have invested in the production. In this metanarrative, *Nina Wu* draws attention to itself as a film about filmmaking, enabling the audience to challenge the importance of sequential and linear storytelling.

This mode of cinematic storytelling also ensures that the audience is never able to cast a fixed moral judgment when it comes to Nina's predicament and circumstances because of the lack of complete information. As the audience constantly seeks to make sense of the filmic experience, we too regard the events as they unfold in real time. This uncertainty positions the audience not as a disembodied and omniscient viewer who observes from a distance, but a participatory body that has become directly involved in the real-time experience of what happens to Nina. As mentioned, it is only in the final moments of the film that a crucial piece of information is revealed to the audience: Nina was sexually assaulted by the film's executive producer during her audition. I will address this sexual assault in detail in the closing section of this essay. However, in one of the press media interviews later in the film, a reporter asks if Nina was in a relationship with the executive producer because of circulating rumours. This non-linear and somewhat disorienting mode of cinematic storytelling allows the audience to infer that Nina, despite not being favoured by both director and casting director, eventually got the lead role as an unspoken recompense for her being raped. The retrospective pieces of information are also vital as they account for the hostility Nina faced throughout the filming process of *Spy Romance*.

Interestingly, this method of unfolding new information about Nina's circumstances alerts the audience to the ways in which rape culture entails the social, cultural and political condoning and normalisation of violence against women, as well as the blame that is placed onto women (and other victim-survivors) when violence is perpetrated against them (Buchwald et al. 2005; Fileborn and Loney-Howes, 2019). The assumption that Nina got the role because she had willingly slept with the executive producer to get the lead role becomes the unquestioned accusation that Nina carries with her throughout the film. In the end, the shocking revelation that Nina had been raped puts the audience in a position to bear witness not only to the act of sexual violence but other moments where she had been victim-blamed, coerced and mistreated. As with the aforementioned false continuity created by the editing, here again there is an experience of non-linear sense making involved, as the film is recast in retrospect after the revelation of the rape. Eventually, the use of editing discloses the painful reality that Nina was dismissed, invalidated and ignored at multiple stages of her filming experience, leaving her to deal with the aftermath of sexual assault on her own.

The Tracking Shot: Cyclical Repetitions of Abuse, 'I really can't take it anymore'

While the editing helps the audience to piece together Nina's harrowing experiences narratively, the film's form otherwise ensures that audience does not disengage or disconnect from the conversation or affects of rape culture. In particular, the use of long tracking shots compels and forces the audience not to look away and thus to participate in the discourse. In an eight-minute-long take, the shot begins with an unsteady camera tracking toward Nina Wu (Wu Ke-Xi), who stands still in the middle of a corridor with her back facing the camera and her right hand clutching a knife. The camera mimics a first person point of view perspective walking toward Wu, who is clad in a red structured box-shoulder dress with leg-o'-mutton sleeves. The set is decorated with crimson red curtains, a red carpet running down the corridor, while lanterns with red tassels and oriental armchairs sit alongside the walls of the corridor. In terms of film form and style, cinema easily achieves aesthetic design and curation without exploiting the female body. The female body, instead of being static, moves through the screen with autonomy. As the camera inches precariously toward Nina, she pivots anti-clockwise and confronts the audience with a knife pointed directly into the camera (see Figure 11.5). The camera tracks away cautiously as Wu threatens the knife at the camera and takes decisive steps forward. At this moment, the audience identifies with Nina's desperation while backing away. Here the scene encompasses the visual power of identification but the camera further embodies the physical movement of the one being threatened by Nina. At this point, the

Figure 11.5 Nina breaks the fourth wall and points a knife at the camera.

audience is unaware that the subject of frustration is Nina's on set love interest, her lover from the Japanese army. Nina stares resolutely and addresses the audience with increased emotions and frustrations, effectively implicating the audience as a bystander who does not lend a hand in this moment of distress. All the while the camera tracks through an open hall before Nina turns her back to the camera and rushes towards the spacious room.

From off-screen a man in uniform charges into the frame to appease Nina's emotions. He replies with lacklustre energy and conviction, 'I have no choice! We can't leave!' The response results in Nina pointing the knife to her own throat, leaving the man helpless and lost. Both of them continue moving through the set, exchanging the words 'I love you'. Nina's emotions and performance juxtapose to a rational, measured, flat platitude from the male lead, 'We can't. The world does not love us!' Nina makes a sudden run for it after stating that she has no choice but to avenge herself. The camera tracks through various different settings in the span of two minutes, moving between aesthetically curated turquoise blue-themed and red-accented set designs. The camera waits patiently as we get a long shot of the male lead and Nina Wu in a stand-down. Nina points her knife straight at the male lead from a distance.

The scene is interrupted by the director screaming and shouting at Nina, asking her to be more emotive. This instruction is confusing to the audience as Nina had been nothing short of emotive. On the contrary, the male lead's performance pales in comparison to hers. The director relentlessly confronts Nina, asking her to curse as he curses. She is shocked and stunned by that instruction until the director slaps her on the face. Supposedly to evoke deep emotions in Nina, he continues to abuse her verbally, calling her derogatory terms like 'slut' and 'bitch', inciting her to fight back and scream, 'you are a talentless director'. The director grabs Nina by her neck, causing her to suffocate as she stares with fear at him. Her male lead is equally shocked by this moment but does nothing but stand in

Figure 11.6   Director enacting physical and verbal abuse on Nina in order to get her to perform her lines to his satisfaction.

shocked silence (see Figure 11.6). Nina is now on the verge of tears, about to experience a meltdown before the director commands her to recite her lines to his satisfaction. The camera starts rolling and the director shouts 'Cut!' abruptly after he is satisfied with Nina's delivery. Nina is left on set, alienated once more.

This sequence emphasises the constructedness of film sets, as well as the unfair standards of filmmaking that are biased against women to the point where abuse is normalised and unquestioned. While there were camera persons and Nina's male lead on set, none of them did a thing to stop the director, but all stood silently watching the events unfold. The audience is left with more questions than clarity on the reasons for Nina's mistreatment and abuse. Yet, one thing remains clear, from auditioning to actual filming, Nina has had to endure different degrees of abuse. Furthermore, the male lead who accompanies Nina in this scene's silence can be seen as another way in which the film comments on the complexities of rape culture. Nina's screams and protests (even if it were part of method-acting as deliberately induced by the director) juxtapose the silence of her male lead who is complicit in the violence enacted upon Nina. By ensuring that the audience affectively experiences the abuse Nina faces on the set of *Spy Romance* without the option to look away, the audience is made to regard the importance of considering ethical modes of filmmaking that do not condone or remain silent in the face of abuse towards women on set.

Producing Rape Culture: 'Not only do they want to destroy my body, they want to destroy my heart too'

To summarise, the audience consistently experiences *Nina Wu* viscerally, before they are able to make sense of the events that happen in the film. This way, the audience is not given the chance to digest or connect the events in a linear or coherent fashion. Instead, the film increases the degree of intensity and cycles of abuse that Nina endures. To be clear, *Nina Wu* is by no means an easy film to watch. The act of bearing witness comes with continuous discomfort. In terms of identifying with the different degrees of abuse and sexual violence Nina has to endure, the film challenges the audience's ability to know what happened to Nina until the final moments of the film.

The final vignette of *Nina Wu* takes place in a hotel suite '1408'. Nina Wu (Wu Ke-Xi) is auditioning for the leading role in a 1960s spy thriller, and is welcomed at the door by the executive producer, a bespectacled middle-aged man who goes by the name of Fat Cat. He appears gentlemanly, professional and unassuming in a suit blazer as he invites Nina into his suite, exchanging pleasantries before politely telling her to wait as he finishes his dumplings for he has had a long day of auditions. Fat Cat switches on the camera that is propped up on a tripod, to record the session, before casually snacking on peanuts nonchalantly. Meanwhile, Nina is left standing in the middle of the room as she surveys this audition space tentatively. Her gaze finds a bottle of red wine and two wine glasses (one with freshly poured wine), Fat Cat's generous plate of dumplings, and two audition photographs of 'Candidate 3' spread on an adjacent glass table. All this while the subjective camera shifts between Nina's point of view before moving in and holding focus on a visibly nervous, and a medium close-up of an increasingly concerned and anxious, Nina in a continuous tracking shot.

Fat Cat urges with flat affect, 'Please, if you could try your audition lines', interrupting Nina as she tries to orientate herself in this foreign location. At the sound of the producer's voice, almost mechanically, she abruptly snaps into action, breaks into a wide warm smile, and abides obediently. 'Yes', she exclaims with feigned confidence as she closes her eyes for an extended moment to regain composure, takes deep mindful breaths, and conscientiously adjusts her micro-expressions before delivering the same set of lines to an offscreen Fat Cat. Nina's performance is imbued with a sense of long-suffering pain, lines delivered through quivering lips and helpless eyes, increasing in measured intensity as she pleads with her imagined audience for an escape. Nina signals the end of her audition by snapping out of her audition character as quickly and smoothly as she transitions into her role as she once again flashes her wide pageant smile. The juxtaposition is stark as her facial expression is void of joy or any visible feeling while she waits for Fat Cat's feedback. The camera pans left down to Fat Cat on his leather armchair who instead nonchalantly requests that Nina mimics an animal of her choice. Clarifying his next instructions, Fat Cat elaborates 'I mean, a performance or mimicry of an animal that you like, or even a pet that you own at home. Either way, it's all right. Please try.' He ends this inappropriate request with an earnest smile. While clearly confused, Nina gathers herself, her face focused with concentration as she crouches down on all fours, presenting herself as a dog.

A high-angle shot frames Nina as she readies herself for her performance. Her mimicry of a dog is realistic and impassioned, down to the micro-gestures such as tail-wagging and other animalesque movements across the floor. She prances around the floor like an excited puppy, inching closer to Fat Cat as she barks, growls and yaps enthusiastically. With each second Nina's performance grows in believability until she raises her right hand as an imagined paw to beg for Fat Cat's validation only to be interrupted yet again by Fat Cat who has at this point gotten up from his seat to offer her a glass of wine. Nina's face of disbelief and forlorn resignation is palpable as the wine glass is placed near her lips. He insists that Nina has been performing too rigidly, and wine helps one to express our inner emotions. Reluctantly, and left with no other real option, Nina winces as she finishes the wine, looking up again at Fat Cat with eager and sincere puppy eyes.

The next scene opens with a closeup of Nina lying unconscious, her left cheek pressed against the crimson red hotel room carpet. Her eyeliner and mascara have run, her lips slightly bruised and lipstick smudged; her hair no longer flawlessly styled. Her body rocks rhythmically and forcefully for a few moments as tears well up in the corner of her eyes. Nina eventually comes to with her eyes wide open, her forehead crinkled as we see her facial expressions shift from a state of shock, to disorientation, pain and finally fear. She attempts to look back at what is being done to her but she has been rendered completely defenceless. Her eyes well up with tears, her nostrils flare, and the camera lingers on her as the horrific rape persists. She eventually musters enough strength to turn her head to see her dress on the ground in front of her, the wine glass toppled on the ground where she last remembered standing. It becomes obvious at this juncture to both Nina and the audience that the wine Nina drank had been spiked, and that she has no capacity to resist the sexual assault that is happening to her at the moment. As she turns her head back and tears stream down her face, Fat Cat's hand grasps tightly at her neck, stopping her from moving any more than she already struggled with. The relentless camera cuts to a long shot of Fat Cat with his trousers pulled down to his ankles as he climbs over Nina who now remains visually obscured by the obscenity of Fat Cat's violent movements of sexual assault. The interminable rape scene slowly goes out of focus with the non-diegetic sound of a burning flame amplifying before the scene cuts to black.

The sequence of events leading up to this point leaves the audience in complete disbelief, shock, and utter disgust at Fat Cat's perverse sense of entitlement, while the audience every so often shuffles between the point of view of Nina's helpless situation and the omnipresent camera visually observing the abusive events that have just unfolded. In a film that addresses the different structures that perpetuate rape culture, the disturbing and startling closing sequence is the most narratologically cogent moment of the entire film. It is also the most discomforting, painful and unsettling sequence to sit through because of the certainty that Nina had been indisputably raped. Here, the experience of cinema is deliberately unbearable – psychologically, emotionally and physically – as the audience is made to endure the intense affects evoked in the last ten minutes of the film. Yet, the unbearable nature of this scene lies in the way the camera subverts the phallic power of cinema by exposing its grotesque preoccupation with the visual which the film had painstakingly chipped away prior to this scene. By removing any visual pleasure that may be evoked from this scene, a powerfully ethical moment in the film is constructed where the camera resists subjecting the female body to visual exploitation. As a result, the 'to-be-looked-at-ness' of passive women on screen – and the visual-centric mode of epistemology – is destabilised through affective modes of sense-making that map out systemic levels of microaggression, covert and overt coercion, and collusion surrounding issues of embeddedness of rape culture within Taiwanese media industry that is otherwise easy for one to turn a blind eye to. As Greg Forter suggests, a focus on linear modes of speaking out might overlook the 'mundanely catastrophic', where 'the trauma induced by patriarchal identity formation rather, say than the trauma of rape, the violence not of lynching but of everyday racism'. Indeed, he continues, that 'such traumas are chronic and cumulative, so woven into the fabric of our societies' as they are (Forter 2007: 260). Insofar as the final scene reveals the despicable act of rape, the film highlights the other unspeakable but equally complicit moments that also perpetuate rape culture.

 Throughout the film, skewed camera angles, deliberate camera movements, lighting, and film edits constantly blur the distinction between memory, real life, or the manifestation of Nina's psyche. Yet, any doubt tied to the unreliability of Nina's subjectivity is continually suspended because the question is not so much the authenticity of Nina's point of view which should be accounted for, fleshed out and analysed in strict sequence. Instead, cinema constructs the (after-)affects of coercion and pressure that constitute Nina's lived experiences as a struggling media talent trying to break into the Taiwanese film industry. By drawing attention to its own film-making processes, *Nina Wu* fleshes out the production of rape culture on screen. Rape culture is embedded within the decentralised spaces of cinematic and/or media environments through a combination of carefully constructed film sets and colour design, extended camera work and movement, non-linear visual montage with continuity sound editing. Most importantly, Nina's interactions with stakeholders involved at different junctures of filmmaking (managing agent, executive producer, casting director, directors, production crew, fellow cast members, audience and press media) and her everyday life outside filming are presented non-chronologically as a series of vignettes. These evoke an affective mode of cinematic address, which works via non-linear sense-making; one which locates rape culture within the production-assemblages of the media and film industry.

NOTE

1. This emancipatory power of the #MeToo movement may be historised in relation to the women's movement in the 1970s, where Judith Herman sought to 'speak out against the denial of women's experiences in [her] own profession [within psychiatric work] and testify what [she] had witness[ed]' (1992: 1). Within the next two decades, Herman's work influenced other survivors of sexual and domestic violence to share their own experiences of war and political terrors in the West. Similarly, speaking out and exposing horrendous sex crimes on social media echoes Roger Luckhurst's theory on the 'shock' factor which has become synonymous with how modern society manages trauma, by a causing sense of disruption and temporal dislocation in dominant discourse or ideology through technology (20).

REFERENCES

Barker, Jennifer. (2009). *The Tactile Eye:* University of California.
Beller, Jonathan (2006), *The Cinematic Mode Of Production*, Lebanon: Dartmouth College Press.
Bowdler, Michelle (2021), *Is Rape A Crime?*, New York: Flatiron Books.
Boyle, Karen (2019), *#MeToo, Weinstein And Feminism*, Glasgow/Cham: Palgrave Macmillan.
Buchwald, Emilie, Pamela Fletcher and Martha Roth (2005), *Transforming A Rape Culture*. Minneapolis, MN: Milkweed Editions.
Choi, Jinhee and Mattias Frey (2014) *Cine-Ethics Ethical Dimensions Of Film Theory, Practice, And Spectatorship*, London: Routledge.
Christians, Clifford, Mark Frackler, Kathy Richardson and Peggy Kreshel (2020), *Media Ethics: Cases And Moral Reasoning*, 11th edn. New York and Abingdon: Routledge.
Dempsey, Michelle Madden (2021), 'Coercion, consent, and time', *Ethics*, 131: 2, 345–68, doi:10.1086/711212.
Downing, Lisa and Libby Saxton (2010), *Film And Ethics*, London: Routledge.
Fanghanel, Alexandra (2020), *Disrupting Rape Culture: Public Space, Sexuality And Revolt*, Bristol: Bristol University Press.
Fileborn, Bianca and Rachel Loney-Howes (2019), *#MeToo and the Politics of Social Change*, Cham: Palgrave Macmillan.
Forter, Greg (2007), 'Freud, Faulkner, Caruth: Trauma and the politics of literary form',. *Narrative*, 15: 3, 259–85. doi:10.1353/nar.2007.0022.
Frater, Patrick (2019), 'Midi Z on "Nina Wu": "I'm aiming for a new cinematic language' – Variety', *Variety.Com.*, <https://variety.com/2019/film/news/midi-z-nina-wu-screenwriter-star-wu-ke-xi-1203220095/>.
Freeman, Elizabeth (2010), *Time Binds*, Durham, NC: Duke University Press.
Gage, Carolyn (2021), *Intimacy Coordinator*, Morrisville, NC: Lulu Press.
Gill, Rosalind (2007, 'Postfeminist media culture', *European Journal of Cultural Studies*, 10: 2, 147–66, doi:10.1177/1367549407075898.
Gill, Rosalind and Christina Scharff (2011), *Postfeminism, Neoliberalism and Subjectivity*, Basingstoke: Palgrave Macmillan.
Grosz, Elizabeth A. (1994), *Volatile Bodies*, Bloomington: Indiana University Press.

Guan, Zexu (2020), 'Chinese beauty bloggers: amateurs, entrepreneurs, and platform labour', *Celebrity Studies*, 12: 2, 326–32, doi:10.1080/19392397.2020.1737154.

Herman, Judith (1992), *Trauma and Recovery*, New York: HarperCollins Publishers.

Horeck, Tanya (2021), 'How to solve the problem of sexual misconduct in film and TV', *The Independent*, <https://www.independent.co.uk/life-style/women/sexual-misconduct-film-tv intimacy-coordinator-b1847485.html>.

Marks, Laura U. (2000), *The Skin of the Film*, Durham, NC: Duke University Press.

Marks, Laura U. (2002), *Touch: Sensuous Theory and Multisensory Media*, Minneapolis: University of Minnesota Press.

Mulvey, Laura (1975), 'Visual pleasure and narrative cinema', *Screen*, 16: 3, 6–18, doi:10.1093/screen/16.3.6.

Schwab, Gabriele (2006), 'Writing against memory and forgetting', *Literature And Medicine*, 25: 1, 95–121, doi:10.1353/lm.2006.0026.

Sinnerbrink, Robert (2015), *Cinematic Ethics: Exploring Ethical Experience Through Film*, New York: Routledge.

Sinnerbrink, Robert and Lisa Trahair (2016), 'Film and/as ethics', *Substance*, 45: 3, 3–15, doi:10.3368/ss.45.3.3.

Sørensen, Inge Ejbye (2021), 'Sex and safety on set: intimacy coordinators in television drama and film in the VOD and post-Weinstein era', *Feminist Media Studies*, 1–16, doi:10.1080/14680777.2021.1886141.

Szlawieniec-Haw, Danielle I. (2019), *Fiction's Truth*, New York and London: Routledge.

Yueh, Hsin-I Sydney (2016), *Identity Politics and Popular Culture in Taiwan*, London: Lexington Books.

Z, Midi (2019), *Nina Wu*, Film, Taiwan: Seashore Image Productions.

INDEX

Aaron, Michele, 178
Act of Killing, The, 61–3, 64, 70, 73, 77
Agamben, Giorgio, 42, 44, 51, 58
Akomfrah, John, 3, 13, 118, 129, 131–2, 144
Alter, Nora, 117–18, 129
Anthropocene/capitalocene, 5, 8, 14, 118–19, 121, 123–4, 130–2, 134–5, 142–3, 145
Ashton, Zawe, 14, 151, 153, 157–8, 160, 165
attention economy, 210
Austin, Thomas, 155, 166
Avatar, 133–4, 139, 142, 148–9

Beller, Jonathan, 210, 223
Beyoncé, 12, 83
Bian, Zhangyun, 45–6, 48–9, 50–1, 52–4
BlacKkKlansmen, 199
Black Panther, 100, 104
Boltanski, Luc, 177, 185
Bolton, Lucy, 5, 12, 14, 57
Brazilian cinema, 23

Carne y Arena, 3, 15, 176–7, 179, 185–6
Carroll, Noël, 9, 16–17, 155, 166
Chthulucene, 119, 155
cognitive mapping, 118, 123, 128, 130–2
colonialism, 6, 23, 39, 89, 92, 119, 196
Coogler, Ryan, 100, 112
'colour-blind' practices, 191
consumer capitalism, 137–9, 147, 180, 185, 191, 210
Cove, The, 145
Cubitt, Sean, 134, 142, 149, 171, 186
Cultural Revolution, 12, 42, 44–7, 50–5, 58–9
Currie, Gregory, 155
Cynn, Christine, 61

Day After Tomorrow, The, 144
Deller, Rose, 164–5
Deleuze, Gilles, 4, 7–9, 11–12, 42–4, 47, 49, 52, 57–8, 119, 121–4, 125–6, 127–9, 130–1

INDEX

Deleuze, Gilles and Felix Guattari, 119, 121–2, 124, 126, 128, 131
Demos, T. J., 118–19, 124–5, 129–30
digital media, 1, 171, 172–4, 178, 207–8
digital visuality, 14–15, 172
Dillard, J. D., 100–4, 108, 111
disidentification, 83, 85, 87–9, 90–3, 94–6
documentary, 2–3, 8, 10, 12, 15, 28, 42–52, 55–6, 60–3, 64, 66, 70, 73, 74–8, 109, 145, 152, 154, 174, 196, 200
  perpetrator, 62, 77
  re-enactment, 12, 62–3, 71, 74–7, 156
drone warfare, 172, 184
du Bois, W. E. B., 109, 195, 198
Duras, Marguerite, 127

Eliasson, Olafur, 117

Fanon, Frantz, 25, 92
Flusser, Vilem, 172
Freyre, Gilberto, 25, 27

gender, 5, 6, 8, 9, 40, 85, 89, 96, 110, 161, 164, 206
  and class, 2, 23–6, 31, 38–9, 143, 151, 161, 164
  and colonialism, 24
  and race, 2, 6, 13, 24–6, 38–9, 85, 89, 96–7, 143, 151, 161, 164
  and sexuality, 11, 24
  and violence, 14–16, 204–5
  inequality, 31, 206
Get Out, 188
González, Lélia, 27
Google Earth, 3, 15, 172, 179–81, 183–5
Grønstad, Asbjørn, 119, 129
Guattari, Felix, 119, 121–2, 124, 126, 128, 131
Gutiérrez-Rodríguez, Encarnación, 32

Hadjioannou, Markos, 171
Halligan, Fionnuala, 155
Hands Across America, 110
Hamington, Maurice, 164–5
Hankivsky, Olena, 14, 164
Haraway, Donna, 119, 130, 188
Hill Collins, Patricia, 164
history
  Brazilian, 28
  cinematic, 195
  Chinese, 46–7, 49–50
  colonial, 2, 4, 11
  global, 64, 119
  media, 174
  military, 184
  natural, 117, 130
  political, 52–3, 65
  racist, 94–5, 201
  visual, 195
  world, 2–3, 42, 47, 54–6, 119
Hongisto, Ilona, 157, 166
hooks, bell, 85, 192, 195, 199
housemaids, 3, 11, 24, 26–7, 28, 30, 31–2, 35, 37
horror, 3, 15, 103, 106, 108, 188, 191–2, 200
  black, 108, 191
  social, 200
Hu, Jie, 12, 42, 45
Huillet, Danièle, 127

identification, 12, 86–7, 91–2, 94–5, 97, 191, 217
  racial, 84–5
imaginary, 85, 87–8, 94–6, 97–8, 174
  Brazilian, 38
  racial, 12, 83, 200
immersion, 121, 127, 172, 174, 176–8
indexicality, 142, 171
Irigaray, Luce, 4, 13, 83, 85–8, 92–3, 95–6

Jameson, Fredric, 117, 118, 123–5, 128–9, 130–1
Jelin, Elizabeth, 47, 56

Khmer Rouge, 3, 12, 72–6, 78
Kinkle, Jeff, 124
Kierkegaard, Søren, 4, 14, 134, 141
Koutsourakis, Angelos, 129
Kubrick, Stanley, 127, 128

Last Goodbye, The, 175, 179
Latour, Bruno, 13, 117
Look of Silence, The (2014), 3, 12, 60–4, 66, 68, 70–7
love
 romantic, 13–14, 29, 50, 53, 97, 133–5, 139, 141–6, 148, 165, 200, 215, 218
 preferential, 139, 141
 universal, 135, 141
Luka-Cain, Alix, 153–4
Lugones, María, 4, 11, 24, 34, 38, 40

Manovich, Lev, 175
Marks, Laura, 9, 209–10
Martin-Jones, David, 12, 119, 148
May, Vivian M., 161–2
#MeToo movement, 2, 204–6, 223
Meillassoux, Quentin, 143
Mermaid, The, 14, 133–9, 142–8
Mey, Chum, 72, 75–6
Midi Z, 3, 15, 204–5, 215
mimicry, 83, 221
Mirzoeff, Nicholas, 123–4
Moore, Jason W., 126, 130
Morley, Carol, 14, 151, 161, 163–5
Morton, Timothy, 123
Mulvey, Laura, 97–8, 209
Muñoz, José Esteban, 4, 13, 85, 88–93

Nath, Vann, 63, 72–7
Nilsson, Jakob, 13–14, 15, 131

Okja, 3, 14, 134–42, 146–8
Omielan, Luisa, 12, 83, 85–7, 93, 94–6
Oppenheimer, Joshua, 12, 61–3, 67, 73–4, 78

Panh, Rithy, 3, 12, 62, 70–4, 77
Peele, Jordan, 3, 13, 15, 100–1, 103, 105, 107, 108–11, 188, 191–2, 195, 200
perpetrators, 44, 62–4, 66–9, 70–7, 205–6
photograph, 28–9, 45, 48–9, 52–5, 63, 74–5, 76, 139, 152–3, 154–5, 156–7, 163, 165, 173, 180, 182–3, 190, 194–6, 201, 216, 220
Pick, Anat, 119
Pol Pot, 66, 71
Ponech, Trevor, 155
psychoanalysis, 87–91

race, 2, 4, 6, 8, 9, 11, 13, 14, 23, 24–6, 28–9, 31, 38, 85–9, 94–5, 100, 103–5, 108–11, 119, 143, 151, 161, 164, 188, 194, 200
racism, 23, 84, 96, 101, 105, 162, 190–1, 200, 222
Rajchman, John, 125
Rancière, Jacques, 4, 11, 24, 124
Rankine, Claudia, 84–5, 96–7
rape culture, 15, 204, 217, 219, 221–3
recognition, 11–13, 34, 39, 49, 63–4, 66–7, 69–70, 76–7, 96–8, 151–2, 164, 166, 191–2
re-enactment, 12, 60, 62–3, 71, 74–5, 76–7, 156
responsibility, 16, 62, 68–9, 70, 72, 73, 77, 102, 134, 147, 160, 178, 213
Rodowick, D. N., 8, 9, 43, 130
romantic comedy, 134, 142, 143–5, 146
Rukun, Adi, 64, 66, 70
Rukun, Ramli, 64, 67, 68, 70

227

S21: The Khmer Rouge Killing Machine, 3, 12, 60, 62, 70, 78
Serra, Richard, 117
Seshadri-Crooks, Kalpana, 68, 86, 95
Sinnerbrink, Robert, 5, 12, 15, 43, 206
slavery, 23, 40, 71, 103, 128
Sleight, 13, 101, 102–4, 107, 108, 111
song, 23–4, 40, 53, 71, 74, 86, 130, 189, 199
Song, Binbin, 57
Sorry to Bother You, 199
Spinoza, Baruch, 122
Straub, Jean-Marie, 127
Suharto, General, 62, 65–6
Sutton, Damian, 49
Syberberg, Hans-Jürgen, 127

Taiwan
  film and media industry, 15, 204–7, 208–9, 211, 214, 222
Treachery of the G30S/PKI, 66
Torchin, Leshu, 69, 78
Toscano, Alberto, 124
trauma, 12, 46, 62–4, 67, 69–70, 72–7, 109, 144, 162, 189, 205, 222–3
Trump, Donald J., 2, 13, 100, 101, 104, 106, 109, 110

Us, 3, 13, 101, 105, 107–9, 109–10

Vertigo Sea, 3, 117–20, 126–30
Vincent, Joyce, 14, 151, 153, 155–7, 159, 161–6
virtual reality, 1, 3, 15, 172, 173, 174, 181
violence, 39, 40, 47, 68–9, 138, 146, 163, 182, 194, 206, 219, 220, 223
  Cultural Revolution, 51, 53, 55–6
  domestic, 163, 223

economic, 40
gendered, 2, 14–16, 204, 217
historical, 62, 64, 76–7
implicit, 39, 68
institutionalised, 73, 75
memories of, 12, 69
of oppression, 33, 65, 71
police, 101–2, 200–1
political, 2, 4, 11, 12, 61–4, 66, 70, 74–7
racial, 15, 222
re-enactments of, 71
screen, 8
sexual, 2, 5, 14,–16, 204–6, 211, 217, 220, 222
social, 39, 62
traumatic, 63, 74, 76–7

Walcott, Derek, 121
WALL-E, 133–4
Wang, Jingyao, 45–9, 50–7
'war on terror', 103, 110
whiteness, 85–8, 93–6, 190–2, 194, 197, 199
Williams, Serena, 12, 83–4, 96
witnessing
  ethical, 2, 11, 12, 62–6, 68, 76–7, 174
world of cinemas, 10, 42, 43–4, 56–7
world simulation, 172
work, domestic, 23, 24–9, 30–3, 35, 164
Wu, Nina, 3, 15, 204, 205, 207–8, 211, 214, 216, 218–19, 220, 222

Yuk-wa Law, Fiona, 135

Žižek, Slavoj, 4, 14, 97, 134, 141
zombies, 192, 193, 194, 196, 199, 201

EU representative:
Easy Access System Europe
Mustamäe tee 50, 10621 Tallinn, Estonia
Gpsr.requests@easproject.com

www.ingramcontent.com/pod-product-compliance
Lightning Source LLC
Chambersburg PA
CBHW071709160426
43195CB00012B/1624